CBar

STIMULATING INNOVATION IN INDUSTRY

STIMULATING INNOVATION IN INDUSTRY

THE CHALLENGE FOR THE UNITED KINGDOM

EDITED BY
ALEX BOWEN AND MARTIN RICKETTS

KOGAN
PAGE

First published in 1992

Apart from any fair dealing for the purposes of research or private study, or criticism or review, as permitted under the Copyright, Designs and Patents act, 1988, this publication may only be reproduced, stored or transmitted, in any form or by any means, with the prior permission in writing of the publishers, or in the case of reprographic reproduction in accordance with the terms of licenses issued by the Copyright Licensing Agency. Enquiries concerning reproduction outside those terms should be sent to the publishers at the undermentioned address:

Kogan Page Limited
120 Pentonville Road
London N1 9JN

in association with the

National Economic Development Office
Millbank Tower
Millbank
London SW1P 4QX

© National Economic Development Office 1992

British Library Cataloguing in Publication Data

A CIP record for this book is available from the British Library.

ISBN 0 7494 0446 9

Printed and bound by in the UK by
Clays Ltd, St Ives plc

Contents

List of Figures

List of Tables

About NEDO

This book has been prepared for publication by the National Economic Development Office.

The National Economic Development Council (NEDC) brings together representatives of government, management, trade unions and other interests to assess economic performance and opportunities for improvment. NEDC meets quarterly, under the chairmanship of the Chancellor of the Exchequer and other secretaries of state.

There are 18 sector groups and working parties, covering different parts of industry or working on practical industrial issues. The sectors covered include, construction, electronics, engineering, and tourism & leisure. Working parties are studying traffic management systems and the European public sector market.

The National Economic Development Office (NEDO) supports the work of the Council and its sector groups and working parties. It carries out independent research and provides advice on ways of improving economic performance, competitive power and the efficiency of industry and stimulating new ideas and practical action.

Note

The National Economic Development Office organised the policy seminar on *Stimulating innovation in industry* to improve the level of understanding of the issues involved, and we are grateful to the authors for the time they have devoted to the project. Their articles are, of course, entirely personal and it should not be assumed that any part of this book reflects the opinions or judgements of the National Economic Development Council.

Notes on the Authors and Discussants

Dr Alex Bowen is Head of Policy Analysis and Statistics at the National Economic Development Office. He studied economics at Clare College, Cambridge and won a Kennedy Scholarship to the Massachusetts Institute of Technology, where he obtained his PhD. He has worked as a lecturer in economics at Brunel University, a research officer at the London School of Economics, and as a consultant to the World Bank, joining the National Economic Development Office in 1987.

John Burke is Director and Chief Operating Officer of Porton International Ltd. Having trained as an organic chemist, Mr Burke joined ICI Dyestuffs Division, Research Department, in 1962. He joined Beecham Laboratories in 1967 as Marketing Director, before becoming Vice-President Europe of G D Searle (USA) in 1978. In 1982 he became the first non-American UK Chairman and European Vice-President of Merck Sharp and Dohm. He was appointed a Main Board Director of Glaxo Holdings plc and Chairman of Glaxo Pharmaceuticals Ltd in 1985.

Tony Buxton is an Economic Adviser at the National Economic Development Office. He has a particular interest in industrial economics and has published in the field of innovation studies.

Professor Tom Cannon is the Director of Manchester Business School. He has extensive experience and training in small business management and enterprise development work, education and training, and has been involved in the development of such programmes as EXPORTS, Graduate Enterprise and Gateway Overseas. He was the Founding Director of the Scottish Enterprise Foundation.

John Chisholm is Chief Executive of the Defence Research Agency. He began his career as a graduate apprentice at Vauxhall Motors in Luton, in 1968. He moved to become an analyst programmer at Scicon Ltd in London, in 1969, remaining there until 1979 when he left to form a new company — CAP Scientific. As Managing Director of CAP Scientific, he steered the company until it merged with Sema Metra SA in 1988 when he became UK Managing Director of the new group. He joined the Defence Research Agency in 1991.

Ninean Eadie is President of ICL Europe. During his 30 years with ICL, Mr Eadie has, in turn, held responsibility for product marketing, small systems product development, customer services, international operations, including the Eastern Bloc and the United States of America, and most recently ICL's continental European operations.

Walter Eltis, D Litt, became Director General of the National Economic Development Office in November 1988, after two years as Economic Director. He was a consultant to the National Economic Development Office from 1963 to 1966. From 1963 until 1988 he was Official Fellow and Tutor in Economics at Exeter College, Oxford.

Douglas Fraser was appointed Industrial Director of the National Economic Development Office in 1988. After graduating from Manchester Business School, he spent 12 years with EMI Ltd where he held a number of management positions before joining the National Economic Development Office in 1979, where he has been responsible for work in information technology and engineering.

Fiona Gilmore is Managing Director of Springpoint Ltd, a European brand and corporate identity design consultancy based in London. She spent seven years in advertising before entering the design industry. She became Managing Director of Michael Peters and Partners in 1987 and later a partner and Managing Director of Lewis Moberly.

Professor John Kay is Professor of Economics at the London Business School and Chairman of London Economics, a leading independent specialist economic consulting group which he co-founded in 1986. Educated at Edinburgh University and Nuffield College, he was elected to a fellowship in economics at St John's College, Oxford in 1970. In 1979 he was appointed the first Research Director and subsequently Director of the Institute for Fiscal Studies. From 1986 to 1991 he was Director of the Centre for Business Strategy at the London Business School.

Mike Kirk is Managing Director of SPS Technologies, TJ Brooks division, one of the world leaders in the manufacture of aerospace fasteners. TJ Brooks was formerly a subsidiary of GKN plc.

Professor Colin Mayer is Price Waterhouse Professor of Corporate Finance at City University Business School. Before that he was Fellow in Economics at St Anne's College, Oxford. He is co-director of the Centre for Economic Policy Research's programme in applied microeconomics and Chairman of the European Science Foundation network in financial matters.

Professor Stan Metcalfe has been Professor of Economics at Manchester since 1980. He is a Director of PREST, a rapidly growing research group within the University of Manchester concerned with the evaluation of science and technology policy and the study of the economics of technology strategy in major British corporations.

Professor Martin Ricketts is Economic Director at the National Economic Development Office. He is on two year's leave from the University of Buckingham where he was Dean of the School of Accountancy, Business and Economics. He took his BA in Economics at the University of Newcastle and his Doctorate at the University of York with a thesis on the UK housing market. He has been a Visiting Professor in the Virginia Polytechnic Institute.

Richard Rooley is Senior Partner of the Project Management Partnership. A Partner of Donald Smith Seymour and Rooley, consulting engineers for 20 years, he has been responsible for the design of enviromnental services in major projects, including hospitals and industrial buildings. He is particularly responsible for project and construction management in the refurbishment of complex buildings, and has served on committees and councils of professional institutions across the building and engineering industries in the UK and America.

Dr Fiona Steele is currently Head of the Technology Group of the Confederation of British Industry (CBI). She took a PhD at the University of Sheffield where her research provided some early background for the technology of fibre optics. After post-doctoral research, she joined the Science Research Council and then moved to the Council of Engineering

Institutions. After four years in the gas industry, she was seconded to the recently formed Fellowship of Engineering to set up an engineering policy unit, until 1987 when she was invited to join the CBI.

Professor Paul Stoneman is currently Research Professor and Director of The Research Bureau at Warwick Business School, University of Warwick. His main research interests centre upon the economics of technological change and technology policy and he has published extensively on the determinants and impacts of technological change.

David Thompson is Chairman of Rank Xerox (UK) Ltd. He joined Rank Xerox in 1965 after seven years with IBM in the UK and the US. He was responsible for Rank Xerox in Holland, the Far East and Latin America before returning to the UK in 1983, where he is currently responsible for operations in Central Europe, the CIS, South Asia and Africa.

Professor Christopher Voss is BT Professor of Total Quality Management at the London Business School. He was formerly Professor of Manufacturing Strategy at the University of Warwick. He has researched and taught for many years in the fields of manufacturing strategy, technology management and Japanese manufacturing methods. His recent work has been in the field of technology implementation, particularly in the area of CAD/CAM. He is Chairman of the UK Operations Management Association.

Dr Norman Waterman is Chief Executive of Quo-Tec Ltd, a consultancy company which assists its clients to create new business from new and improved technologies. He is Chief Technical Adviser on two current major Department of Trade and Industry programmes; and is also retained by a number of multinational companies to advise on new product development and business diversification. Quo-Tec developed the Innovation Management Toolkit for the National Economic Development Office.

Dr Howard White is an Economic Adviser at the National Economic Development Office. His research interests lie in the area of the economics of development.

Seminar participants

The editors would like to thank the other distinguished participants in our policy seminar for their valuable contributions. In addition to the authors and discussants of the papers published in this book, they included:

Mr M Beck Deputy Head of Work-related education, Strategy and Further Education Branch, Employment Department Group

Professor P J Buckley Management Centre, University of Bradford

Dr D W Budworth Co-ordinator, Joint ESRC-SERC Committee

Mr J Chowcat National Officer, Manufacturing Science & Finance Union

Mr A Francis Head of Business Policy and Marketing Group, The Management School, Imperial College

Dr P Geroski Professor of Economics, Centre for Business Strategy, London Business School

Dr J D Giachardi Research Director, Courtaulds plc

Dr C Greenhalgh Fellow and Tutor in Economics, St Peter's College, Oxford

Mr E A B Hammond OBE, General Secretary, Electrical, Electronic, Telecommunications and Plumbing Union

Dr I Harrison Senior Principal, Research & Technology Policy Division, Department of Trade and Industry

Mr P Hayward Director, International Intellectual Property Law Centre, St Peter's College, Oxford

Dr A E Hughes Director of Programmes, Science and Engineering Research Council

Mr D Lobley ACOST Secretariat, Cabinet Office

Mr J C Chow Consultant

Mr K Mayhew Fellow and Tutor in Economics, Pembroke College, Oxford

Mr R Maconachie Technology Unit, Industry Department, Scottish Office

Mr G A McLaughlin Technology Unit, Industry Department, Scottish Office

Mr A J Meyrick Senior Economic Adviser, HM Treasury

Mr D M Moffat Corporate Service & DCM Director, Unipart Group of Companies

Mr B Nixon Department of Accountancy and Business Finance, Dundee University

Mr A Owen Director, SciTec Management Consultants Ltd

Professor K L R Pavitt Science Policy Research Unit, University of Sussex

Mr M Phelps Economic Adviser, Department of Trade and Industry

Mr J Pilditch CBE, Author, *Winning Ways*

Mr M J Pratt Manager, Industrial Finance Division, Bank of England

Mr H Ross Innovation Grants Unit, Scottish Office

Mr S Seymour Manager, Marketing and Business Development Division, Price Waterhouse

Ms M Sharp Science Policy Research Unit, University of Sussex

Dr F Steward Director of the Technology Policy Unit, Aston Business School, University of Aston

Dr P Swann Department of Economics, Brunel University

Dr N von Tunzelman Science Policy Research Unit, University of Sussex

Mr J G Walshe Science and Technology Secretariat, Cabinet Office

Dr D H Watts Geography Department, University of Sheffield

Mr I Yates Vice President, European Aerospace Association (AECMA)

Introduction

Innovation and its promotion are vital to economic success. In 1991 the Rt Hon Peter Lilley MP, the then Secretary of State for Trade and Industry, remarked that there are companies in the electronics industry where half of all sales consist of products that were not made at all in 1988. World trade grows fastest for successful new products. The companies that create them enjoy monopoly opportunities until patents expire, which can enable them to earn exceptional profits. New processes to manufacture conventional products offer similar opportunities: firms that make advances acquire monopoly rights over the sale of the machinery and equipment that is required to exploit them.

While the development of new products and processes is the aspect of innovation that offers by far the highest returns, and, at the national level, the best prospects for export growth, a successful reorganisation of the manufacture of traditional products can also be innovative. Superior quality control, the more effective organisation of production, superior marketing techniques, and more effective partnerships between management and labour to raise productivity can all be innovative. The UK needs to become more innovative both in the way in which production is organised and in the creation of new products and processes.

The research and development required to evolve new products can be extremely expensive to finance. Money needs to be committed many years before new goods can actually be marketed, and a ten year gestation period is common in many sectors of industry, which adds a very substantial interest burden to what is actually spent on research and development. Moreover, only a small fraction of the ideas explored will actually prove financially viable, so very great risks are involved which are compounded because the first comers gain the main fruits of temporary monopoly situations and a fairly successful team can emerge second or third. Because of these risks, most research is undertaken by established companies with money generated from their own cash flows supplemented by outside borrowing to provide the seed corn for future market security and dominance.

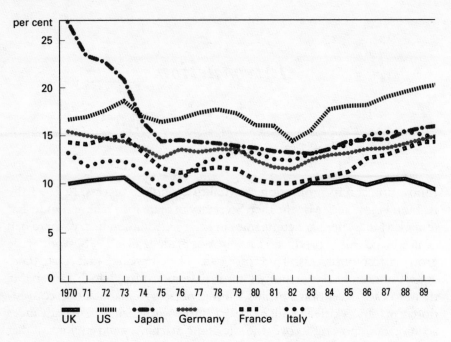

Figure 1 The real rate of return to capital in the business sector Source: OECD

Because the financial basis for R&D is profits from existing production, a fundamental explanation of the UK's weakness in comparison with Germany, the US and Japan is readily evident. OECD data show that the real rate of return on capital in the UK business sector has been substantially lower than in these other leading countries in the last 20 years. (Figure 1). If existing UK capital earns a lower rate of return, there is less scope for the provision of internal funding of future products.

Retained earnings can be supplemented by borrowing and UK companies now pay approximately the same real interest rates as companies in Japan, Germany and the US, because real rates have converged since the freeing of exchange controls in 1979. The key consideration in borrowing for R&D is the margin by which profits can be expected to exceed interest because most such financing will require an above average risk premium. Since the average UK rate of return is substantially lower than returns in these overseas countries, while the real interest rates UK businesses have to pay are approximately the same, the excess of profit rates over interest rates has been far narrower in the UK. The details are set out in the charts below which show a far smaller excess of profit rates over interest rates in the UK, whether money is borrowed short term as in Figure 2 or long term as in

20

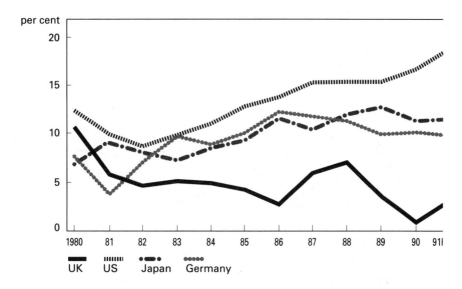

Figure 2 The real rate of return less the short-term real rate of interest
Source: OECD

Figure 3. Because profit rates are so much closer to interest rates here, lending money to finance research and development is very much riskier. The City and industry can both be expected to respond to an unacceptable level of risk by avoiding it and therefore aborting ideas by UK scientists and engineers when equivalent ideas are sensibly encouraged and developed in Germany, Japan and the US. Nobody thanks banks for losing shareholders' money through loans that fail to be repaid, and no-one thanks managements, such as those who ran Rolls Royce until 1971, that invest in the development of marvellous new technologies that fail to be financially viable. The prudent in UK industry and in the City have responded to the small excess of average profits over interest by only encouraging proposals for research and development that offer the prospect of a rate of return far above the UK average.

A good deal of the UK chemicals and pharmaceuticals sector has achieved rates of return well above the national average, which has permitted substantial research and development to continue. The occasional firm outside this area, such as JCB, has achieved a return sufficiently over the odds to permit the development of world leading products. But in the bulk of British industry and especially in most of the physics based industries, with the exception of the aircraft industry which has until recently been heavily dependent on government support and contracts, UK rates of return have been at or

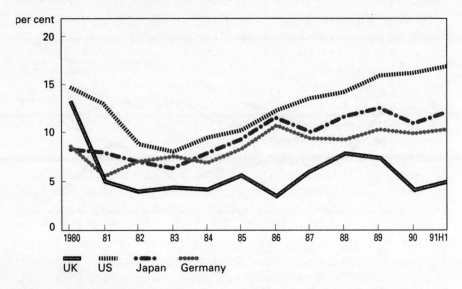

Figure 3 The real rate of return less the long-term real rate of interest
Source: OECD

below the dismal British average, which in any case offers an inadequate margin over interest costs. These industries have generated fewer and less effective new products and processes and continually lost market share; they have failed to generate the returns which would enable them to invest sufficiently in research and development to reverse their decline.

Worse still, because the bulk of our production in these industries is either of traditional products or of products designed outside the UK where others own monopoly rights, our profits have necessarily remained far lower than those that the originators of the successful new products enjoyed. There is a clear danger that our comparatively low profitability in these industries will persist, and that we shall continue to lack the financial underpinning to move up-market whenever this involves heavy capital costs.

During the 1960s and the 1970s, many UK economists and a good many of our predecessors in the National Economic Development Office will have seen greater State help for industrial research and development as an obvious response to this problem. If the private sector cannot find the funding for such a vital economic activity, there is an evident market failure; it used to be argued that government should be brought in to do what private industry and the City would not. The weaknesses and embarrassments in that approach have not been its theoretical unacceptability, but its evident practical failures in the UK. Sir Euan Maddock, a government chief scientist of the 1970s, has shown that in the 1950s we spent three per cent of our national income in order to generate three per cent of our energy through the development of nuclear power station processes which have as yet led to the sale of only two British-designed power stations overseas. There has been no net nuclear pay-off in the short term, the medium or the long term, and the nuclear dinosaurs proved an expensive embarrassment to the Department of Energy in the evolution of the privatisation programme. The vast sums poured into the aircraft industry culminating in the Concorde fiasco proved an equal embarrassment. Because of these errors and innumerable others, there are few today who believe the government should try to pick winners and judge which of the private sector's market failures (and its unwillingness to finance Concorde and the nuclear energy programme were regarded as market failures by the economists and Civil Servants of a generation ago) should receive state assistance.

An alternative approach is to provide blanket subsidies for areas of activity such as industrial research and development that are expected to offer exceptional benefits to the economy at large and which are extra or 'external' to those that investing firms obtain. The objections to this approach are not as obvious as those to trying to pick winners. One clear difficulty if R&D capital is allowed to be written off at a rate of over 100 per cent so that there is a tax subsidy (as has been proposed in Australia) is that this would provide a good deal more employment for our already overworked accountants, who would be asked to ascribe the greatest possible amount of company activity to research and development. The thrust of UK policy in the last thirteen years has been to simplify corporate taxation, to remove subsidies, and to leave it entirely to companies to determine how the profits that remain after the payment of the lowest rate of corporation tax in Europe can best be deployed.

The embarrassments associated with the state directed control of R&D activity in Eastern Europe underline the difficulties in proposing a return to that approach in the UK. So how can the UK escape from the trap that is described in Figures 2 and 3, which indicate that most of our industry earns lower profits but has to pay the same real interest rates as the industries of our leading overseas competitors? Some would seek the solution of lower real interest rates than our European competitors. A naive attempt to bring UK interest rates below Germany's would produce a collapse of sterling within the ERM, devaluation and an acceleration of inflation, and the inevitable re-emergence of UK interest rates several percentage points above Germany's, as was the case throughout the period when inflation was significantly faster in London than in Frankfurt. Economies with first division currencies have about the same inflation and interest rates, nominal and real, as Germany. Economies with second division currencies, such as Italy and Spain, pay between one and three percentage points more interest than Germany to reflect a greater inflation and exchange rate risk. Economies with third division currencies, such as the UK in the 1970s, have to pay five or more per cent interest above German rates. Any effort to get our interest rate down below the German level would lead to the relegation of sterling to the second or third divisions and an eventual return to an interest differential over Germany of five or more percentage points. We have succeeded in joining Germany, France, Belgium, the Netherlands, Japan and the US in the first division with a level of nominal interest rates which is about the same as theirs, based on the expectation that we shall continue to achieve the same low inflation as the world's leading economies. Any premature attempt to get industry's interest rates down would prejudice our chance of remaining in the first currency division of sound inflation economies. Such an attempt would put us back into a world where UK interest rates and inflation rates were far higher than those of our competitors, and where the financing of R&D was therefore considerably riskier and subject to far more cyclical and liquidity vicissitudes than in the economies which are now enjoying the benefits of currency stability. So we cannot escape from the profit rate/interest rate trap by unilaterally lowering UK interest rates in the manner that some advocate.

The only viable way out of the British trap is to raise the rate of return on capital in UK industry towards the levels that have been achieved in the last several decades by our leading competitors. If they can earn higher industrial rates of return, then so can we. This suggests that the vital way forward for UK industry has to be innovation within the firm, in order to use resources more effectively and to cut costs and improve cash flows. Several papers in this volume cover ways in which more innovatory approaches can improve the performance of individual companies. Our productivity is lower in mechanical engineering, clothing and many other sectors than in leading competitor countries. By raising productivity we can cut costs and enhance cash flows and profitability. Some of the benefits from higher productivity must go to the employees responsible for the improvements, and higher pay is an integral element in most successful company reorganisations, but it is vital that a good deal of the gain should go towards correcting the discrepancies in profitability that the OECD data describe. Successful innovation at the company level should sustain a significant increase in both pay and profitability. The task of raising the rate of return in UK industry towards the levels of our competitors must be a precondition for the attainment of the research and development levels we wish to see. This adjustment ought to be made in the course of the next cycle, for profits and wages can both be raised substantially in the recovery phase of the cycle. If this can be achieved in the next prolonged period of economic expansion we shall establish the foundations for a revival of industry- and City-financed R&D, and all the benefits of new product development and enhanced world market shares that follow from this.

The present volume includes important papers on the conditions that will promote the development of new products and processes, on the reorganisation of production and marketing within companies, and on what help can sensibly be expected from government. The contributors include academic economists and some of the industrialists who plan and implement successful policies to promote innovation. It is mainly the responsibility of those who manage and control our companies to assess the weaknesses of UK industry and to correct them.

The articles in this volume will clarify some of the issues that are central to an understanding of why we have underperformed as innovators since the Second World War, and what we now need to do.

Walter Eltis
Director General
National Economic Development Office

Part 1
Why Innovate?

1
Overview

Why innovate?

Innovation is crucial to survival, competitiveness and growth. British companies must innovate and manage the process of innovation well if they are to prosper. David Thompson, the Chairman of Rank Xerox (UK), illustrates the importance of innovation by describing the failure of the UK motorcycle industry and the near failure of the Xerox corporation. The motorcycle industry in the UK did not fail because of technical inadequacy, but because it did not innovate to match changes in the market, in particular, changes in demography and social attitudes towards motorcycling. Xerox lost its market share when its plain paper copying patent expired and the Japanese entered the market. This was not because of a failure to invest in research and development; indeed, Xerox's research establishment at Palo Alto has been a source of technical inspiration to much of the office automation industry. Xerox failed to innovate where innovation mattered most — in serving its customers. The Japanese produced copiers which were simpler to use, more reliable and cheaper. Xerox's patent monopoly had encouraged a protectionist and complacent attitude and its recovery from near failure was based upon continuous innovation and a renewed dedication to finding out about its customers' needs.

Alex Bowen, Tony Buxton and Martin Ricketts of the National Economic Development Office describe attempts to measure the effects of innovation by looking at economic growth and taking away the part which can be attributed to growth in labour and capital. They report on the work of Maddison, which suggests that 65 per cent of growth in the UK between 1913–84 resulted from innovation.

Innovation depends very much upon the actions of individual companies; Paul Stoneman of Warwick University discusses incentives to innovate and how companies try to benefit from innovation. The prime incentive is to increase profits over the long term and this can be done by improving product quality or customer service (for example, through achieving a shorter delivery time or increasing the flexibility of use of the product), or by reducing production costs. However there is no simple model of the innovator, always first to market with new products — followers can be equally innovative and successful. A company needs to decide where to position itself, as a 'global innovator' first into the market place with a new product, or as a 'local innovator' constantly improving its products and processes.

There are three advantages in being the leader:

- A temporary monopoly can be created through the use of patents.
- A leader can take control of resources in situations where they are limited (for example, the best location for a new leisure facility).
- The first into a market sets the rules and standards to which others then have to respond.

Sky Television took the early UK market for satellite broadcasting and its customers invested in equipment which matched its broadcast standards. British Satellite Broadcasting entered the market shortly after with a technically superior but incompatible system, but the customers had already made their choice.

Being first is not necessarily best. The first entrant to a market faces uncertainty and makes mistakes from which competitors can learn; the Boeing 707 benefited from the experience of the Comet with metal fatigue. As an innovation spreads, knowledge about its application increases: subsequent users can incorporate it more rapidly and more cheaply than the pioneers. An infrastructure of specialist suppliers starts to spring up and standards emerge, the market becomes more developed and distribution channels and complementary products are established.

Fiona Steele of the Confederation of British Industry describes the work of the CBI in encouraging firms to be forward looking and argues that 'a company with a future' should be spending 10 per cent of its revenue on innovation. In the case of industries such as electronics, where product life times are short, the figure should be very much higher. The CBI has instituted a survey of innovation trends: in March 1991, two-thirds of manufacturing industry surveyed in the UK was spending less than 5 per cent of its sales revenue on innovation and only 10 per cent of firms were spending more than 10 per cent of their revenues.

Do UK companies innovate sufficiently? If not, why not? R&D is only part of the story, but it is measurable and as Bowen, Buxton and Ricketts demonstrate, there is a correlation between R&D investment and economic performance. This is brought out most graphically by looking at R&D as a capital stock of knowledge which can be built up over time but which depreciates. In terms of the proportion of Gross Domestic Product (GDP) spent on R&D, the UK has fallen from second to fifth place among the six leading industrial countries over the last 20 years. This is of greater concern when it is realised that, in the UK and the US, industry itself funds only two-thirds of business directed research and development, compared with 98 per cent for Japan, and a substantial part of the government funded element is for application in defence industries. One measure of the impact of research and development investment is in the number of patents taken out in the United States. Of the five leading industrial countries, excluding the US itself, the UK with 40.5 patents per million population in the period 1980-85, although still occupying a mid point in the ranking, was the only nation to reduce its patenting activity over the 30 years quoted in the paper.

Stoneman takes up the argument that innovation is a major contributor to economic well-being, but points out that customers, government and other firms are likely to share in those benefits. The benefit to the individual firm is therefore less than the benefit to the economy as a whole. He quotes Mansfield's estimate, based on a study of innovation in the US, that the social return to innovation may be twice the private return to the innovating firm. In addition, the economy as a whole can absorb risk that might deter the individual enterprise. On the other hand, where innovation is used to create market power, there may be a social cost. Stoneman concludes that the poor research and development performance of UK companies might be associated with the differences between social and private benefits, but considers that the evidence is inadequate and since all nations face the same dilemmas, this does not explain the specific under-performance of the UK. He goes on to argue that the answer is more likely to be found in the institutional and macro-economic environment. The difference between private and public returns is used in all nations to justify government support for technology, but in the UK that support has tended to take the form of 'mission oriented' support for R&D, with a preference for high technology expensive projects which have often failed.

This approach contrasts with German and Japanese policy which has been oriented towards diffusion. Stoneman also relates the short termism argument to both the UK capital markets and management incentives. He argues that the instability of the UK economy has worked against the development of long term investment.

The short term argument is also picked up by Steele, who says that traditional performance measures which focus on competitive bench marking, stock levels and inventory control, are too narrow, particularly for the new manufacturing environment. The CBI is working with the Department of Trade and Industry and the Chartered Institute of Management Accountants to see whether more useful performance measures can be evolved, which could be recognised by both the manufacturing and the finance sectors.

Bowen, Buxton and Ricketts discuss education and training. They argue that a more educated and skilled workforce is better able to implement innovation in the work place and note that between 1985 and 1989 63 per cent of the UK workforce had no vocational qualifications; in West Germany only 26 per cent had none. They go on to discuss a number of other issues, including appropriation of the benefits of R&D, the role of the size and structure of firms and the importance of labour contracts and industrial relations.

They also point out that although the UK can only reasonably be expected to originate a small percentage of all innovations, its companies have a poor record of importing technology from overseas. David Thompson said that the challenge for British companies is to get into international joint ventures and to lead them aggressively.

Innovation offers the key to success: the 'company with a future' must rise to the challenge of managing it well if it is to compete and grow into the next century.

2

*The Economics of Innovation: Setting the Scene**

Alex Bowen, Tony Buxton and Martin Ricketts

Introduction

The importance of innovation to economic development is difficult to over-state. Firms must introduce new products, processes and organisational struc-tures if they are to be successful; economies cannot rely upon increases in the quantity of capital and labour alone to improve living standards and com-petitiveness. The papers presented to this seminar consider many of the ele-ments in the chain linking new ideas to success in the international marketplace. To provide a background to the other contributions, this paper illustrates the quantitative importance of innovation to economic growth. It argues that measures of traditional R&D activities help to explain pro-ductivity growth and international competitiveness, despite their drawbacks. The trends revealed by these measures are presented and compared with the experience of the UK's main competitors. Traditional R&D activity is designed to generate innovations, but its success in so doing depends on many other factors including the labour force and the financial markets. These are discussed briefly. Finally, some questions are raised which read-ers may wish to consider when thinking about how government, managers and workers can stimulate innovation in British industry.

* The views expressed are the authors' own and should not be attributed to NEDO. Thanks are due to several colleagues, particularly Marco Pianelli and Martha Prevezer, for their comments and assistance.

The contribution of innovation to economic growth

The importance of innovation can be illustrated by 'growth accounting' exercises, while sidestepping an evaluation of more ambitious theories of economic growth. The basic approach is to calculate the growth of labour input and the physical capital stock; the growth in output in excess of the growth of measured inputs provides a measure of the importance of innovation, albeit adulterated by measurement error, omitted inputs, and index number problems. This approach suggests that the contribution of innovation can be very large indeed. Robert Solow (1957) drew attention to this in the 1950s; his calculations suggested that only around 10 per cent of labour productivity increases in the US non-farm economy could be attributed to increases in capital per person, leaving a residual of 90 per cent to be explained by innovation. Subsequent work[1] has attempted to account for growth in more detail, but refinements in the measurement of inputs and allowance for factors such as economies of scale have not diminished greatly the proportion of growth broadly attributable to innovation. To take a recent example, Maddison (1987) tries to estimate the contribution of 14 components to output growth, including capacity utilisation effects and measures of structural change as well as inputs.[2] Three components are clearly related to innovatory activity: capital quality, 'catching up' with the US (the technological leader), and the residual (as a measure of factors like improvements in work organisation which are 'disembodied'). Table 2.1 tabulates estimates of these factors' contributions to growth over the long term; innovatory activity appears to account for over 60 per cent of British growth.

Table 2.1 Sources of GDP growth, 1913–84

Country	GDP Growth (Average annual rate) (1)	Innovatory activity (2)	100x(2)/(1)
UK	1.81	1.17	65
US	3.01	1.15	38
France	2.54	1.65	65
Germany	2.83	1.54	54
Japan	4.74	1.16	24

Source: derived from Maddison (1987), Table 20, using geometric averages of components for 1913–50, 1950–73, 1973–84. (2) is the annual average percentage point contribution to the growth rate.

This sort of exercise can only assign rough orders of magnitude to the various components of growth. It may underestimate the role of innovation in providing the impetus for capital accumulation, training and structural change. Even so, it demonstrates clearly the quantititive importance of innovation in explaining any one country's economic growth.

At the same time, variations in economic growth across countries are larger than the variations in the rough measure of innovation's contribution, so this may not be the key to why growth rates differ. Indeed, if innovations could not be appropriated by their originators, their contribution to growth would be very similar across all countries. Should a country, therefore, avoid devoting resources to increasing innovatory activities like R&D? This depends on whether a direct link can be established between those activities on the one hand and productivity growth and international competitiveness on the other. Innovation encompasses much more than purely technological change and even this is broader than R&D. However, there have been many econometric studies of the impact of R&D spending on measures of output, holding other inputs constant (in other words, investigations of the contribution of R&D to total factor productivity growth). The level of analysis — firm, industry, country — has varied, as has the precise definition of the R&D variable used.[3] The results provide considerable evidence that R&D is positively related to total factor productivity. One study, for instance, found elasticities of output with respect to R&D of 7–14 per cent in the UK, 14 per cent in the US, 16 per cent in Japan, 10 per cent in France and 19 per cent in West Germany (Soete, Turner and Patel, 1983, quoted in Stoneman, 1987).

The rates of return implicit in most of the results, for both the private investor and society as a whole, appear to be quite high (in the range of 10 to 20 per cent). American evidence suggests the benefits of both R&D and patents are reflected in the stock market valuation of firms which perform R&D activities (Griliches, 1984). On average, R&D activities seem to be a good investment. One should be cautious about this conclusion. For instance, the estimates may not be a good guide to returns at the margin, the contribution of imported new technology may be underestimated, and the costs of diffusion of new techniques ignored. However, the evidence is sufficient to warrant investigation of trends in R&D activities.

Studies of international competitiveness point in the same direction.[4] Research by one of the authors suggested that, in 1983 values, a £0.3 billion increase in UK R&D spending (about five per cent more than the actual figure) would improve the balance of payments and GDP by £0.4 billion (Buxton, Mayes and Murfin, 1991). The relationship is complex, and the study stressed that it is not simply R&D spending which counts, but investment in R&D relative to that undertaken by competitors. Nevertheless, the evidence requires one to ask if the UK does enough R&D.

Trends in R&D activity

In 1989, the estimated total amount spent on R&D in the UK was £11.5 billion (this compares with nearly £100 billion spent on investment in fixed capital).[5] GDP in that year was about £510 billion, so 2.2 per cent of this was allocated to R&D. Compared with the previous 20 years, this fraction has remained reasonably stable. Table 2.2 shows where this research was carried out and how it was funded. Private industry performs two thirds of research, but funds only half of it, the rest coming mainly from government. The government spends more on R&D carried out in private industry and other places (eg universities) than it does on R&D carried out within government.

Figure 2.1 puts the UK position into the international context by comparing the ratio of R&D[6] to GDP with those of our main competitors, the other 'Group of Six' countries. It shows that they have tended to raise their R&D ratios while the UK has not, and has fallen from second to fifth in the R&D league table.

Table 2.2 UK R&D in 1989

	Performed by (%)	Funded by (%)
Business	66	50
Government	14	36
Other	20	13

Source: CSO

In the UK, the business sector finances a relatively low proportion of the R&D which it actually carries out, as Table 2.3 below indicates.[7] This should give cause for concern if the willingness of industry to finance its own R&D is taken as an indicator of its confidence in the benefits of R&D. However, the share has increased significantly in the 1980s. Non-manufacturing business R&D is substantially higher as a percentage of the total in the UK than in the rest of the Group of Six. Since utilities and construction employ little R&D, most of the resources are taken up by the business services/banking sector.

Table 2.3 Industry funded business R&D (1987), as a percentage of:

	Germany	France	Italy	UK	Japan	US
Total business R&D	86.5	85.2	71.7	68.2	98.0	66.8
Business output	2.2	1.5	0.6	1.5	2.1	1.6

Source: OECD *Main Science and Technology Indicators*

The UK tends to have a higher proportion of business R&D in sectors such as drugs, aerospace, electronics and computers, at the expense of 'other' manufacturing such as shipping, metals, ceramics, textiles, plastics, food and drink. A common way of comparing business R&D across countries is to relate it to value added. Those sectors that have a significant share of total business R&D also tend to devote a higher proportion of value added to R&D. Only Italy does worse than Britain here, and it still has comparative strengths in sectors with a traditionally low R&D intensity (see Archibugi, 1986). Some industries, such as pharmaceuticals and electrical equipment, have relatively high R&D spending in most countries; others, like textiles, food, drink and tobacco tend to devote little to R&D anywhere. The UK is actually ahead of the field in some high R&D areas, such as drugs, but the research effort in some US and Japanese industries is very much

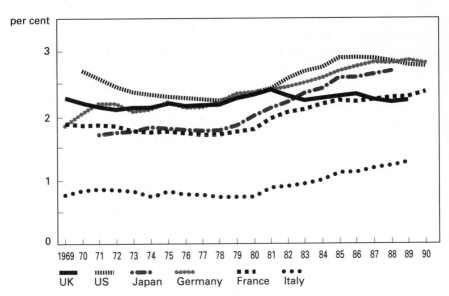

Figure 2.1 Total R&D as a fraction of GDP
Source: OECD *Main Science and Technology Indicators*

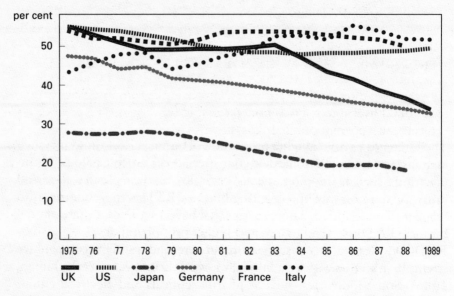

Figure 2.2 Fraction of total R&D financed by Government
Source: OECD

higher (eg instruments). Unfortunately, countries differ in the industrial breakdown which they use when collecting statistics.

Indicators of R&D expenditure seem to suggest a position of relative weakness for the UK. One of the factors that has contributed to the relative reduction in R&D expenditure in the UK has been the decline in the government contribution to both business and total expenditure on R&D, as shown by Figure 2.2. The fall in government R&D as a fraction of GDP comes about partly because public spending has been reduced relative to GDP, but also because government finance for R&D has taken a rapidly falling share of public spending since 1981. Does this matter? The economist usually seeks to justify government intervention by invoking market failures. There are many reasons why a market economy may not achieve an optimal allocation of resources. Amongst these are the presence of monopoly power, uncertainty, and inappropriability. All three of these can apply in the case of innovation. Invention of a new product by a company gives it market power, the extent of which depends on how much it differs from existing products. Uncertainty about the outcome of expensive research programmes and the activities of rival companies may lead to underinvestment in research by risk averse firms or overinvestment where oligopolistic behaviour is possible (eg patent races). Inappropriability of ideas reduces

38

the incentive for firms to try to come up with new ones. Yet some methods of restoring appropriability can reduce the rate at which innovations are disseminated through the economy; new knowledge is a form of public good, so secrecy and refusal to licence other users can reduce welfare. In principle, well-informed and motivated government action can help to rectify the sort of failures listed above, so market failure provides a pretext for government intervention. However, improving economic efficiency is not the only government goal; non-economic objectives, like defence and culture, also prompt public R&D activity.

Table 2.4 provides more comparative evidence about government funding for R&D. In the UK, it is significantly higher than in Japan, where two per cent of national resources is put into R&D by industry. It is noticeable that a large share of UK R&D funded by government is devoted to defence, especially compared with Japan, West Germany and Italy. The Japanese example demonstrates that high government spending is not necessary for good R&D performance, but leaves begging the question of why other funds are more forthcoming there.

Table 2.4: R&D expenditure relative to GDP (%), 1988

	Government funded R&D:		
	Total	Defence	Civil
UK	0.96	0.42	0.54
France	1.37	0.51	0.86
Germany	1.05	0.13	0.92
Italy	0.80	0.08	0.72
Japan	0.47	0.02	0.45
US	1.23	0.83	0.40

Source: OECD *Main Science and Technology Indicators*

So far, R&D spending has only been compared with measures of value added. It is also possible to look at real spending on R&D if one is satisfied with using the GDP price deflator to convert the nominal data. Total R&D was about 50 per cent higher in real terms in 1989 than in 1969. This is made to look paltry by international comparisons of total, business and non-business R&D. Japan is the outstanding leader in all three measures, with business R&D about five times higher. The UK performs the worst in the three indicators over the period.

The yearly flow of R&D output adds to the existing stock of knowledge and techniques which generate added value. The concept of a stock of knowl-

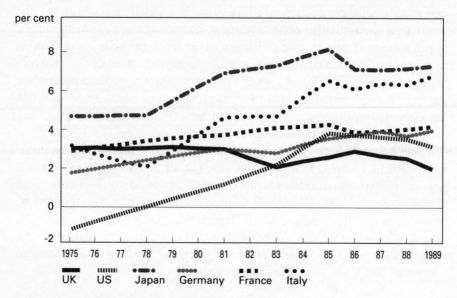

per cent

| | | | | | | | | | | | | | | |
|1975|76|77|78|79|80|81|82|83|84|85|86|87|88|1989|

■■■ UK　　▮▮▮ US　　•▬• Japan　　◆◆◆ Germany　　■ ■ ■ France　　•• • Italy

Figure 2.3 G6 growth of total R&D 'capital stock'
(based on R&D growth from 1969–75)
Source: NEDO, OECD *Main Science and Technology Indicators*

edge or of R&D 'capital stock' is more useful than the incremental flow if one is seeking to explain productivity levels. The practical difficulties include obtaining a consistent long run series of constant price R&D figures and choosing an appropriate depreciation rate[8]. Using a depreciation rate of 10 per cent, the stock of R&D capital in 1989 in the UK was £74 billion (1985 prices). This compares with an estimated stock of net fixed capital excluding dwellings of about £730 billion. The equivalent real numbers in 1975 were £50.6 billion and £614 billion; the stock of R&D capital has grown faster than the stock of fixed capital. However, the R&D capital stocks of other countries have grown more rapidly, as Figure 2.3 demonstrates.

Another way of looking at R&D effort is to consider the manpower devoted to it. Figure 2.4 shows UK R&D employment and its distribution in the 1980s. Numbers have, if anything, fallen whereas in Italy, West Germany, France and Japan, annual growth has been 2.9 per cent, 3.3 per cent, 1.9 per cent and 4.7 per cent respectively. Taken as ratios of the labour force, the UK figures for total R&D personnel, business R&D personnel and the numbers of research scientists and engineers are well below the G6 average. Figures 2.5 and 2.6 illustrate some international comparisons.

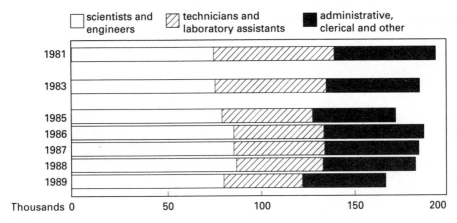

Figure 2.4 R&D employment in the UK
Source: CSO

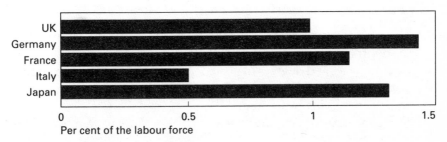

Figure 2.5 Total R&D personnel, 1987
Source: OECD *Main Science and Technology Indicators*

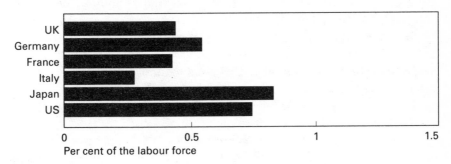

Figure 2.6 Research scientists and engineers, 1987
Source: OECD *Main Science and Technology Indicators*

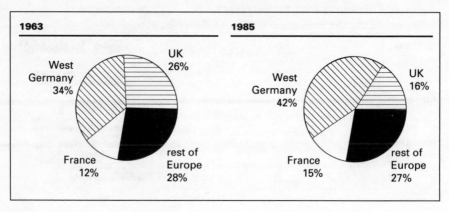

Figure 2.7 US patents taken by west European companies
Source: SPRU Database

The number of patents is frequently used as a proxy for the output of R&D activities. However, several factors concerning patents affect comparisons:

- The ratio of patents applied for to patents granted varies from country to country.
- Patenting fees and degrees of protection vary from country to country.
- There are some significant lags between the time a patent is applied for and when it is finally granted.
- There are variations amongst technical fields, due to differences in protective measures.

Because of these factors, it is preferable not to use patenting data on their own for comparisons, but to compare external patents, or better, patents taken out in the US classified by country of origin. Figure 2.7 shows the share of West European patenting in the US.

The UK's failure to keep up with its major competitors is also shown by trends in per capita patenting. This is illustrated in Table 2.5 above. The US has been excluded because its firms have a naturally higher propensity to patent in their own country. The reduction in UK per capita patenting in the US since the period 1963–8 contrasts dramatically with figures for Japan, where the increase has been more than 600 per cent.

The UK record in producing technology for sale compares well with the rest of the Group of Six. Figures for the technological balance of payments (ie, money balances for the use of patents, licences, trademarks, designs, inventions, know-how and closely associated technical services) produced by the OECD are shown in Figure 2.8. Until very recently, the UK was a

Table 2.5 Trends in per capita patenting in the US by major OECD countries (Patents per million population)

	1963–8	1980–5
Japan	10.4	79.0
France	26.6	38.8
West Germany	55.3	97.0
Italy	8.1	14.0
UK	44.4	40.5
Western Europe[1]	36.7	51.1

[1] Western Europe is defined as France, West Germany,.Italy, UK, Netherlands, Sweden, Switzerland, Belgium, Denmark and Ireland. Source: Pavitt & Patel, 1988.

net exporter of technology. This compares starkly with Japan and West Germany, which over the entire period have experienced deficits. This may suggest that the view that UK industry is not keen to use processes and products developed abroad may be correct. Figure 2.8 may also reinforce arguments that the UK has generally been good at invention but not at exploitation of technological knowledge. Case studies also suggest that UK firms fail to take up technology as fast as their competitors.

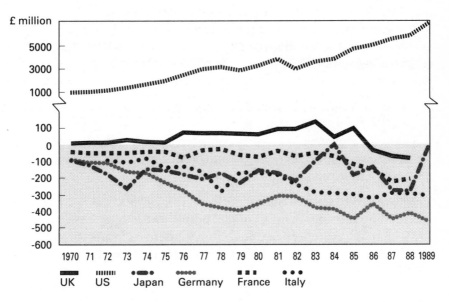

Figure 2.8 Technological balance of payments
Source: CSO, OECD *Main Science and Technology Indicators*

Effectiveness of R&D

Skills

What contribution do workforce skills make to innovative activity in the UK? This question, a theme of a previous NEDO seminar (see Stevens and Mackay, 1991), deserves more attention than can be given to it here. This section simply seeks to rehearse the argument that a more educated and skilled labour force would facilitate innovation, as well as adding to the stock of human capital.

Having a better trained, more educated workforce makes it easier to introduce new technology successfully and to develop techniques by drawing upon workers' informal knowledge and experience. The size of the seedbed for major new ideas is increased. The evidence for these propositions is fragmentary but persuasive. A study for the National Economic Development Council (NEDC/MSC, 1984) compared the effectiveness of vocational education and training systems in the US, Japan and West Germany with the UK's, and recommended that to remain competitive, British companies must develop amongst their employees the ability and habit of learning, plus an ability to behave in a self-reliant way. These abilities are necessary to cope with a wide variety of changes, in competitive conditions as well as in technological possibilities, and the strategy of product and process innovation will be inhibited without them.

The importance of having a skilled labour force has also been stressed in analysing industry productivity differences across countries and different countries' education and training achievements. It has been suggested that Germany's superior range of craft level skills has helped German firms to:

- produce more differentiated product ranges (and by implication, more product innovation)
- introduce information — processing technology and integrated microprocessor controlled machinery into production earlier (diffusion of process innovations).

The work of the National Institute of Economic and Social Research on skills and training provides many examples of this sort.[9]

Much of the evidence referred to above is derived from case studies and the observation of best practice. In the United States, Bartel and Lichtenberg (1987, 1991) have examined some aspects of the issue by econometric analysis of industry costs and employee wages. Their data corroborated three hypotheses:

1) The successful application of new technology requires significant learning on the part of employees.
2) Highly educated employees enjoy a comparative advantage in on-the-job learning.
3) Innovative firms pay higher wages to employees of a given age, educational attainment and sex, in order to satisfy their increased requirement that workers learn following the introduction of new technology.

Bartel and Lichtenberg write:

> Government subsidies and other policies which tend to encourage the acquisition of education and increase the relative supply of highly-educated workers will be expected to accelerate the rate of diffusion of new industrial technologies by lowering the cost of adjustment and implementation.

Better educated individuals tend to adopt innovations sooner. In their study of wage structures and labour turnover in the United States and Japan, Mincer and Higuchi (1988) concluded that the low labour turnover and the importance attached to on-the-job training in Japan is a response to actual and anticipated rapid technological change. The relationships of productivity, wages and separation rates with job tenure in the two countries are consistent with this hypothesis, and the authors argue:

> Introduction of new technologies requires complementary, growing, and changing worker skills on the job, as well as a strong basic educational system which promotes continued learning skills.

Given the importance of acquiring a more educated and skilled workforce, the UK has some cause for concern. Evidence is brought together in NEDC (1991) which shows that, although the level of qualifications being achieved by successive age groups has been improving, Britain suffers in international comparisons. West Germany brings more than twice the proportion of young people to the standard of A-levels or their vocational equivalent (nearly 90 per cent compared to about 40 per cent). At graduate level, particularly in producing scientists and engineers, the UK is competitive, but at intermediate level, it is at a considerable disadvantage. This is illustrated in Table 2.6.

Table 2.6 Vocational qualifications of the workforce, 1985–89

Selected countries (%)	UK	Netherland	West Germany	France
University degrees and higher voc. diploma	17	18	18	14
Intermediate vocational qualifications	20	44	56	33
No vocational qualifications	63	38	26	53
Total	**100**	**100**	**100**	**100**

Source: NIESR (data provisional)

In 1989–90, 53 per cent of 16 year olds stayed on in full-time education in Britain. This is a low figure in comparison with other major economies, including West Germany(69 per cent), France (78 per cent), the US (94 per cent) and Japan (92 per cent).

Trade unions

There has been a considerable debate amongst economists recently about the role of trade unions in promoting or hindering productivity growth. Some American evidence suggested that unionised firms are more productive and thus are able to pay a union wage premium (see Freeman and Medoff, 1984). The argument, which pits the advantages of a collective voice against the disadvantages of restrictive practices and skewed relative factor prices, still rages (for instance, Addison and Hirsch, 1989). One of the ways in which trade unions can affect productivity is by regulating the introduction of new technology; the British Workplace Industrial Relations Survey of 1980 showed that 65 per cent of unionised establishments had bargaining over major change in production methods (Daniel and Milward, 1983). Some forms of technical change can reduce employment, at least in the short run.[10] If unions try to maintain previous employment levels, they can render innovations unprofitable and inhibit their adoption. The extent to which this happens is an empirical issue. Daniel (1987) found a *positive* association between union presence and technology change. Nickell, Wadhwani, and Wall (1989), using company-level data, found that union firms experienced faster total factor productivity growth than did their non-union counterparts during 1980–84. This could have been due to the weakening of trade unions' ability to influence the introduction of new technologies, although union firms did not appear to suffer a slower growth of total factor productivity in the late 1970s. Metcalf (1988) places considerable weight on changes in industrial relations in the 1980s as an explanation of improved productivity growth, emphasising 'the consequence of management being in the saddle coupled with yielding unions'.

The impact of collective bargaining on innovation should be judged on a case-by-case basis. The relationship runs both ways, and there is a voluminous literature about the impact of technological change on industrial relations and the extent to which the desire to regulate labour provides an incentive to innovate. The debate extends to whether technical change is 'skilling' or 'deskilling'.[11]

Finance for innovation

Finance for R&D has to be raised in the wider market for finance, which is governed by a complex institutional and legal framework; companies and individuals compete for debt and equity funds to serve different purposes. Is the raising of finance for research and development inherently different from funding other investment projects? R&D projects are typically characterised by higher risk and lengthy time periods before returns are expected. These factors raise the required rates of return for funding R&D projects. If private required rates of return are so high that the R&D is not undertaken, this may indicate a market failure. Investors with no expertise in a project area suffer anxiety because they cannot assess the likelihood of success. The firm has more information at its disposal; this often leads to R&D being funded entirely from within the company using retained earnings. This has further consequences. To diversify the risk within the company, a wide portfolio of R&D projects often has to be undertaken, which in turn raises the total cost of undertaking R&D. The fungibility of external finance makes the linking of the fundraising process to the expected returns of a particular project hard to establish. It may be easier to raise new equity for acquisition purposes than for internal research; nevertheless, partitioning of funds for particular purposes is not common practice. It may make more sense to think of the cost of finance as being calculable only in relation to a particular company rather than according to the project or sector for which the funds are intended.

The stock market does, however, have some influence on how much R&D is undertaken, through its assessments of the extent to which R&D is intrinsic to success in a particular sector. It tends to favour R&D investment in certain sectors, such as pharmaceuticals, at the expense of those in which the need for R&D is not recognised. These perceptions have consequences, in that there will be greater pressure on company performance at the expense of R&D projects, the more unfavourable the stock market rates the worth of R&D in that sector or company. The market may of course turn out to be vindicated, but its judgement plays a part in that vindication process by making R&D more difficult and expensive.

The venture capital market has developed over the 1980s in the US and UK to provide a vehicle through which long term high risk projects may be financed, particularly in small companies. The ease with which this market operates for high risk projects is increased when larger companies enter the field alongside the venture capital companies; this helps to establish the credibility of the small company and provides the specialist expertise necessary to judge particular projects. Venture capital financing is also eased by the ability of such small companies to make initial public offerings at a relatively early stage in their life cycle, well before the fruits of the research have begun to be marketable, thus offering the venture capital funds an earlier exit route. These features are present in the US to a much greater extent than in the UK.

Some questions and answers

It is now widely accepted that innovation is important to the growth of productivity and hence higher living standards. There is an evident link between the general level of innovative activity and the level of R&D expenditure or patents applied for. The UK's recent record raises questions about its ability both to generate innovations and to make full use of their potential. However, statistical associations do not necessarily tell us anything about cause and effect. If the figures quoted in earlier sections do reflect a poorer climate for innovation in the UK, the natural response is to seek for plausible explanations.

Appropriability and market failure

Innovation concerns the use of new information and knowledge; economists have traditionally focused on the difficulties of trading in information, both to explain why markets may 'fail' and to consider the pros and cons of government policy. The main problem, according to this approach, is that it will often be costly to control the availability of valuable information and that people will therefore 'free ride' on the innovative efforts of others. The social return from innovation will be greater than the private return, and less innovation will occur than is ideally desirable. Where innovation requires financial backing from an outside source, further problems are encountered. No-one will supply finance for undisclosed purposes, but disclosure involves risking exposure to competitors. The very process of conveying the relevant information to sources of finance and convincing them of the viability of an innovation may also be costly. The greater these costs, the more uncertain the outcome; the less secure the relevant information, the more innovation will be discouraged. Attempts to provide property rights and hence incentives to innovation via the patent system introduce further problems. Innovators may 'race' each other for patent rights, rather as mineral prospectors will invest in 'confirming' a natural resource deposit far in advance of exploitation. There is at least the possibility, therefore, of over-investment in innovation in some circumstances. These traditional economic considerations give rise to some obvious questions.

- Do weak property rights represent a serious discouragement to innovation in the UK?
- Does the problem of appropriability influence some forms of innovation more than others — perhaps, paradoxically, the forms in which the UK has historically had an advantage?

It is usual to distinguish between pure science, invention and development. Results in the purely scientific field are not patentable but may eventually have great practical and commercial influence. It is for this reason that government involvement in pure science can be defended, although its ideal extent seems incapable of rational calculation, especially as the benefits may spill over to other countries. At the other end of the spectrum, some forms of development to product, process or organisation may be the outcome of conditions so specific to a particular firm that the danger of imitation is considered unimportant or irrelevant.

- If the 'market failure' notion is important to understanding innovation, why should the UK suffer more than other countries from this problem?

At least two responses to this question are possible. We can look for failures in government policy in the UK and argue that foreign states have developed better instruments for coping with innovation — better patent systems, different tax systems, more sophisticated appraisal systems, more or less generous funding policies, more or less vigorous competition policies and so forth. Alternatively we can conclude that the relative failure is an institutional one and only indirectly related to failures in government. In this view, business institutions in the UK have not succeeded in adapting to the problems of handling change as successfully as their foreign counterparts.

Stimulating innovation in industry

Innovation and the structure of the firm

The generation, control, and use of information play a central role in the modern view of the firm. For example, multinational firms are observed to be highly innovative, to employ more scientific staff than other firms, to spend more on R&D, and to advertise more. The ability to make use of internally generated information within the firm, and thus to increase the returns to innovation without having to resort to external markets with their associated hazards, has been considered an important force leading to this form of enterprise.

Similar arguments can be used in favour of close associations between buyers and suppliers if innovation is to be successful. The innovation process requires good communications between upstream and downstream operations. It may sometimes involve a supplier investing in special capital to facilitate a buyer's plans. Without great trust between buyer and supplier, the supplier may be unwilling to take part, fearing the ultimate failure of the scheme, or be unable to negotiate a contract giving sufficient assurances on the distribution of any profit (Teece, 1988). In 1964, Kindleberger suggested that the German and Japanese bettering of the UK could be linked to 'the organisation of British industry into separate firms dealing with each other at arms' length' (p146) and he provided many historical examples of the problems of securing innovation in the iron and steel and textile industries around the turn of the twentieth century.

The close associations that exist between buyers and suppliers in Japan, although short of full vertical integration, facilitate the country's capacity to innovate. Where innovation requires restructuring before it can be implemented, the process will be slowed down and possibly inhibited altogether.

The questions arise as to how far it has been necessary to adopt different business structures recently in the UK so as to secure the benefits of innovation, and whether this has been a significant factor in restricting progress.

Innovation and labour contracts

Innovation requires a flexible labour force; this is not simply a matter of formal skills and training. It also concerns the accumulation of non-patentable 'know-how' in the workforce — information which is valuable to the firm although not immediately transferable to other companies. Because it is not easily pirated and because it facilitates innovation, companies might be expected to encourage this form of expertise. Such encouragement may be given by raising wages over time in line with growing productivity. However, this incentive relies on firms and employees expecting their association to continue for a long time. If the employee expects to get no long run reward for flexibility and alertness, there will be no incentive to develop skills which have a value mainly to a specific firm.

The importance of these labour issues to effective innovation is illustrated by the case of General Motor's high technology Hamtramck factory.[12] This attempted to outdo the Japanese in automated methods with the use of robots and other advanced techniques. It proved to be far less reliable than the lower technology Japanese factories which relied more heavily on the skills of the workforce. Although the Japanese use more robots than other countries, they make use of features such as record and playback programming, by which the robot reproduces the actions of an operator; individual skills are used to facilitate smooth rather than highly disruptive innovation.

To what extent do labour relations in the UK still inhibit the development of positive attitudes towards innovation?

Finance and innovation

It is often claimed that financial markets underestimate the importance of innovation or R&D expenditure to future profitability. There is clearly a communications problem to overcome, but investors would be foolish to overlook the problems of these investments. Judgements are required on matters such as the associated risk, the length of time before commercially viable results can be expected, and the rate of depreciation of their economic value. These judgements will depend upon complex issues such as the quality of management and other personnel, the activities of other competing companies, the likely strength of patent protection and so forth. It would not be too surprising if in these circumstances capital markets adopted crude rules of thumb to assess companies' prospects. Nevertheless, the constraint on R&D expenditure resulting from a falling share price is more pronounced in the UK than elsewhere. How significant is this as an explanation of the UK's R&D performance?

Innovation and the size of firms

The debate about the role of small versus large firms in the process of innovation has a long history. Joseph Schumpeter saw the large firm 'ousting the entrepreneur' and institutionalising economic progress while Galbraith, in a famous quote, argued that the role of the small firm was a fiction.

> Technical development has long since become the preserve of the scientist and the engineer. Most of the cheap and simple

inventions have, to put it bluntly, been made. Not only is development sophisticated and costly but it must be on a sufficient scale so that successes and failures will in some measure average out... Because development is costly, it follows that it can be carried on only by a firm that has the resources associated with considerable size. (Galbraith, 1952)

John Jewkes, David Sawers and Richard Stillerman, in a survey of the major inventions of the twentieth century, countered this view by arguing that the source of most inventions could be traced back to particular individuals and small firms, even if subsequent development was taken over by a larger corporation (1969). Clearly, the most appropriate organisation for purposes of invention may be different from that for the conduct of pure science or for the perfection or further development and refinement of established techniques. On the other hand, the interdependence of these activities makes it difficult to state that entirely different and independent institutions for each type of activity would be appropriate. The possibility that vertically integrated structures may favour innovation has already been mentioned, and this is not likely to favour small scale.

These issues raise the general question of whether the size distribution of firms in the UK has permitted innovation, and whether the role of small scale enterprise in innovation has been undervalued.

Government funding of R&D

The positive statistical association between R&D spending and productivity per capita revealed in international comparisons might suggest that government action to increase R&D (if necessary by funding it directly) would improve the UK performance. However, the same international comparisons suggest that the government share is not the important factor. As pointed out in Table 2.4, the Japanese government contribution is low by international standards. Critics have suggested that government spending has been focused too heavily on defence and that, more generally, government involvement leads to a change of attitude by executives in companies. Lobbying for funds and favoured projects, or predicting government attitudes and political exigencies, become as important to company profitability as attention to product markets and the efficient conduct of R&D.

Effective defence will continue to require R&D, however, and problems of appropriability suggest a continuing major role for government at the pure science end of the research spectrum. Two questions therefore arise:

- Have government resources been effectively allocated towards R&D over recent years?
- Do better procedures for allocating these resources exist?

The use of innovations from overseas

As economic development occurs in other countries, more R&D will take place overseas. This implies that, as time advances, more potentially useful ideas will originate overseas than in the UK. Being attuned to these influences may be at least as important to successful innovation as developing new ideas from scratch. Using foreign ideas requires investment in R&D to tailor them to local conditions or adapt them to different purposes, but the Japanese have shown that the return to this type of innovation can be substantial.

Does Figure 2.8 suggest that the UK pays too little attention to developments in foreign technology? If so, what can be done to increase the take-up of opportunities originating overseas? Government encouragement of foreign multinational enterprise does not merely encourage employment but, in the long run, could be regarded as an important component of innovation policy. The recent history of the motor car industry in the UK indicates the enormous innovatory impact of foreign firms.

The questions and issues raised in this section are intended to be suggestive rather than exhaustive. There are many other possible influences on innovation, including market structure and the legal background of patent and copyright protection. However, persuasive explanations of the UK's record on innovation are unlikely to emphasise a single major factor but may incorporate a range of related influences.

Notes

1 Examples include Denison (1967), Matthews, Feinstein and Odling-Smee (1982) and Maddison (1987).
2 The 14 components are: labour quantity, labour quality, labour hoarding, residual capital quantity, non-residential capital quantity, capital quality, capacity use effect, catch up effect, structural effect, foreign trade effect, economies of scale, energy effect, natural resource effect, costs of regulation and crime.
3 Griliches (1984) contains a good selection of these studies.
4 Greenhalgh et all (1991) provide a useful survey. They conclude 'the evidence from both the literature review and the new empirical work is that both product quality and price competitiveness contribute to trade balance improvement and that continuous innovation in both products and processes are vital to success'.

5 In the UK, R&D expenditure data are collected by surveying samples of firms and institutions annually (triennially before 1985). International use of the so called Frascati manual (OECD 1981) has helped make the results of surveys in different countries reasonably comparable. R&D data may under-estimate true expenditure levels as some areas of design (especially in small firms), product in engineering and software development may be left out. Pavitt and Patel (1988) discuss this issue.

6 Gross expenditure on R&D in current prices.

7 The Frascati manual defines the business sector as: all firms, organisations and institutions whose primary activity is the production of goods or services for sale to the general public at a price intended approximately to cover at least the cost of production; and the private non-profit institutes mainly serving them. This is not coterminous with the private sector or production industries.

8 The method adopted here is that used by Griliches (1980) and Suzuki (1985) among others. This involves computing the stock in the initial year, 1975, by assuming that up to that point R&D expenditure had increased by the average rate of growth it showed previously [over 1969–75] and then depreciating it at a fixed rate. R&D capital for any further year, RDC_t, can then be calculated in the normal way by depreciating stock and adding the new expenditure, RD_t.

$$RDC_t = (1 - d) RDC_{t-1} + RD_t$$

where d is the rate of depreciation.

The crucial element here is the choice of d, the depreciation rate. There is no agreed estimate for the rate available from existing sources and the appropriate rate is likely to vary substantially both by industry and according to the type of innovation. The 'capital' involved is to a large extent human knowledge and experience. It is usually argued that the depreciation rate is low, and that the increase in knowledge remains useful for long periods. Griliches (1984) actually assumes a zero rate, but the compromise adopted here is 10 per cent. Clearly the lower is the rate, the greater is the error should the assumption be wrong. The actual values are therefore likely to have variances which might not be small. But the trends they show are unlikely to be systematically biased.

9 See, among others, Steedman and Wagner (1987 and 1989) and Steedman, Mason and Wagner (1991).

10 Sinclair (1982) and Stoneman (1983) examine the circumstances in which this can happen.

11 Braverman (1974), Piore and Sabel (1984) and Freeman and Soete (1987) provide an introduction to the large literature on the subject.

12 A report on this case appears in The Economist, August 10, 1991, pp. 62–63.

Chapter bibliography

Addison, J T and Hirsch, B T (1989) 'Union effects of productivity profits and growth: has the long run arrived?' *Journal of Labor Economics*, vol 7, no 1, January, pp77–105

Archibugi F (1986) 'Sectoral patterns of industrial innovation in Italy: an analysis of Italian patenting in the USA', Technical Report, Rome, CNR

Arrow, K (1962) 'Economic welfare and the allocation of resources for inventions', in Nelson, R R (ed) (1963) *The rate and direction of inventive activity*, Princeton, Princeton University Press

Bartel, Ann P and Lichtenberg, Frank R (1987) 'The comparative advantage of educated workers in implementing new technology', *Review of Economics and Statistics*, vol 69, no 1, February, pp1–11

Bartel, Ann P and Lichtenberg, Frank R (1991) 'The age of technology and its impact on employee wages', *Economics of Innovation and New Technology*, vol 1, no 3, pp215–232

Braverman, H (1974) *Labor and monopoly capital*, New York, Monthly Review Press

Buxton, A, Mayes, D and Murfin, A (1991) 'UK trade performance and R&D', *Economics of Innovation and New Technology*, vol 1, pp243–55

Daniel, W and Millward, N (1983) *Workplace industrial relations in Britain*, London, Heinemann

Daniel, W (1987) *Workplace industrial relations and technical change*, London, Frances Pinter for the Policy Studies Institute

Denison, E F (1967) *Why growth rates differ*, Washington DC, Brookings Institution

Freeman, R and Medoff, D (1984) *What do unions do?* New York, Basic Books

Freeman, C and Soete, L (1987) *Technical change and full employment*, Oxford, Basil Blackwell

Galbraith, J K (1952) *American capitalism*, Boston, Houghton Higgins

Greenhalgh, C A, Suer, B, Taylor, P and Wilson, R A (1991) 'Trade performance and innovatory activity: a review', mimeo, Institute of Employment Research, University of Warwick, January

Griliches, Z (1980) 'R&D and the productivity slowdown', *American Economic Review*, vol 70, no 2, February, pp343–48

Griliches, Z (ed) (1984) *R&D patents and productivity*, Chicago, University of Chicago Press for NBER

Hay, D A and Morris, D J (1991) *Industrial economics and organisation: theory and evidence*, 2nd edn, Oxford, Oxford University Press

Jewkes, J, Sawers, D and Stillerman, R (1969) *The source of invention*, 2nd edn, London, Macmillan

Kindleberger, C P (1964) *Economic growth in France and Britain 1851–1950*, Cambridge, Mass., Harvard University Press

Maddison, A (1987) 'Growth and slowdown in advanced capitalist economies', *Journal of Economic Literature*, vol 25, no 2, June, pp649–698

Matthews, R C O, Feinstein, C H and Odling-Smee, J C (1982) *British economic growth, 1856–1973*, Oxford, Clarendon Press

Metcalf, D (1988) 'Water notes dry up', Discussion paper no 314, Centre for Labour Economics, London School of Economics, July

Mincer, J and Higuchi, Y (1988) 'Wage structure and labour turnover in the United States and Japan', *Journal of the Japanese and International Economies*, vol 2, no 2, pp97–133

NEDC/MSC (1984) *Competence and competition: training and education in the Federal Republic of Germany, the United States and Japan*, London, National Economic Development Council/Manpower Services Commission

Nickell, S, Wadhwani, S and Wall, M (1989) 'Unions and productivity growth in Britain, 1974–86: evidence from UK company accounts data', Centre for Labour Economics discussion paper no 353, London School of Economics, August

OECD (1981) *The measurement of scientific and technical activities (the Frascati manual)*, Paris, OECD

OECD (various years) *OECD Main Science and Technology Indicators*, Paris, Organisation for Economic Cooperation and Development

Pavitt, K and Patel, P (1988) 'The international distribution and determinants of technological activities', *Oxford Review of Economic Policy*, vol 4, no 4, Winter pp35–55

Piore, M and Sabel, C (1984) *The second industrial divide*, New York, Basic Books

Sinclair, P J N (1981) 'When will technical progress destroy jobs?' *Oxford Economic Papers*, vol 33, no 1, March, pp1–18

Soete, L, Turner, R and Patel, P (1983) 'R&D, international technological diffusion and productivity growth', Mimeo, SPRU, University of Sussex, August

Solow, R M (1957) 'Technical change and the aggregate production function', *Review of Economics and Statistics*, vol 39, no 3, pp312–320

Steedman, H and Wagner, K (1987) 'A second look at productivity, machinery and skills in Britain and Germany', *National Institute Economic Review*, no 122, November, pp84–96

Steedman, H and Wagner, K (1989) 'Productivity, machinery and skills: clothing manufacture in Britain and Germany', *National Institute Economic Review*, no 128, May, pp40–57

Steedman, H, Mason, G and Wagner, K (1991) 'Intermediate skills in the workplace: deployment, standards and supply in Britain, France and Germany', *National Institute Economic Review*, no 136, May, pp60–76

Stevens, J and Mackay, R (1991) *Training and competitiveness*, London, Kogan Page for National Economic Development Office

Stoneman, P (1983) *The economic analysis of technological change*, Oxford, Clarendon Press

Stoneman, P (1987) *The economic analysis of technology policy*, Oxford, Clarendon Press

Suzuki, K (1985) 'Knowledge capital and the private rate of return on R&D in Japanese manufacturing industries', *International Journal of Industrial Organisation*, vol 3, no 3, pp293–305

Teece, David J (1988) 'Technical change and the nature of the firm', in Dosi *et al* (eds) *Technological change and economic theory*, London and New York, Pinter Publishers

3

Why Innovate?

Paul Stoneman

Introduction

As with many areas of academic enquiry the best questions are the obvious ones. 'Why innovate?' is one such obvious and basic question. The literature in economics has imputed many motives to economic actors that cause them to innovate (many in the best economic traditions can be simply summarised as to maximise profits), but this basic question is rarely itself addressed.

In answering this question, many fruitful avenues of enquiry open up. This paper not only tries to answer the question but also to draw out some implications from that answer. Although these implications are not new in terms of the discussion of economists, they are drawn from an approach to the issues that is somewhat different.

This paper is concerned with the implications that relate to the apparently poor technological performance of the UK economy and the appropriate policy response to this performance. It is thus useful to present some data on UK technological performance before proceeding too far. This is done in an appendix to this chapter (further detail can be found in Stoneman (1991)).

Given the data in the Appendix as background, a good place to start the analysis is with some definitions. The paper is restricted to a discussion of technological innovations. Technological innovations relate to new products, new production processes, new raw materials and new management methods (Schumpeter,1942). There are of course many innovations that occur everyday outside this list, but they are not the main interest of this paper. There are some problems even with this definition, for it is not clear what exactly is meant by new. For example, is a fifth generation computer to be defined as a new technology or is it no more than an improved fourth generation computer? This paper assumes that improvements are innovations but that some innovations are more innovative than others.

It is necessary to define exactly what is meant by 'innovate'. The term is commonly used to encompass several related but different concepts and it is useful not only to separate these concepts but also to talk about each.

First, innovation is sometimes used to refer to an action that has never been performed before. Thus one might think of innovation as relating to the first use anywhere of a new process of production, or the first introduction anywhere of a new product. This is labelled here as 'global innovation'.

Second, innovation is sometimes used to refer to the first time that an activity has been undertaken by the unit of analysis under observation. Thus a firm that installs a robot for the first time, even if other firms have already installed robots, under this definition is said to be an innovator. For this activity the term 'local innovation' is used. It is clear that the very first economic actor to undertake local innovation of a particular technology is the global innovator.

The term innovation is sometimes used to refer to the whole process of technological change, encompassing not only the first (local or global) use of a new technology but also the process whereby that technology spreads widely within and across economies. The reason for introducing this meaning of the term is that it is commonly observed that the process of innovation (local or global) will have little impact on the economy unless the innovation introduced is used or introduced widely. For example, if a firm is a global innovator, then unless it is particularly dominant in the economy its innovation will have little impact unless other firms copy (undertake local innovation). Similarly, if a firm undertakes a local innovation, that innovation will have little impact on the firm unless it is applied widely within the firm. The installation of one robot may be a local innovation, but one robot is unlikely to have much affect on a firm's production costs. Only if the firm's output is fully robotised will there be much impact. The process whereby a technology spreads after a global innovation is known as the process of diffusion. This process of diffusion will involve a series of local innovations as other firms do what the global innovator has already done (known as inter firm diffusion). It will also involve a process of intra firm diffusion as firms, after a local innovation, use a new technology more intensively. Limitations of space and time prevent detailed discussion of intra firm diffusion in this paper. However, by looking at local innovation, inter firm diffusion will also be covered.

The structure of the paper is as follows: first, the issue of why firms might wish to locally innovate is discussed. This then leads on to a discussion of firms' preferences over the timing and order of local innovation (which also covers global innovation) prior to a consideration of preferences relating to the amount of innovation. This is followed by a discussion of the consumer and government views of innovation. The general issue of differences between the private costs and benefits and the social costs and benefits of innovation is addressed next. This leads into a discussion of innovation policies. Some conclusions are presented in the final section.

The innovating firm

Local innovation

Why should a firm wish to do something new? The simple answer to this hides many complexities. The simple answer is that by doing something new the firm will generate a net benefit stream over time (for shorthand, we will consider these firm-level private benefits to be profits) that is preferred to the net benefit stream that would have arisen if the innovation had not been undertaken. To clarify issues, this statement does not say that innovation will increase profits today. In fact, innovation may reduce profits today but increase profits tomorrow. By talking of preferred benefit streams, the intertemporal nature of the costs and benefits of innovation are catered for. Innovation will involve costs. These costs might be R&D costs, or the costs of acquiring new types of capital goods and perhaps adaptation costs, or training costs. The innovation will only be undertaken if expected benefits at least offset these costs (with due account taken of discount factors). The expected benefits from innovation may arise from reductions in production or other costs or increases in revenues. Reductions in costs may take many forms. There may be reductions in labour inputs per unit of output, reductions in work in progress, reductions in raw material costs, reductions in set up costs or reduction in capital costs to mention just a few. These cost reductions, however, need not be immediate. A firm might, for example, invest in new technology to learn about it with a view to cutting costs in the distant future. The principle is clear, however, in that innovation may reduce production costs (generally defined) either now or at some time in the future.

The impact of innovation on revenues is a more involved topic. There are obvious ways in which innovation may affect revenues:

- by improving product quality and/or reliability, it may be possible to charge higher prices or achieve greater sales;
- improvements in delivery dates, product flexibility, or customising may have a similar effect;

- reductions in production costs may enable price to be reduced, market share to be increased and revenues to be increased.

All such effects are obvious and important.

Economics has concentrated more on the indirect routes by which innovation may affect revenues. There has been particular interest recently in the way in which innovation can be used to manipulate the competitive environment and in the impact that this will have on profitability. For example, an innovation might make the market less competitive and increase the firm's margins, leading to increased profitability.

A simple example will illustrate the point: a number of potential competitors for a firm may enter the market and compete if that firm does not innovate. If, by innovating, it deters the potential entrants from entering the market, then the market structure will be more concentrated as a result of the innovation than it would otherwise have been, and there will be a profit gain to the innovating firm. An alternative example of the same phenomenon could be where a firm installs a new technology that enables it to drive another firm out of the market, thereby gaining increased margins from the reduced competition. Again, a firm might also adopt new technology in order to prevent itself being driven out of the market.

A useful classification for this discussion is one proposed by Freeman (1965) that distinguishes between offensive, defensive and protective innovation. Offensive innovation is an innovation undertaken by a firm in order to attack the market of others or to generate or capitalise upon market expansion. Defensive innovation is innovation undertaken in reaction to other firms' offensive innovation. Protective innovation is innovation undertaken to forestall or pre-empt innovation by others that would harm the firm. Given that firms compete in markets, the incentives for a firm to innovate arise from a desire either to improve its market position, restore its market position or forestall an attack on (protect) its market position. Each type of action generates a net benefit flow superior to that in the no-innovation case.

The date of local innovation

Although innovation may be discussed as an almost atemporal event, every innovation has a time dimension. The decision the firm faces is not only whether to innovate but also when to innovate. In this paper, a (rather unrealistic) distinction between the date of innovation and the order of innovation is deliberately drawn, although it should be clear that the earlier innovation occurs, the higher up the order of innovation is the innovator likely to be.

Stimulating innovation in industry

In modelling the choice of a date of innovation, the economics literature moves towards an approach based on optimisation. Basically, the date of innovation is chosen as that date that yields the best outcome (as opposed to just a profitable outcome). Given that, for the moment, the question of the order of innovation has been set aside, it is here only necessary to address questions as to why early rather than late innovation may be preferred. There are a number of factors that may be taken in to account.

- It is often argued that the cost of undertaking an innovation increases the more quickly the innovation is undertaken. Thus the cost of research and development may increase if a result is required sooner rather than later. (This story has empirical support from Mansfield (1971) and is often backed up by reference to the race to put a man on the moon.)
- It is also often argued that if innovation involves the acquisition of new capital goods, then those capital goods may be expected to improve in quality over time or reduce in price over time.

Both of these effects would tend to delay the optimal date of innovation.

- On the other hand, if innovation is delayed then the firm will forego the extra profits that would have arisen from having the innovation in place. This factor would argue for early innovation.

The optimal date of innovation would be when the expected benefits arising from a further short delay exactly equal the expected costs of a further short delay.

The order of local innovation (global innovation)

The timing and the order of local innovation have been separated in this paper. This is purely an analytical device, but it is now time to look at the order. The question here is whether it is better for a firm to be one of the first local innovators or one of the last innovators. If one can determine the factors that influence the ordering of innovation, one will also gain insight into the determination of global innovation, for the first local innovator is the global innovator.

What would influence a firm in its choice of order of innovation?

- If a firm is undertaking R&D to develop a new technology, the patent system works so as to give the advantage to the first discoverer. The patent system produces a competition between firms that is like a race; the first to the post wins all. Thus one advantage of being first is that the first firm wins the prize of the value of a patent. One should note, however, that the empirical literature — eg the discussion in Stoneman (1987) suggests that the actual value of a patent in most cases is quite small and that the patent system does not generally result in a situation in which winner takes all.

- The firm that innovates first may be able to pre-empt the best resources. In a situation in which there are limited resources, the first innovator may well be able to acquire those resources earlier than others. Thus for example, a firm may take the best geographical locations if it is first to innovate, or it may employ the limited pool of skilled labour. There may also be other more general forms of pre-emption (see Tirole,1989).

- In many models, especially game theoretic models of firm behaviour, there are first mover advantages. In principle these may exist in models of the adoption of new technology and thus yield advantages to being high in the order of adoption. The argument is as follows: a low order adopter must take the earlier adoption by preceding adopters as a datum in making innovation decisions and, being low in the order, cannot influence the choice of order of earlier adopters. However, higher order adopters may be able to influence the choice of the order, or date, of adoption of lower order adopters to their own advantage (see Dixon,1988). This gives earlier adopters a first mover advantage. An example is satellite television in the UK. The early launch of Sky television had a considerable impact through programming and compatibility issues on the potential market for BSB and basically made the continued existence of BSB unfeasible.

These three factors encourage firms to be high in the innovation order. However, there may be counteracting forces.

- Low ranking innovators may well be able to learn from the experience of high ranking innovators. The pioneers may face considerable uncertainty and need to acquire knowledge when generating or introducing an innovation. Later innovators may well be able to learn from this experience. The example of the Comet and the Boeing 707 is often quoted here. The experience with the Comet led to increases in knowledge about metal fatigue; overcoming the problem delayed the launch of the modified Comet sufficiently long for the Boeing 707 to capture the larger part of the market—a classic case, referred to in this context by Mowery and Rosenberg (1989). Of course, low rankers can only learn if there are cross firm information flows, but these never seem to be completely zero.

- Low ranking adopters may also benefit from more indirect externalities. As an innovation spreads, it is quite likely that the industry producing the capital goods which embody that innovation will learn from experience and thus have lower costs. Thus innovations may well be available to low rankers more cheaply than high rankers.

- As an innovation spreads, there may be a more supportive infrastructure than was available to high ranking adopters. For example, the question of standards and compatibilities may well have been sorted out by the time low rankers adopt (see David,1991). Thus, for example, early users of personal computers had to make decisions about the software standards that would later dominate the market whereas late adopters found this problem solved. In addition, for late adopters there may well be more developed markets for the product or for the specialised inputs that support the new technology.

These factors might encourage low ranking against high ranking adoption. The optimal rank of adoption would depend on the trade off of these two competing effects.

These arguments apply to all firms and so there is a problem in determining which firm will adopt first and which last. Similarly, if the arguments in the previous section apply to all firms, then all firms will wish to innovate at the same time. However, if the above arguments are allied with the view that potential innovators differ from one another in various ways, then one can predict that firms will have different preferred innovation dates and also different preferred positions in the order of adoption. Examples of dimensions in which firms might differ include size, particularly relevant to technologies with scale effects, attitudes to risk, information, past experience and expertise.

The amount of local innovation

Should firms undertake a lot or a little local innovation? Any answer is implicitly preceded by a discussion of the costs and benefits of making a specific innovation, the speed at which this innovation should take place and the order a firm should choose in the adoption ranking for the innovation. There is another question: how many innovations should a firm introduce? One answer is that the firm should introduce any innovation that, with an optimal order and speed, would improve its benefit flow relative to what it would be without the innovation. This, however, is not really a complete answer to the question. It ignores:

- Any interaction between different innovations (it is clear that individual innovations may be complements or substitutes). Two innovations may reinforce the effect of each other, in which case there is an advantage to undertaking both jointly rather than either in isolation. By the same token some innovations may compete with each other. In general, a firm would not wish to introduce such competing technologies, but this might not always be the case. If one is talking of product innovations, there may be two new products that compete in some segment of product space. The firm might not wish to have both products on the market but if there was an expectation that the resultant market gap might be filled by a product from another firm then it might well launch both new products. There may also be disincentives for a firm to innovate if such activity hit an existing profitable product. Again, however, potential competition might lead to such an innovation.

- Any impact upon the innovator of the total investment in innovative activities. Is there any reason why the firm should be limited in the total amount of its innovative effort, even if all innovations are profitable? The point to realise here is that innovation represents an investment. Such investment will mean that the firm will experience reduced current period profits. These lower profits (although offset by the prospect of higher future period profits) will mean either lower dividends or higher net borrowing. How will this impact on the firm's total innovative spend?

  — This is in fact quite a complex area and the answers are involved with the operation of the financial markets. As the financing of innovation is discussed elsewhere only a few comments are made here, and these by no means exhaust the analysis of the issue.

  — First with regard to financial markets: as innovation and thus investment increases, the probability increases that the firm is spending more on innovation than its shareholders may wish. The shareholders' rate of time preference (preference for current as opposed to future dividends) may be less than the firm's. The increases in innovation spending may thus lead shareholders to sell and generate a fall in the share price. This makes the firm more liable to take-over and the introduction of a new management that would cut back the innovation programme.

  — Innovation is an inherently uncertain activity which could increase the riskiness of a firm's activities. Shareholders could also react to this. As the riskiness of the firm's activities increased, the cost of borrowing would also increase and this may limit the profitability of innovative activities (Nickell, 1978).

  — Second, there may be internal incentive mechanisms in the firm that have the same effect. For example, managers' pay incentive schemes that relate salary to current profits may well limit the totality of innovation spending that occurs in the firm. Managers' attitudes to risk may also have the same effect, as may the nature of the managerial labour market (see below).

— Finally, the total amount of innovative activity may be limited by other mechanisms within the firm. Change requires management. It may be argued that the amount of management required increases more than proportionally with the amount of innovation (Penrose, 1959). If so, then the management and co-ordination costs of change could well limit the amount of innovation. Similarly, if innovation causes labour redundancy, there may be limits to the rate at which redundancy can be made effective. Moreover, greater innovation and greater change may well require more recruitment of new skills and retraining, the speed of which may be limited.

Overall, therefore, there is an extra dimension over and above that seen from a single innovation perspective and that dimension has particular implications of its own for the extent of innovation in the firm. These issues are explored in the discussion of private and social benefits and incentives below.

The consumer viewpoint

So far, only the costs and benefits of innovation to the firm have been discussed. It is now time to consider a wider perspective, starting with the consumer: why should consumers welcome innovation? The answers to this are quite clear. Consumers benefit from innovation in a number of ways: to the extent that innovations lead to cheaper and/or better products they benefit; to the extent that new products enable the satisfaction of outstanding desires and needs they benefit; to the extent that innovations increase the extent of consumer choice they benefit. It should be immediately clear, however, that such benefits will arise from innovations made overseas as well as at home and thus consumers are not interested in the origin of the innovations.

This is not to say that there is no limit to the extent to which consumers welcome innovations. There may well be limits on this. This question is worth approaching from two angles. The first is that innovation may lead to a degree of dissatisfaction among consumers. Continued innovation may lead to obsolescence of existing products; the buyer of a new car that is quickly superseded may well be dissatisfied . Similarly, anyone with a collection of old 78s may find it hard to buy a suitable record player. Thus there may be costs to some from innovation. There may also be costs resulting from the wrong decisions made during innovation, as any purchaser of a Video 2000 VCR will know. This is an example of how innovation can create uncertainty for and may impose costs on the consumer. As new products appear on the market, there are extra search and information costs that consumers must bear as part of the costs of enjoying the benefits of those innovations.

The second way one might approach the question as to the desirable limit on innovation from a consumer point of view is to return again to the fact that innovation is an investment. In a reasonably static economy, investment can only be financed at the macro level by a reduction in current consumption. As investment in innovation increases, the surplus available for consumption decreases. Consumers may prefer goods today, without the expense of innovation, to better goods tomorrow. Finally, consumers may view innovation as undesirable if it leads to increased market power for some producers.

Overall, however, despite what has been said above, the net benefits that consumers enjoy from innovation (in terms of the benefits available with innovation compared to those on a counter factual path without innovation) largely have a zero cost for them.

Government viewpoint

Why should government want innovation? To answer this, it is necessary to think of government in three guises.

1) In the first guise, government is a producer (either of products distributed through markets or in other ways), and as a producer, although it might have different objectives (for example, service instead of profit), it will behave in a similar way and for similar reasons as do firms. For example, in trying to maximise the flow of health services for a given budget, the government will wish to innovate. It should be noticed, however, that as technology improves then, just as with a private firm, the pressure on government to innovate can also increase. As technological change extends the ability to provide health services of various kinds, so the pressure actually to provide those services increases.

2) Government is a purchaser, and as such it may be treated in the same way as a consumer (as in fact can any firm that is also a purchaser of products subject to innovation). The government as a purchaser will thus benefit from cheaper products or better products that arise from innovation elsewhere in the economy. Thus, for example, technological advances in the defence industries enable the government to protect the UK more adequately or more cheaply. In fact, this defence example illus-

trates how innovation elsewhere can drive innovation, even in a non-market sector such as defence. Technological advances by hostile nations in their defence capabilities drive forward similar developments of domestic defence capabilities.

3) The government has a remit to improve the general welfare of the nation. In the long run one of the few ways of achieving such improvements is through innovation. Governments are thus concerned with the innovative success of the economy for this wider reason. However, this particular subject is perhaps best treated as a topic in its own right and represents the task of the next section.

Social costs and benefits and the efficiency of market forces

Measuring the benefits

Innovation can yield benefits to producers in terms of extra profits, to consumers in terms of better or cheaper goods, and to government in terms of cheaper or better services. However, it is not costless. Firms bear the costs of innovation and consumers may also do so. Innovation is an investment in the future and there is always a cost in terms of foregone current consumption. The presumption is that innovation can yield benefits that exceed the costs and is therefore a desirable activity.

There are some estimates of returns to innovation that may be worth presenting at this time. The calculation of benefits can take place on a number of different levels of aggregation. On one level, one may look at the economy as a whole and attempt to measure the impact of innovation or technological change on total output, the growth of output or the trading performance of the economy. On another level, one may look at industry data or firm-level data and attempt to measure the impact of innovation on firm or industry-level output or profitability.

At the aggregate level, the early work of Solow (1957) established the overwhelming importance of technical change rather than capital and labour growth as a source of output and productivity growth in the US economy. Later work by Matthews (1964) and Denison (1962) amongst others has replicated the result for the US and for other economies including the UK. Pavitt and Soete (1982) and Fagerberg (1987) present evidence to support the view that the growth performances of economies are significantly related to differences in their technological performance. There is now also a growing literature illustrating how the trading performances of economies depend significantly on their technological performances — eg for the UK, Buxton, Mayes and Murfin (1990) and Greenhalgh (1990).

At the lower levels of aggregation there is further evidence illustrating the importance of technological change. Griliches (1988) argues that, using time series data on individual US companies, one may estimate that a one per cent increase in R&D by a company will increase its output by between 0.06 per cent and 0.1 per cent . Using line of business data and industry aggregates yields an estimate in the 0.2 per cent to 0.5 per cent range (higher estimates are expected due to spillovers of various kinds). It should, however, be noted that Griliches argues that it is likely that such figures seriously underestimate the contribution of R&D because of the researchers' inability to measure properly both spillovers and productivity. Other work in the US by Griliches (1984) shows significant positive relationships estimated at the company level between equity values and patenting activity. There is also work by Mansfield (1977) relating to the US, showing private (and social) rates of return to innovative activity considerably in excess of the cost of funds for that activity.

The Innovation Advisory Board (1990), in addition to quoting the Griliches 0.2 per cent to 0.5 per cent elasticity estimates, argues on the basis of data in *Business Week* that 'the relationship between research and development spending and growth of output is strong and enduring', and then presents a number of short case studies that further support the view that technological performance is an important, if not the most important, contributor to the economic performance of companies and economies.

The empirical evidence thus supports the view that innovation or technological change is a major contributor to economic well being. That is why there is so much concern about the apparently poor technological performance of the UK economy.

Incentives

Innovation is a desirable activity from many points of view. An economy should undertake a desirable activity to the point where the marginal social benefit of an extra unit of such activity equals the marginal social cost. It is should be clear, however, that the actors in the economy in general react to private benefits and costs rather than the social benefits and costs. If the private benefits and costs differ from the social benefits and costs, then the amount of innovative activity undertaken will not be optimal (see Stoneman and Vickers,1988, for more detail).

Return then to the case of the local innovating firm. The innovating firm will bear costs for its innovative activity. It will also generate some extra revenues or reduced production costs either today or in the future that will yield, for a successful innovation, an increase in the profit stream. This increase in the profit stream is the private incentive to innovate. However, the firm's innovation will also yield some benefits to consumers in that they will be able to buy better or cheaper products. The innovation may also yield some benefit to government on the same grounds. There may also be some spin-off to other firms as they learn from the innovator's experience. The extra benefits are socially desirable benefits, but do not go to the innovating firm. Thus we have a situation where the returns to society as a whole, firms, government and consumers, are greater than the returns to the local innovator who bears all the costs. In such a situation, the incentives to the innovator are less than the social value of the innovation and, as a result, the amount of innovation that occurs will be sub-optimal. In support of these arguments one may quote the seminal work of Mansfield (1977) who has provided estimates relating to a number of US innovations that suggest that the social return to innovation may well be twice the private return to the innovating firm (55 per cent compared to 25 per cent on average).

This is not to argue that all the costs and benefits are as unequally weighted as this example suggests. The innovating firm does not bear the costs of the increased uncertainty that consumers might face, nor the costs of the obsolescence that innovation might generate, nor the reduction in profits of other firms that might result from the innovation (which factors are not all included in Mansfield's calculations). The point is, however, that in general one might well expect that the private incentives to innovate differ from the social ones.

One can address this issue from another viewpoint: in the above discussion of local innovation, the incentives to firms to choose particular positions in the order of innovation were considered. From most viewpoints, society is not particularly concerned which firms are first in the order of innovation but to individual firms this may matter a great deal. The incentives to a firm may thus differ from those that reflect society's preferences. Whereas firms may well devote resources to being high in the adoption order, society will not view that as a desirable use of resources. One can make a similar case relating to the dates of local innovation, and in fact there is a large literature relating to what are called patent races (Dasgupta, 1987), that points out that such races often produce socially undesirable outcomes.

This particular discussion can be taken further into a slightly different dimension: although society may not normally be concerned whether firm A or firm B makes a particular innovation first, it may well be concerned if firm A is a UK firm and firm B is a foreign firm. For consumers, it does not really matter if new products originate from the UK or elsewhere, but from the points of view of labour and of social welfare, it may well matter if overseas firms are innovating and UK firms are not (or more generally if overseas firms innovate before domestic firms). A similar sort of argument can be applied to other aspects of the topic. It may be in a firm's private interest to undertake its research and production overseas, or to undertake its research in the UK and base its production overseas. It may not be socially desirable for this to happen, as it may reduce employment and production in the UK (which may be only partially offset by any repatriated profits). Many thorny questions and issues arise once the global nature of technology sourcing is fully realised.

Innovation may be used as a means of obtaining market power. As far as society is concerned, market power is often considered undesirable. Innovation driven by incentives that arise from the gain in market power is not necessarily driven by incentives that are compatible with social preferences. One does have to be careful with this argument, however. It is often asserted, and the patent system is built upon such a view, that the monopoly power generated by innovation is what provides the incentive to innovate. This is not in dispute. There are, however, costs to monopoly power in terms of higher prices and restricted output that are socially undesirable. If, as in the case of the patent system, these monopoly costs are transitory and evaporate as the innovation spreads, then there is no long term problem. However, if innovation is being used as a means of preserving existing monopoly power, or if it will generate monopoly power in perpetuity, then there may be some conflict between private and social incentives.

Finally, in discussing private and social incentives, one should address risk and uncertainty which are inherent to the innovation process. In a world of incomplete insurance markets, which is the world in which we live, the innovator in most cases will have to carry a considerable burden of risk (Arrow, 1963). The innovator's attitudes to risk will thus considerably influence his/her behaviour. A very risk-averse innovator will undertake less risky innovative activity than someone more prepared to take chances. If society is less risk-averse than private innovators, then the private sector will undertake less innovation than is socially desirable. The question then arises, why should society be less risk-averse than private innovators?

There is first a question of the ability to spread risk. Society as a whole may carry a portfolio of projects, the overall riskiness of which will be less than the riskiness of the highest risk private project. Society may thus be more willing than the private sector to carry a marginal project with higher risk. Secondly, the downside risk for society as a whole may be much less than for an individual actor in the economy. As far as the whole economy is concerned, the failure of one firm (resulting from unsuccessful innovative activity) may not be too large a burden to bear, but for the owners, workers and managers of that firm that will not be the case. Such factors as these may argue for a difference between the riskiness that firms are willing to bear and that which society will tolerate or would prefer. Arguments like these have been used to justify the Launch Aid scheme in the UK. One must note, however, that this is not the whole story. It may be the case that a government taking an attitude to risk that reflects social preferences may still not wish to help a private sector project for which a firm requests support. The problem here, however, may not be so much to do with attitudes to risk as with information asymmetries. A firm may have a project that it thinks is viable, but before offering support, a government will assess the incentives to the firm to bias the information it provides, and it may then turn down a seemingly viable project.

One could continue to illustrate differences between private and social costs and benefits and incentives; the point is, however, already well made. The next step is to ask why all this should matter. The reason for going through this explanation of incentives is that it is argued that in general that one can explain sub-optimal innovative performance by these incentive problems. In essence, one might attribute the poor R&D performance of the UK to the differences between private and social benefits and incentives. Unfortunately, the argument is not that convincing.

- Poor performance in innovation is often diagnosed by drawing international comparisons. However, the economic reasoning above is supposed to be universal and thus applies to all economies. It cannot, therefore, be used alone to explain poor UK performance.
- The arguments above imply that the differences between net social benefits and net private benefits may be either positive or negative depending upon the circumstance. If one is to use these arguments to explain poor UK performance one must assume that in general the balance is one where private net benefits are less than social net benefits. This needs more supporting evidence than is currently available.

If such arguments rest on weak foundations, how is the apparent poor UK performance to be explained?

The institutional and macroeconomic environment

The arguments relating to the causes of the poor technological performance of the UK economy have been addressed in another paper (Stoneman,1991) and are not repeated in detail here. There is, however, some need to address the topic if one is going to reject the arguments based on market failures, as has been done in the previous section. Before doing this, it is worth noting that successful innovation requires not only new technologies but also new skills in the labour force. This means training. The training and skill problems of the UK labour force are not the major topic of concern here, although there is ample evidence of the deficiencies in the UK relative to other economies. Skill and training acquisition is as much a long term investment as is innovation, and as subject to market failure. So although these are not explicitly addressed here, the discussion of innovative activity may be extended to skills and training without much variation.

Four main arguments are put forward here about the causes of the poor UK technological performance.

1) The first grows out of the market failure arguments presented above. The argument is that in all economies there are market failures and that these tend to reduce technological activity below its optimal level, but other economies are more successful in terms of their government policies in overcoming these market failures. This argument can be illustrated either by reference to the differing nature of technology policies in the UK relative to other economies, or by a detailed analysis of institutions. Supporting evidence concerning the UK emphasis on defence R&D in the government's R&D spending, or on expensive failures (eg Concorde and nuclear energy) in the government sector is put forward. Ergas (1987) successfully illustrates how UK policy has concentrated on 'mission orientated' support for R&D with a preference for high tech expensive projects (which have often failed), in contrast to German and Japanese policy which has been orientated towards diffusion. Such diffusion orientated policies emphasise knowledge, standards and training and the use of new technologies rather than the development of high technologies.

2) The second argument relates to UK institutions. This argument can be allied with the market failure discussions or stand alone. The institutions currently in the spotlight are those relating to the capital market. The argument is that the operation of UK capital markets in terms of the attitudes of funding sources and the nature of the market for takeovers and mergers discourages long term technological activities. It is further argued that different institutional structures in Germany and Japan produce the opposite result. However, there is not complete agreement on this. Although Mayer and Alexander (1990) support the argument, Marsh(1991) tends to disagree, emphasising the issues in the next paragraph. It is noticeable however that since the IAB conference on short termism (IAB, 1990a), there has been an increasing emphasis on this attitude as a reason for the UK's poor technological performance.

3) The third, apparently convincing, argument is again one of institutions but at a more micro level. It is argued that, for example, managerial incentive structures discourage long termism, which discourages innovation. If managerial salaries are based on current profits then there is an incentive to maximise them, perhaps at the expense of future profits. Given that innovative activities imply costs today and returns in the future, such incentives are hostile to R&D. The argument can be taken further: even if managerial pay schemes are not constructed in this way, if the managerial labour market assesses the abilities of managers by the current profits of their employers, then the incentives are opposed to long term behaviour. In this sense, jobs for life in Japanese companies may have a lot to do with their more long term attitudes.

4) It is often argued that the instability of the UK economy is harmful to long termism and investment in technological activities in particular. Periodic spells of high interest rates punish those who have invested in technological activities and the prospect of high interest rates discourages those who are thinking of doing so. One can further argue that the instability results from the inherent inability of the UK economy to generate high employment or growth without inflation or balance of payments problems, and this leads to a vicious circle. The instability results from the incompatibility of low inflation and high employment and growth, but this incompatibility in turn is the result of poor innovative performance, which the policy reaction actually worsens.

Conclusion

This paper did not set out to present a set of policy prescriptions. In the presence of a large range of possible reasons for poor UK performance, it is difficult to select one policy instrument in preference to any other. What is clear, however, is that the effectiveness of any policy instrument will depend not only on the nature of the cause of the poor UK performance, but also on the behaviour of the economic actors in the economy. This paper has tried to give some insight into the behaviour of and incentives to firms, consumers and governments when considering innovation, and it has illustrated how private and social incentives may differ. Only by understanding these issues may reasonable predictions be made as to how the economy may react to policy interventions. If one can understand why firms innovate, one may then proceed to ask why they do not undertake sufficient innovation, and then ask whether particular policy measures will encourage more innovation. It is in the light of this reasoning that the paper has been written.

Appendix: UK technological performance

This appendix provides some statistics on UK technological performance. It concentrates on R&D as an indicator of performance, although it should be realised that R&D is not a good reflection of all technological activity nor necessarily the best indicator of innovation *per se*. The advantage of using R&D as a measure is that the numbers are freely available and people are familiar with the use of R&D data for this purpose.

In Table 3.1, some data on Gross Expenditure on R&D (GERD) on an international comparative basis are presented. This is supplemented in Table 3.2 by data on GERD relative to GDP.

Table 3.1 Gross expenditure on R&D (£billion at ppp)

	1981	1983	1985	1986	1987	1988	1989
Italy	2.4	2.9	4.0	4.3	4.9	5.6	6.4
France	5.5	6.2	8.3	8.8	9.6	10.6	11.8
FRG	7.9	9.2	11.4	n/a	13.6	15.0	16.6
Japan	12.8	15.8	21.3	22.4	25.3	29.1	33.7
US	39.9	50.0	66.0	70.7	76.5	84.1	89.8
UK	6.1	6.8	8.2	8.9	9.4	10.3	11.5

Source: OECD

Note: Purchasing Power Parity (ppp) is an exchange rate that equates the costs of purchasing a representative bundle of goods and services between any two countries; thus a bundle of goods costing $100 in the US and £62.50 in the UK would yield a ppp exchange rate of £1=$1.60. The use of such rates is intended to remove the short term fluctuations in international comparisons that would be introduced by using actual (more volatile) exchange rates. In the data here, the ppp exchange rates have been calculated by the OECD, and relate to a bundle of goods covering all of GDP and not just R&D inputs.

Table 3.2 GERD as percentage of GDP

	1964	1981	1983	1985	1986	1987	1988	1989
Italy	n/a	n/a	1.0	1.1	1.1	1.2	1.2	1.3
France	1.8	2.0	2.1	2.3	2.2	2.3	2.3	2.3
FRG	1.6	2.5	2.5	2.7	n/a	2.9	2.8	2.9
Japan	1.5	2.4	2.4	2.6	2.6	2.7	2.7	n/a
US	2.9	2.5	2.7	2.9	2.9	2.9	2.9	2.8
UK	2.3	2.4	2.3	2.3	2.3	2.2	2.2	2.3

Source: OECD

It is common to undertake a comparison of such R&D figures concentrating upon the ratios to GDP. This is inappropriate: first, it is not at all clear that a small economy needs less R&D in total than a large economy (or more weakly, proportionately less R&D) to maintain competitiveness; secondly, good performance of R&D relative to GDP could be the result of declining GDP.

The data on levels of R&D indicate that during the 1980s the UK had a performance very similar to that of France but has spent considerably less than Japan, Germany and the US. The data relative to GDP show the UK in a better light, although again behind the USA, Germany and Japan. These data, to some degree, paint a too optimistic picture of UK performance, for two reasons.

- Some data for 1964, in Table 3.2, illustrate that whereas in 1964 the UK devoted 2.3 per cent of GDP to R&D and still devoted a similar proportion in 1989, Germany and Japan devoted a considerably smaller proportion of GDP to R&D in 1964, but have not only increased that proportion to UK levels over the years but actually surpassed the UK proportion by 1989. The latest data thus hide the extent to which Germany and Japan have been increasing the share of GDP devoted to R&D whereas the UK share has remained constant (or even fallen).
- The data aggregate both civil and military R&D. Although it is not possible to get a precise measure of total defence R&D, it is clear that in the UK this is about 25 per cent of the total, whereas in Germany and Japan it is near zero. Many would argue that military R&D will not contribute to economic performance to anything like the same degree as civil R&D and as such the above international comparisons are overly favourable to the UK. Even if one does not accept this argument, there is the other argument that UK defence R&D spending is considerably overstated (House of Lords, 1990) and thus again the reported figures are flattering to the UK. Whatever the true position, the data suggests that, in aggregate, UK R&D performance is poor by international standards.

Table 3.3 presents data on industrial R&D in the UK. Industrial R&D is that part of GERD performed (although not necessarily financed by) industry.

The first column of Table 3.3 shows intramural expenditure on R&D in the UK at constant 1985 prices. These data are, however, misleading for prior to 1986 the UKAEA was not included as part of the industrial sector whereas after 1986 it was. Making a correction to the data for this gives column two. In these corrected data one may see that UK industrial R&D has remained an approximately constant share of GDP, and over the period from 1981–9 industrial R&D increased by 19 per cent. However, if one removes the chemicals sector from the data, as in column 4, the increase in industrial R&D (excluding chemicals) over the same period is only 9 per cent. Such a small rate of increase is a matter for concern.

The data in this appendix illustrate that the technological performance of the UK has been poor relative to international competitors, especially Japan and Germany, and in the industrial sector has not grown at an impressive rate.

Table 3.3 Industrial R&D in the UK, 1981–9 (£m at 1985 prices)

Year	Raw data	With UKAEA correction	As % of GDP	Excluding Chemicals
1981	4752	5141	1.6	4368
1983	4605	5007	1.5	4194
1985	5122	5486	1.5	4544
1986	5750	5750	1.6	4747
1987	5828	5828	1.5	4629
1988	5962	5962	1.5	4607
1989	6129	6129	1.5	4764

Source: Cabinet Office, 1991.

Chapter bibliography

Arrow, K (1963) 'Economic welfare and the allocation of resources to invention', in Nelson, R R (ed) (1963) *The rate and direction of inventive activity*, Princeton, Princeton University Press

Buxton, A, Mayes, D and Murfin, A (1991) 'UK trade performance and R&D', *Economics of innovation and new technology*, vol 1, no 3, pp243–255)

Cabinet Office (1991) *Annual review of government funded R&D 1991*, London, HMSO

David, P A (1990) 'The economics of compatibility standards: an introduction to recent research', *Economics of innovation and new technology*, vol 1, no 1–2, pp3–42

Dasgupta, P (1987) 'The economic theory of technology policy: an introduction', in Dasgupta, P and Stoneman, P (eds) *Economic policy and technological performance*, Cambridge, Cambridge University Press

Dixon, H (1988) 'Oligopoly theory made simple', in Davies S and Lyons, B (eds) *The economics of industrial organisation*, Harlow, Longman

Denison, E F (1962) *The sources of economic growth in the United States*, New York, Committee for Economic Development

Ergas, H (1987) 'The importance of technology policy', in Dasgupta, P and Stoneman, P (eds) *Economic policy and technological performance*, Cambridge, Cambridge University Press

Fagerberg (1987) 'A technology gap approach to why growth rates differ', Research Policy, vol 16, no 2, pp87–99

Freeman, C (1965) 'Research and development in electronic capital goods', *National Institute Economic Review*, no 34, pp40–91)

Greenhalgh, C (1990) 'Innovation and trade performance in the UK', *Economic Journal*, supplement, vol 100, no 400, pp105–18)

Griliches, Z (1980) 'Returns to R&D in the private sector', in Kendrick, J and Vaccara, B (eds) *New developments in productivity measurement and analysis*, Studies in income and wealth, no 44, Chicago, Chicago University Press

Griliches, Z (1984) 'Market value, R&D and patents', in Griliches, Z (ed) (1984) *R&D. Patents and Productivity*, Chicago, University of Chicago Press

Griliches, Z (1988) 'Productivity puzzles and R&D: another non-explanation', *Journal of Economic Perspectives*, vol 2, no 4, pp9–21)

House of Lords (1990) Select Committee on Science and Technology, *Definitions of R&D*, London, HMSO

Innovation Advisory Board (1990) *Innovation and growth*, London, Department of Trade and Industry

Innovation Advisory Board (1990a) *Innovation: City attitudes and practices*, London, DTI

Mansfield, E (1971) *Research and innovation in the modern corporation*, New York, W W Norton

Mansfield, E (1977) *The production and application of new industrial technology*, New York, W W Norton

Marsh, P (1991) *Short termism on trial*, London, International Fund Managers Association

Matthews, R C O (1964) 'Some aspects of postwar growth in the British economy in relation to historical experience', *Transactions of the Manchester Statistical Society*, Session 1964–5, pp1–25

Mayer, C & Alexander, I (1990) 'Banks and securities markets; corporate financing in Germany and the UK', CEPR Discussion Paper, no 433, London, Centre for Economic Policy Research

Mowery, D, and Rosenberg, N (1989) *Technology and the pursuit of economic growth*, Cambridge, Cambridge University Press

Nickell, S (1978) *The investment decisions of firms*, Welwyn, Cambridge University Press

OECD (various years) *OECD Main Science and Technology Indicators*, Paris, OECD

Pavitt, K and Soete, L (1982) 'International differences in economic growth and the international location of innovation', in Giersch, H (ed) *Emerging technologies: consequences for economic growth, structural change and employment*, Tubingen, JCB Moir

Penrose, E (1959) *The theory of the growth of the firm*, Oxford, Basil Blackwell

Schumpeter, J (1942) *Capitalism, socialism and democracy*, New York, Harper

Solow, R W (1957) 'Technical change and the aggregate production function', *Review of Economics and Statistics*, vol 1, no 3, pp312–20)

Stoneman, P (1983) *The economic analysis of technological change*, Oxford, Oxford University Press

Stoneman, P (1987) *The economic analysis of technology policy*, Oxford, Oxford University Press

Stoneman, P (1991) 'The promotion of technical progress in UK industry: a consideration of alternative policy instruments', Warwick Business School Research Papers, no 11, University of Warwick

Stoneman, P and Vickers, J (1988) 'The economics of technology policy: the assessment', *Oxford Review of Economic Policy*, vol 4, no 4, ppi–xvi

Tirole, J (1989) *The theory of industrial organisation*, Cambridge, Mass., MIT Press

4

The CBI and the Promotion of Innovation

Fiona Steele

The CBI's recognition of the crucial importance of innovation to company competitiveness goes back a number of years: companies need a continuous commitment to innovation, and the CBI has maintained a similar commitment in its policy portfolio. The CBI's role is essentially one of promoting awareness of the value of innovation, both directly to companies and through its lobbying of Government (and increasingly the European Commission) to obtain an infrastructural climate in which innovation can thrive.

Innovation — the ground rules

The CBI's 1986 leaflet *Innovation — the ground rules* was designed as a checklist of the key factors contributing to a continuously successful company, and of the corresponding key questions a company should pose to itself and respond positively to.

While the leaflet was primarily addressed to manufacturing industry, its message equally applied to the service sector, and is one which is just as relevant today. Companies must make, sell, supply, generate cash and innovate. 'Not carrying out the first four effectively will put the company out of business today — failing to achieve the fifth will push it out of business tomorrow'. Not content with a general message, the leaflet went on to suggest some percentage guidelines (see Figure 4.1) to demarcate the company with a future from the one with a past.

Innovation trends

To what extent are UK companies meeting these guidelines? The CBI's next move was to propose an innovation trends survey to complement its

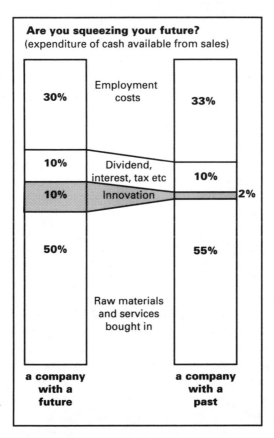

Figure 4.1 Are you squeezing your future?

Industrial Trends, which over the years has built up a reputation for its accurate reflection of the state of the UK's industrial economy as a whole. *Innovation Trends* was not an easy concept to translate into reality, not least because of the need to develop a comprehensive but user-friendly questionnaire, and to attract sufficient resources to guarantee production over a long enough period to predict real trends. Commitment to the task bore fruit in 1989 when a pilot survey was introduced which was able to demonstrate proof of concept and led to the first full survey in 1990. Generous support from the National Westminster Bank's Technology Unit has underwritten production for five years, by which time it should be firmly on the map as an indicator of national innovation performance, a peer review mechanism for companies themselves, and as a benchmark for government in the development of innovation support services.

Stimulating innovation in industry

As Table 4.1 shows, few UK firms are meeting the ground rule of 10 per cent of expenditure of sales on innovation for 'a company with a future'.

Table 4.1 Expenditure on innovation

Expenditure on innovation as a percentage of sales	*Percentage of companies responding*	
	Total manufacturing	Total non-manufacturing
0–2	32.8	50.0
2–5	45.2	27.3
5–9	13.9	12.1
9–14	4.6	1.5
14–20	0.8	4.5
20–30	1.5	3.0
>30	1.2	1.5

Source: *CBI Innovation trends* survey, Issue 2, 1990, published March 1991

A sub-sectoral variation might be expected and this is indeed the case (Table 4.2). Although there was a change in 1991 in the basis of the percentage presentation to provide greater disaggregration at the sub-10 per cent level, and accepting that the difference between the 5–9 per cent and 5–10 per cent ranges could be significant, even so there was a noticeable drop in the percentage of companies spending more than 10 per cent of sales on innovation in the electrical and electronic-based industries from 22.5 per cent in 1990 to 9.6 per cent in 1991. By contrast the chemical industry, traditionally regarded as a good UK performer, showed a consistency of around 11–12 per cent, this despite the recession. However it may be noted that the chemistry-based industries enjoy longer product and process life cycles: this and other factors as well as absolute expenditure may contribute to success .

Innovation trends also develops some of those 'other' factors. It analyses:

- where innovation expenditure is being directed;
- the aims of innovation expenditure;
- the incentives and constraints to innovation;
- where sales are going;
- where competition is coming from; and
- what is of most importance to customers.

Table 4.2 Sub-sectoral expenditure on innovation
(percentage of companies responding)

Expenditure on innovation as a % of sales	Chemical industry	Manufacture of unspecified metal goods	Mechanical engineering	Electrical and electronic engineering	Food drink and tobacco
1990					
10–15	9.5	0	5	17.5	0
15–20	2.4	0	0	2.5	0
20–25	0	0	0	2.5	0
25–30	2.4	0	0	0	0
>30	0	0	0	0	0
Total >10	**11.9**	**0**	**5**	**22.5**	**0**
1991					
9–14	5.7	0	6.1	5.4	0
14–20	2.9	0	0	0	0
20–30	2.9	4	0	0	0
>30	0	0	0	0	5.9
Total >9	**11.5**	**4**	**6.1**	**8.3**	**5.9**

Source: *CBI Innovation trends* survey, Issue 2, 1990, published March 1991

This detailed survey is paralleled by a single general question on innovation expenditure in the *CBI Quarterly industrial trends* survey, and it is interesting to compare the data obtained so far, both with the annual innovation trends results which might be said to reflect a deeper company perspective, and with the general current business situation of which the Quarterly trends is a recognised snapshot. It is particularly enlightening to look at the comparison between the trend in innovation expenditure intentions and that of general business optimism (Figure 4.2). Whereas the downward trend in the innovation expenditure is discouraging, no doubt reflecting the recession, there is some encouragement in the more positive balance of firms planning to increase innovation expenditure compared with the balance of confidence about the business situation as a whole.

The Silver Jubilee programme

1990 was the CBI's Silver Jubilee year, and it was entirely appropriate that a special programme on innovation should be mounted with a look to the future while celebrating the successes of the past. Invaluable support from

AEA Technology, demonstrating its own dedicated commitment to the

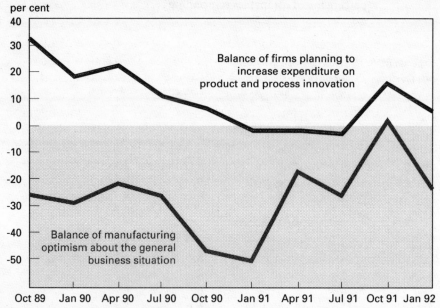

Figure 4.2 Changes in investment plans and business confidence
Source: CBI quarterly *Industrial Trends* survey

importance of innovation, enabled the CBI to mount a series of seminars with accompanying publications, aimed particularly at encouraging smaller and medium sized companies to improve their competitive position through innovation and providing them with ideas on where they could obtain tangible outside help. This exercise was also a demonstration of the CBI's close liaison with the DTI, which provided the valuable added dimension of designating the seminars and publications as 'training' opportunities for its Enterprise Counsellors, thus magnifying the potential audience many times over.

Technology and enterprise

In parallel with the Silver Jubilee programme, the CBI was also working with the DTI in following up the recommendations arising from a survey of CBI members' views on the DTI's own innovation support schemes and technology in particular. For this exercise, the CBI was indebted to British Telecom for the loan of a secondee who was able to carry out detailed on-site interviews of CBI members across the country. The resulting recommendations centred on ways in which the DTI's support could be made more effective and on gaps in provision which, if filled, would offer considerable added value. The suggestion fell on receptive ears and 1991 saw a succession of announcements relating to improving the effectiveness of schemes, for example reducing the bureaucracy of the LINK programmes for support of collaborative research. New initiatives were also introduced, such as the SPUR scheme for single company R&D support for smaller firms, and a Technical Action line leading to consultancy help for solving more immediate problems. In May there was a major speech by Peter Lilley, the Secretary of State for Trade and Industry, wholly devoted to the Government's commitment to innovation, in which he described more new schemes and how the entire programme would be packaged and focused, including an innovation 'Hot Line' to point people in the direction of the most appropriate support mechanisms.

Innovation on the political agenda

The CBI is delighted that 1991 and 1992 is finding innovation in its rightful place high on the political agenda. The Labour Party came out with a strong policy statement in spring 1991. The Government followed with its May announcement and the launching of a further raft of schemes in spring 1992, and the Liberal Party put out its proposals in July 1991. Underlying these was the very timely report of the House of Lords enquiry, *Innovation in Manufacturing Industry*, which was published in March 1991. This major enquiry had been amassing a very impressive volume of evidence since 1989, and has since made a significant contribution to increasing awareness. The tenacity of its members will no doubt ensure that the political pressure will be maintained. The CBI was very pleased both to provide written evidence to this enquiry and to give oral evidence, firstly by members at the sharp end, and secondly by the CBI President himself, who was able to provide the wider dimension of a City as well as a CBI hat.

Short-long termism

During the course of the Technology and Enterprise Review, many CBI members commented that the high cost of capital, coupled with the perceived emphasis of the UK stock market on short-term performance, impedes investment in innovation by companies, particularly investment in technology and research and development.

The temperature of the short/long termism debate was raised following the publication of a report by the DTI's independent Innovation Advisory Board in June 1990. This identified a need for strong action in three key areas: communications, corporate manager/shareholder relationships and investment management objectives. The IAB chose to follow up the need for better relations between industry and its investors, particularly in the communication of innovation plans, and set up an 'Action Team' to develop guidelines on best practice, on which the CBI has been represented.

More generally, the CBI President announced at the CBI's National Conference in November 1990 that he had invited the Chairmen of the International Stock Exchange, the Association of British Insurers, the National Association of Pension Funds and the Institutional Fund Managers Association, together with the DTI and the Bank of England, to join with the CBI in setting up a Steering Group on Long-Termism and Corporate Governance. The objective was to coordinate individual activities in this field and to suggest new initiatives as appropriate.

There has been a close synergy between the DTI's Action Team and the CBI President's Group, the latter having followed the progress of the development of innovation plans guidance with strong interest, culminating in detailed comment on the final draft of the guidance booklet which was finally published by the DTI in September 1991. This has been given a very wide circulation, not least by the CBI.

The DTI's Action Team has commissioned the production of an R&D Scoreboard, similar to that produced by *Business Week* in the US. The Scoreboard was published in *The Independent* in June 1991 and will be repeated annually. Again it is intended as a peer review mechanism for companies and to provide investors with another indicator of performance.

The perception of short-termism hindering investment in R&D was also the subject of a report from the management consultancy Sciteb and the CBI followed the progress of this study with considerable interest. It proposed that short-termism is more of a problem for physics-based industries than chemistry-based ones; this is reflected in a poorer stock market performance by the former, particularly in electronics.

R&D expenditure is a very imperfect measure of innovation performance but it is the only factor to which absolute values are regularly ascribed and which must now, save for some exceptions, be reported in company accounts. The correlation between R&D input and output in the form of marketable products and services has intrigued policy makers for years, and it will be looked at in CBI's next major study of innovation which will be carried out in 1992. With the publication of the third annual *Innovation*

Trends survey, it is timely to test the methodology of this and also take advantage of the unique data base which *Innovation Trends* respondents provide for a deeper study of innovation practice in companies. Again there will be close cooperation with the DTI with its Innovation Unit's business secondees acting as the interface with the respondents. It is planned that face-to-face interviews will draw out some valuable insight into the do's and don'ts of innovation best practice across a range of companies of all sizes, and across a large number of sectors in both manufacturing and services. The study will complement the work of other organisations, and both the Advisory Council on Science and Technology and the Central Statistical Office will be actively involved.

There will be further synergy with the DTI through parallel testing of the effectiveness of the *Innovation plans* handbook referred to above. Copies of this were sent out with the 1991 *Innovation Trends* Questionnaire and it is intended to gauge the extent to which the Handbook is being used and by whom.

Allied with this and of crucial importance in helping to communicate the importance of innovation to the financial function within companies themselves, as well as to outside investors, are the broader performance measurements used by industry. Recent work has suggested that the traditional performance measures which concentrate on competitive benchmarking, stock levels and inventory control are too narrow, particularly for the new manufacturing 'Just-In-Time' and simultaneous engineering environment. The DTI has embarked on a study, which is being managed by the Chartered Institute of Management Accountants, to see whether the performance measures currently used can be packaged to provide more effective tool-kits that can become industry-accepted norms, recognised by both the manufacturing and finance sector, or whether new measures are needed. The CBI is associated with this project as a 'collaborator', adding a further dimension to its portfolio of innovation-related activity.

Innovation trends, investor/industry relations, performance measures, and the promotion of technology transfer are receiving an even higher profile in the CBI, not least as a consequence of the formation of a National Manufacturing Council under the CBI umbrella. This was a key recommendation in the CBI's *State of the manufacturing nation* report, published in October 1991, which was debated at the National Conference and endorsed by the CBI Council at the end of November 1991. The CBI hopes that its commitment will be reflected in a much better innovation performance by the UK across the board, such that many more companies can match the performance of the best and become world-class operators.

Part 2

The Management of Innovation

5

Overview

The management of innovation

John Burke, Director and Chief Operations Officer of Porton International plc, says the management of innovation should start with the identification of a market need which requires a technical solution. The chosen project should be tackled by a team, since few individuals have the creative ability to come up with all the right answers. Production people should be brought in at a very early stage, and the team should be ruthlessly managed to rein in technical hobbyhorses. Successful teamwork depends on the recruitment, selection and development of open-minded, creative, committed staff and on clear lines of communication. Burke notes that unsuccessful, inflexible systems have inflexible managers. Creating the right environment for successful innovation may involve blending demonstration with formal teaching and adapting material from academia and other businesses.

It is no coincidence that this sounds like a recipe for good management in general. The London Business School's John Kay argues that the lesson to be learned from successful innovators both here and abroad is that if you get the other aspects of management right, the capacity to handle innovation follows. Norman Waterman of Quo-Tec, reporting on his research for NEDO, says that a major finding is that the most successful innovatory firms are first and foremost well managed. However, good management alone is not enough. Richard Rooley, senior partner of the Project Management Partnership, says thet firms sometimes try to innovate their way out of trouble and that 95 per cent of innovation fails because the function and the consequences of modes of failure have not been analysed correctly. Successful innovation demands more than the right technology and a sprinkling of serendipity — appropriate managerial strategies are crucial.

Kay cites Marks and Spencer and Liverpool Football Club as examples of organisations which have got it right. Architecture is the quality which makes a body greater than the sum of its parts, a dynamism which follows the establishment of a productive equilibrium. When that balance is achieved, the returns to a firm are appropriable at the level of the organisation rather than to groups or individuals within it. This makes innovations hard to pirate and copy; active innovation within an effective architecture can be the key to success.

Kay proposes an investigation of the role of innovation built upon the model of a firm as a set of relationships or contracts; these are both formal and informal and give a firm a distinctive identity and capability when some feature distinguishes it from the contract sets of other firms. He claims a firm's architecture is its most subtle aspect, suggesting that it is a feature of a set of relationships taken as a whole; architecture is the dynamism of the inter-reaction between departments and employees, the firm's activity rather than its formal hierarchy. Successful high-tech firms always have healthy architecture: they often have informal organisational structures and flat pay structures, related to the company's performance rather than that of individual employees. This dynamism, which is hard to copy, is what makes a successful company 'greater than the sum of its parts'.

The ideal innovation is appropriable — it can be made one's own. In product innovation this can be difficult; although the copyright and patent systems provide a degree of legal protection, comparatively few products are entirely appropriable. Investment in firm-specific process innovations carries the least risk: a custom-designed robotic car assembly line delivers benefits only to the company — not to individuals and obviously not to competitors. If innovation is not firm-specific it is risky, and where there are no legal safeguards managerial strategies are particularly important. As Kay points out, Sony was unable to protect the concept of the Walkman, but has maintained its market edge because it does not rely on innovation alone; its architecture prompts a continual flow of innovations, and its reputation ensures a market for whatever it produces.

Chris Voss, of the London Business School, says that discussion of innovation has focused on products, 'despite the fact that in many cases one person's product is another person's process'. He emphasises that process rather than product innovation has been responsible for a great deal of Japan's industrial success, and cites the introduction of 'lean production' into the country's car industry in support of this. He asserts that the traditional distinction between process innovation and adoption leads to the mistaken assumption that the implementation of a successful innovation is bound to repeat that success.

The notion of 'successful adoption' is critical here; there is plenty of evidence to show that a process innovation can succeed in one installation and fail in another. Thus, the study of implementation is the study of the *process of adoption* of innovations; far from ending at the point of technical attainment, this study must follow the push towards business achievement.

Success is often subjectively measured; where it is not, technical evaluation standards are generally used. Voss emphasises that such approaches are severely limited; to view a process innovation as a success simply because it is up and running and has had its bugs ironed out is to ignore the most crucial aspect of the whole enterprise — the links between technical success and business success. He proposes a three-phase model of the life cycle of the implementation process: the pre-implementation phase involves an evaluation up to the go-ahead point; the installation phase is complete when the process is working successfully and targets are being met consistently; the post-commissioning phase involves technical improvements and the activities needed to move beyond technical achievement to business success — this phase never really ends, as an effective company never stops looking for ways to improve its processes.

The post-installation phase is crucial because the evidence suggests that technical effort alone often fails; business success can be elusive. Voss uses his three-stage life cycle model to examine the divide between technical success and business objectives. Of his conclusions, the most striking is that cross-functional teams boost the chances of successful process installation and implementation. He cites a study (Tidd, 1991) which draws unfavourable comparisons between the organisational contexts of UK and Japanese firms: the UK firms studied are characterised by poorly trained, low-skilled operators, poor communication between design, manufacturing and sales functions and weak relationships with suppliers and customers; the Japanese context features highly skilled operators, good inter-firm communications and close links with suppliers and customers. The lesson to be learned is that cross functional teams help where innovations involving a number of technologies have to be implemented in an existing production environment which is fed by a variety of suppliers.

Turning innovative enterprise into business success demands the organisation of a package of effective managerial strategies. Part of the mystique of innovation is the competitive edge which it appears to generate, but since most innovations can be copied, innovation must be combined with some other distinctive capability if success is to be maintained. It is therefore crucial that innovation is integrated within a package of effective managerial strategies.

How this is done will vary from industry to industry: Rooley points out that the structure and shape of an industry will affect the definition of and practice of innovation. Discussing the construction industry, he notes that any one building project may involve a large number of planning specialists and contractors. These are organised into what, by the nature of the industry, can only be temporary teams which communicate in a mixture of official and informal methods. This gives rise to what Rooley terms 'Fuzzy Edge Disease' in which the potential for misunderstanding inherent in communication becomes a problem. He suggests that effective innovation follows a stringent definition of the function and requirements of the innovation process and an analysis of the ways in which failures occur and of their consequences.

Waterman identifies a number of strategies which are common to successful managements, almost regardless of the industry and the size of the company. These include:

- promoting a positive culture and a sense of mission;
- building strong internal and external communications;
- creating an effective organisation structure;
- fostering close relationships with customers, suppliers and investors;
- analysing competitors effectively;
- nurturing successful new products and processes through the vulnerable early stages.

New enterprises can demand new managerial objectives. If the implementation of innovation involves a series of cycles of adaptation of technology and organisation, then the new objectives can be abstracted from the process. Voss describes a framework for this analysis and goes on to note that managerial control systems no longer recognise the priorities and needs of manufacturing systems. Traditional objectives such as cost reduction and maximisation of output have been subsumed into a range of targets including improved flexibility, cycle time reduction and quality improvement. Mismatches between the objectives of technology and managerial control systems are a major cause of innovative failure. Professor Voss cites a case in which a system installed to maximise medium term product change flexibility had made no product changes at all: the managerial control system emphasis was purely on up-time and output, which were maximised by cutting down on the flexibility of the system.

Thus the choice of performance measures will influence management behaviour. This is as true for the firm overall as for operations within it. John Chisholm, Chief Executive of the Defence Research Agency, says:

Decisions to invest in innovation are nearly always unsafe for the
decision maker, and the degree to which industries and countries succeed in innovation is directly related to the extent to
which they are successful at providing an environment which
redresses that adverse risk-reward ratio.

Chisholm notes that the positioning of a decision-maker depends on the
size of the company and that most innovation occurs in middle sized or large
companies which seek their funds on a corporate basis:

At whatever level, or in whichever organisation he sits, the
decision maker will in the end be motivated by the probabilities
of the project outcome as they relate to himself.

The incentive to put delivery of the annual dividend before research and
development investment was noted in the previous section. Chisholm
suggests that the emphasis placed on competition in the free markets of the
US and the UK favours short-termism, but that it is not so much a lack of
will to finance potentially risky ventures that hinders innovation but poor
risk-reward ratios. While innovators may be able to get hold of funds, their
ventures are still driven by the need to return attractive quarterly or half yearly figures, which restricts the scope for speculative innovatory investment.
Colin Mayer, of the City University Business School, quotes the Innovation Advisory Board:

The company/City interface has resulted in too high a priority
for short-term profits and dividends at the expense of R&D and
other innovative investment.

He goes on to note the view that US companies have been 'hobbled' by a
financial environment which undervalues long-term investment. This
position contrasts with the situation in France and Germany where comparatively few investment institutions make equity-staked long-term loans.
The relative security of this scenario changes the perspective of the individual
innovation decision taker; the investor's long-term commitment of funds
will have followed a thorough analysis of the project and will be reinforced
by a commitment to see it through, and further public support may follow.

Whatever the stresses imposed on innovation decision makers by the
markets may be, a radical restructuring of industrial activity is not going to
happen. Like Mayer, Chisholm sees scope for policy changes to encourage
long-term insider relationships at the expense of pure free market objectives; greater commitment to the plans of innovating companies on the part
of investment bodies would improve the environment for positive decisions.

Stimulating innovation in industry

Before concluding that policy changes could help promote innovation in the UK, Mayer reviews how the activities of small, medium-sized and large UK firms are currently financed. He finds that the most significant difference between the US/UK financial system and European practice is the degree of insider control: our emphasis on the role of the markets has advantages, particularly for small firms, but it makes it harder to retain corporate control. There is scope for policy changes redressing the risk-reward ratio.

6

The Financing of Innovation *

Colin Mayer

Introduction

The financing of industry is a subject that has been of continuing interest and concern: in a recent analysis of the operation of the UK financial system, the Innovation Advisory Board concluded that 'the company/City interface has resulted in too high a priority for short-term profits and dividends at the expense of research and development and other innovative investment' (Innovation Advisory Board, 1990, p.19). In the US, the Office of Technology Assessment described US companies as being 'hobbled' by a financial environment undervaluing long-term investment (US Office of Technology Assessment, 1990).

A difficulty that faces those analysing the functioning of financial markets is that there are well-known problems associated with the financing of innovation. Capital markets may be efficient at spreading risks in general but they are not good at coping with circumstances in which investors are less well informed about investments than managers or entrepreneurs, that is, where there are asymmetries in information between investors and firm.

Innovation is particularly prone to asymmetries in information. By definition, innovative entrepreneurs have an idea that is not evident to others and if they do too much to reveal it to financiers then the idea may no

*This paper draws heavily on work that is being done as part of two international projects: a Centre for Economic Policy Research international study of corporate financing and an Economic and Social Research Council project on capital markets, corporate governance and the market for corporate control (W102251003). I am grateful to members of both projects — Elisabetta Bertero, Jenny Corbett, Jeremy Edwards, Julian Franks and Tim Jenkinson — for advice on this paper. Ian Alexander and Myriam Soria provided valuable research assistance.

   I am grateful to Alex Bowen for having suggested this paper and to Martha Prevezer and Lucinda Francis at NEDO for help at various stages with this project.

longer be theirs alone. Where information is appropriable it undermines incentives to innovate. Where information is not appropriable, it makes innovation difficult to finance.

That there are problems in financing innovation is therefore neither surprising nor informative. The real question is whether there are some institutional arrangements and forms of organization that are better placed at avoiding these market failures than others: are some financial systems better at financing innovation than others? Is innovation best undertaken by the public or the private sector? Are there public sector policies that can be used to rectify capital market deficiencies? This paper will be primarily concerned with the first of these questions. It will have something to say about the third and virtually nothing to say about the second as that is being addressed elsewhere in this book.

The paper is therefore concerned with comparisons of the ways in which innovation is financed in different countries. International comparisons of corporate financing are notoriously difficult, particularly in the area of innovation where questions about the comparability of industries as well as financial systems arise. The paper draws heavily on two international comparisons that are currently in progress, one looking at the financing of industry in different countries and the other at corporate governance and corporate control.

Section 2 examines the way in which innovation is financed. It contrasts three groups of firms: small, medium-sized and large — and notes that the financing of these three groups is quite different. In discussing the financing of innovation, it is therefore important to distinguish between different sizes of firms.

Section 3 describes the concerns that have been expressed about the operation of the UK financial system in financing innovation. These apply to all three size groups but the nature of these concerns differs among groups.

Section 4 examines the validity of these concerns. It looks at evidence on the performance of the UK financial system in financing innovation relative to that of other countries.

Section 5 considers the implications of these observations. It suggests that there is a quite clear pattern to the way in which the UK financial system influences the behaviour of companies. This points to some merits and some deficiencies of the UK system.

Section 6 draws conclusions for the design of policy towards the financing of innovation. The paper suggests that there are some policies that may assist in the financing of innovation which do not require a radical overhaul of our existing system.

The financing of innovation

This section will examine the financing of three groups of firms in the UK: small companies, medium sized companies and large companies. The observations relate primarily to high technology sectors such as electronics, pharmaceuticals and chemicals. However, it is not always possible to identify separately the financing of high technology firms; in that case, reference is made to broader aggregates of firms.

Small firms

Small companies are particularly heavily reliant on external sources of finance. Table 6.1 shows that between 1977 and 1982 small firms in the UK raised only just over half of their total sources of finance from retentions in comparison with over 70 per cent for larger companies.[1] This is as true of the higher technology (electrical engineering and chemicals) sectors as of the economy as a whole. External finance comes almost exclusively from banks and trade credit: over the six years, nearly 50 per cent of total sources came from banks and trade credit. Small companies are therefore particularly dependent on banks as sources of finance.

Table 6.1 Financing proportions of small and other companies in the UK: average 1977–82

	Retentions bank loans	Shares	Other trade credit	Long term debt
All companies				
Small	52.6	45.7	1.3	0.3
Other	70.9	23.2	5.7	0.2
Chemical companies				
Small	50.3	50.5	3.8	-4.7
Other	70.5	20.2	7.6	1.6
Electrical companies				
Small	60.4	37.4	2.4	0.1
Other	79.4	19.4	3.1	-1.9

Source: Mayer, 1990

Information on still smaller firms is available from a study by Oakey (1984) of high-technology firms in the UK and US. On the basis of a sample of 174 firms in Scotland, the south-east of England and the San Francisco Bay area in the US, he found that personal savings were by far and away the most important source of start-up capital. Nearly 70 per cent of start-up capital came from personal savings in the UK and just over 50 per cent in the US.

At the start-up stage, bank finance is relatively unimportant, only accounting for 6–7 per cent of total sources of finance, but in the later stages of development, it becomes more important. This was particularly evident for the sample of Oakey's firms in Scotland which raised 24 per cent of their finance from banks.

One of the main reasons for the lower dependence of the US firms on personal savings was the greater use of venture capital. This accounted for 30 per cent of start-up sources of finance in the Bay area as against 3 and 6 per cent in Scotland and the south-east of England, respectively.

While high by European standards, venture capital finance in the UK is low by US standards. The pool of venture capital funds in the UK in 1984 was around £200 million in comparison with over $16 billion in the US (OECD, 1986).

However, more important than the size of venture capital finance is its composition. Table 6.2 shows the types of investments made by UK venture capital firms over the period 1983–7. It records that only 20 per cent by value (30 per cent by volume) of venture capital finance in the UK went to start-ups and other activities in their early stages of development. Towards the end of the period shown, the proportion of start-up finance actually declined and management buy-outs and buy-ins increased. It is possible now that with a reversal in these activities start-up finance has increased again. However, the emergent picture is one of only a limited amount of venture capital finance being provided at the early stages of development.

Table 6.2 Venture capital in the UK: investment by financing stage

Stage	1983	1984	1985	1986	1987
Percentage of investments by volume					
Start-up	23.5	19.3	19.1	20.8	19.5
Other initial	18.8	13.0	11.2	11.7	8.6
Expansion	33.4	47.5	47.9	43.9	47.0
Buy-out/buy-in	19.6	16.2	15.7	18.8	21.2
Other	4.7	4.0	6.1	4.8	3.7
Percentage of investments by value					
Start-up	14.9	16.7	12.9	15.5	8.0
Other initial	10.3	9.5	6.4	7.3	4.2
Expansion	43.3	40.7	36.1	27.2	22.2
Buy-out/buy-in	24.2	27.9	38.1	43.8	62.5
other	7.3	5.2	6.5	6.2	3.1

Source: Venture Economics

Table 6.3 casts doubt on the notion that venture capital is a high technology activity. It shows venture capital finance over the same period broken down by industry. It reports that the most important destinations for venture capital finance are consumer-related products and other services. It is known that management buy-outs are particularly closely associated with retail sectors but the fact that consumer-related sectors have been so important suggests that the weak association of venture capital with high technology is more deeply rooted than that. In two out of the four years, electronics accounted for less than 10 per cent of the investments made by the venture capital industry by value.

Table 6.3 Venture capital in the UK: investment by main industry sector

Industry sector	Percentage of investments by volume			
	1984	1985	1986	1987
Consumer related	19.7	22.0	26.6	18.6
Computer related	14.8	14.9	13.7	14.3
Electronics	10.4	10.5	7.2	5.4
Medical/ genetics	8.0	4.0	7.0	8.1
Industrial products	8.9	11.9	7.6	6.5
Communications	5.9	6.9	5.7	6.0
Transportation	4.6	3.8	4.7	3.4
Energy/ mining	4.3	2.2	1.4	1.2
Construction	3.7	5.0	2.9	3.8
Other manufacturing	6.3	7.3	4.9	9.7
Other services	13.4	11.5	18.3	23.0

Source: Venture Economics

The other feature of venture capital is well appreciated. Table 6.4 shows just how regionally based venture capital finance in the UK is. The south-east of England has routinely accounted for more than half of venture capital provided in the UK. This may have reflected the relative economic prosperity of different parts of the country at the time, in which case it might reverse as relative fortunes change; on the other hand, it may reflect the concentration of venture capital businesses in the south-east and the limited horizons of venture capitalists.

To summarise: small businesses are dependent on external sources (primarily banks). At the start-up stage, companies are reliant on personal savings. Little venture capital finance is available in the UK. What venture capital there is, goes mostly to relatively low technology, low risk activities situated in the south-east of England. These observations suggest that small high technology firms face a financing problem; we return to this below.

Table 6.4 Venture capital in the UK: regional distribution of investment

Region	Percentage of investments by volume			
	1984	1985	1986	1987
Greater London	22.5	23.2	27.6	24.0
Rest of South East	24.4	23.9	19.4	25.8
South West	5.6	7.3	8.2	6.6
Midlands	10.2	10.5	10.2	10.0
East Anglia	6.1	5.7	7.0	6.9
North	2.2	2.0	3.0	2.2
North West	4.3	2.2	5.3	5.2
Yorkshire and Humberside	3.9	3.7	3.3	4.2
Scotland	13.9	11.7	8.0	6.1
Wales	6.7	8.6	7.5	8.0
Northern Ireland	0.2	1.2	0.5	1.0

Source: Venture Economics

Medium-sized firms

The typical development of a UK firm is that once it has grown beyond a certain size it seeks a quotation on the stock market. This section therefore concentrates on the financing of a group of small quoted companies on the UK stock market. Table 6.5 shows the financing proportions of a sample of 13 small quoted firms with sales of less than £25 million. It records a quite different picture from that of the small companies in the previous section. Firms are still heavily dependent on external sources of finance but for quoted firms, access to the stock markets provides them with an alternative source of external finance: new equity. This accounted for 35 per cent of the gross sources of finance of this sample of firms and 60 per cent of the net sources (net of equivalent purchases of financial assets).

Only a limited segment of the medium size class actually seeks quotation. However, the rate of Initial Public Offerings (IPOs) in the UK over the last few years has been high: around 150 companies a year came to the stock market for the first time over the period 1985–8. The level of IPOs is very cyclical and dependent on the state of the stock market: during the trough of the mid -1970s new listings were running at a level of under one tenth of their peak of more than 200 in 1972. For those firms that do not seek quotation, banks are still the dominant source of external finance.

The picture that emerges is that at some points in time and for some types of firms, the financing constraints of small firms are relieved for medium sized firms by access to stock markets. These firms raise appreciable sums of money on the stock market while others remain reliant on bank finance.

102

Table 6.5 The financing of small quoted companies in the UK electrical engineering sector, 1982–8 (per cent)

	Gross sources of finance	Net sources of finance
Retentions	32.2	62.1
New Equity	35.1	60.2
Medium and Long Term Loans	6.7	16.9
Short Term Loans	3.3	-30.6
Trade Credit	22.7	-8.5

Source: Mayer and Alexander (1990)

Notes:
1. Net sources of finance are defined net of accumulations of equivalent types of financial assets.
2. 'Small quoted' firms are defined as having sales of less than £25 million in 1982. There were 13 firms in the sample.

Large firms

The financing needs of large companies drop appreciably and they gain access to debt as well as equity securities markets. Table 6.6 shows the gross and net financing sources of large electrical engineering and pharmaceutical companies in the UK over the period 1982–8. It shows that retention proportions are higher in large companies.

On a gross basis, retention finance accounted for nearly 70 per cent of large electronics firms' finance and 60 per cent of large pharmaceutical company finance. On a net basis, retentions accounted for considerably more than the investment requirements of both electronics and pharmaceutical firms; in other words, they were net acquirers of financial assets.

Where external finance is raised, most of it is medium and long term in nature: large firms were net acquirers of short term financial assets (ie, deposits and short term securities) over this period. In contrast to the smaller quoted firms, much of the long term finance is debt in nature. The reason for this is that large firms have access to the Eurobond market. Table 6.7 shows that between 1987 and 1989 there were more than 50 bond issues per year. These raised on average more than $100 million per issue. In total, since the inception of the Eurobond market at the beginning of the 1970s, fewer than 150 UK companies have accessed the market. While substantial sums of money are therefore raised on Eurobond markets, they are the preserve of a small number of very large companies.

Table 6.6 The financing of large electronics and large pharmaceutical firms in the UK, 1982–8

	Electronics	Pharmaceuticals
Gross sources of finance		
Retentions	69.0	58.2
New equity	5.6	14.3
Medium and long term loans	6.6	7.9
Short term loans	0.7	1.1
Trade credit	18.1	18.5
Net sources of finance		
Retentions	138.4	112.9
New equity	-2.3	-11.3
Medium and long term loans	13.2	14.1
Short term loans	-34.6	-25.6
Trade credit	-14.7	9.9

Source: Francis (1990) and Mayer and Alexander (1990)

Note: Large firms are defined as having sales in excess of £500 million in 1982. There were four companies in each of the electronics and pharmaceuticals samples.

Table 6.7 illustrates another striking feature of Euromarkets: while bond markets have been important sources of finance for large companies, at least over the last few years banks have been still more important. The form in which large companies generally raise bank finance is syndicated bank credits. The total number of these over the last few years has been of the same order as the number of bonds issues, but the total amounts raised in syndicated bank credits have been much larger. Thus, the average size of issue of syndicated bank credits is larger than that of bonds (see Davis and Mayer, 1991, for an elaboration of this point).

One final feature of large company financing that should be emphasized is that *net* new equity finance is actually negative. This means that on average large companies purchase more equity in other companies than they raise themselves. Much of this purchase of equity is associated with takeovers. The difference between gross and net equity sources of finance is illustrative of the importance of takeover activity to this group of firms. In addition, much of the syndicated bank finance that has been raised by large companies appears to have gone towards financing purchases of other companies in takeovers. We return to this below.

To summarize, it is ironic that precisely those firms that have the best access to financial markets are those that are least in need of external finance. Large companies have access to bond markets and syndicated bank credits as well

Table 6.7 Number and value of Eurobond issues and syndicated bank loans by UK non-financial corporations, 1980–9

	Syndicated credits		Eurobonds	
	Number	Value ($m)	Number	Value ($m)
1980	5	622	12	495
1981	5	882	3	82
1982	5	1048	9	489
1983	2	78	15	763
1984	7	1628	20	1101
1985	4	259	32	2339
1986	8	779	56	5039
1987	53	29532	57	5505
1988	84	33752	57	8769
1989	66	20436	52	7280

Source: Davis and Mayer (1991)

as new equity issues. They therefore face much more competitive markets for the supply of debt finance than small and medium sized firms. Much of their external finance appears to go towards financing acquisitions.

The concerns

A number of concerns have been expressed about the operation of the UK financial market in relation to the financing of innovation. We discuss all three size groups in turn.

Small firms

Small firms are seen as facing an unfavourable climate for raising finance for innovation. Critics point to the high cost of bank finance for small firms and the vulnerability of small companies to the whims of bank managers. One example of this is the ability of banks to raise interest charges to companies that face difficult financial conditions in recessions. Another is the practice of calling in overdrafts at little or no notice.

Banks are thought to be unsympathetic to the financing needs of their small high technology customers: the response of banks to the financing problems of Acorn in the middle of the 1980s can be interpreted in this way (see Garnsey *et al*, 1987). Faced with financial difficulties on the part of their borrowers, banks pursue the simplest course of calling in loans, rather than following more difficult policies of restructuring companies.

Stimulating innovation in industry

Venture capital finance is thought to be in short supply. Critics point to the low levels of venture capital finance in relation to the US and the high proportion of venture capital that goes to activities other than start-ups. They also note that the market for corporate venturing by which large companies support small high technology firms is far less developed in the UK than in the US.

Medium-sized firms

In comparing the UK with Germany, it is frequently noted that there appears to be much less long term bank finance available to UK than German firms (Edwards,1987). This is thought to deter UK companies from undertaking long term investments.

The main drawback that has been associated with stock market finance is loss of control (see, for example, Hay and Morris, 1984). Successful firms are founded by dedicated entrepreneurs who wish to retain control of their managements. Stock market finance can only be raised at the cost of dilution of control.

Large firms

Some of the most serious criticisms of the UK financial system relate to large companies. These concern the supposedly short-term attitude of the stock market and the short term horizons that it imposes on management. Critics point to the short-term horizons of the stock market and to the long gestation that is involved in earning a return on R&D: 10–15 years in technically intensive industries such as aerospace and pharmaceuticals, 4–7 years in less technically complex industries such as cameras, automobiles and domestic goods (Yates,1989).

It is not clear where the short-term horizons of the stock market come from, but rapid turnover of shares and takeovers are most frequently cited. In comparison with the 10–15 year gestation periods on corporate investments, typical holding periods of shares appear short.

The threat of takeovers is thought to force firms to pay undue attention to their share prices (see, for example, Cosh, Hughes and Singh, 1990). If share prices are influenced by short-term considerations, then management has to pursue short-term goals. These include paying out high dividends instead of retaining earnings for the business and trying to smooth reported earnings (Innovation Advisory Board, 1990). Threats of outside intervention appear to make management reluctant to cut dividends in the face of declines in earnings.

There is a formidable array of criticisms of the UK financial system, claiming to identify serious impediments to the financing and implementation of innovation. But are these criticisms valid?

The evidence

It only makes sense to evaluate a financial system in a comparative context. The financing of innovation is almost by definition difficult. The question is, how does the UK system match up with others? A great deal of information has been accumulated from international studies and it will only be possible to highlight some of the main results here. The following sections consider evidence on the financing of small, medium-sized and large firms.

Small firms

Small firms in all countries are heavily reliant on their own sources of finance. This in itself does not mean that they are constrained by their financing resources. However, there is some evidence in favour of this assertion. Blanchflower and Oswald (1990 and 1991) examine the determinants of decisions to become self employed by a cohort of 12,000 people. To evaluate the influence of financial constraints, they consider the effects of gifts and inheritances. They find that the effect is large: a gift or inheritance of £5,000 approximately doubles a typical individual's probability of setting up his or her own business. They conclude that 'British data support the hypothesis that entrepreneurs face capital and liquidity constraints'.

The UK is not alone in this. Blanchflower and Oswald were motivated to perform their study by similar studies in the US that came to the same conclusion. Evans and Leighton (1989) and Evans and Jovanovic (1989), for example, found that imperfect credit markets constrain entrepreneurs.

Similarly, Hunsdiek and Albach (1988) report the results of surveys of problems encountered by samples of prospective and actual entrepreneurs in Germany. They found that finance was ranked either first or second by both groups. They went on to examine the causes of financial problems. They record that financial constraints were primarily associated with a lack of track record on the part of entrepreneurs, insufficient equity capital and inadequate collateral.

While venture capital finance is not as readily available in the UK as in the US, it is in even shorter supply in the rest of Europe. The facts that bank finance is often only available once companies have reached a certain stage of their development and that banks appear conservative in their lending policies have led to calls for the development of venture capital markets in Germany and elsewhere (see, for example, Hunsdiek and Albach,1988).

To summarize, there is evidence of capital market deficiencies in the financing of innovation by small companies. These deficiencies do not appear to be restricted to any single financial system. It is unclear which system is best suited to funding small firms but in view of concerns about its ability to provide risk capital, it is unlikely to be the German one.

Medium-sized firms

Mayer and Alexander (1990) report the results of a comparison of medium sized firms in Germany and the UK. They find that, while medium sized firms in high technology sectors in the UK raise large amounts on stock markets, German firms typically do not. Instead, medium sized German firms are particularly reliant on bank finance.

This would suggest that there is a source of finance in the UK that is not so readily available in Germany. Table 6.8 shows that the number of UK firms coming to the stock market is typically eight times that in Germany. This is reflected in a much smaller stock market in Germany than in the UK with around 500 quoted firms as opposed to over 2000 in the UK and a market capitalization of 26 per cent of GDP in Germany in 1986 as opposed to 86 per cent in the UK.

Table 6.8 Unseasoned new issues by firms coming to the German and UK stock markets for the first time

	Germany	UK
1980	2	21
1981	2	73
1982	2	61
1983	11	113
1984	21	128
1985	11	151
1986	26	159
1987	19	146
1988	13	138

Source: Mayer and Alexander (1990)

On the other side of the coin, UK firms have access to less long term bank finance than German ones. Mayer and Alexander report that two thirds of bank lending in Germany is medium or long term in nature (maturity of greater than one year); the equivalent proportion in the UK is one third.

The greater provision of long term finance reflects longer term relations between banks and companies in Germany.

For medium sized firms, there appears to be a trade-off between the provision of equity finance in the UK and the availability of long-term debt finance in Germany.

Large firms

It is possible to compare the performance of large companies that are quoted on the stock market with those that are not, in addition to comparing finance in different countries. Mayer and Alexander (1991) report the results of a comparison of matched samples of quoted and unquoted firms in similar industries in *The Times* 'Top 100 firms'. They find that R&D is predominantly undertaken by quoted companies: there is a much higher concentration of quoted than unquoted companies in high technology industries. Quoted firms grow more rapidly, earn higher returns on capital employed, raise more medium and long term finance both in the form of equity and debt, and pay a higher proportion of their earnings as dividends than unquoted companies. On all accounts, quoted companies appear to outperform their unquoted equivalents. There appears to be no support for the short-term view of stock markets.

The result of the comparison of large German and UK firms is remarkably similar to that between quoted and unquoted firms. In terms of financing, large German firms look very much like unquoted UK firms. They raise less long term debt or equity finance and pay a smaller proportion of their earnings as dividends than UK firms. All of this suggests that the UK financial system is acting to the advantage of large UK companies.

However, before coming to such a conclusion, it is necessary to consider other aspects of the operation of the two countries' financial systems. Franks and Mayer (1990) emphasize corporate control. They note that the takeover market in the UK is considerably larger than that in Germany. More significantly, there have been just three cases of hostile takeovers in Germany in the whole of the post World War Two period. In the UK, typically one third of takeovers of quoted companies are hostile in nature (ie, initially rejected by the target management).

Franks and Mayer record that one important consequence of this is a high level of executive dismissal in the UK. Within a period of two years after a successfully completed hostile acquisition, between 70 and 80 per cent of the executives of the target firm can expect to have resigned. In addition, there is a high level of asset disposal: one-half of target firms disposed of more than 10 per cent of their assets within two years of a hostile bid. The implication of this is that there are substantial changes in policy associated with hostile takeover markets in the UK. But if takeovers are not used as the method of restructuring poorly performing firms in Germany, what is? Franks and Mayer have performed an analysis of 14 major restructurings in Germany over the past decade. They looked at the factors leading up to the restructuring, the changes that occurred and the consequences of the restructuring.

They find that there are two groups that initiate restructurings. The more common is the management board of the firm itself (the Vorstand); a majority of restructurings did not involve any outside intervention at all. Only in cases of clear financial failure did the supervisory board of the firm (the Aufsichtsrat) intervene. If it did, then the chairman of the management board might be changed but otherwise restructurings were usually initiated by the chairman himself. Restructurings are rarely associated with changes in ownership.

Restructurings of German firms therefore typically appear to involve less change in managerial control than those in the UK. This may be a sign of the inflexibility of the German system in not being able to replace inadequate management. On the other hand, it may reflect a greater stability of the control structures of German firms and the fact that German managers are under less external pressure than their UK counterparts.

There is some evidence in support of the latter interpretation. It was noted above that UK managers appear reluctant to cut their dividends during periods of financial difficulty. Indeed, one of the most common responses of target firms to hostile takeovers is to raise their dividends as a defence tactic (see Jenkinson and Mayer, 1991). That is not true in Germany. During periods of financial distress, firms frequently cut their dividends and often pass them altogether.

Still more strikingly, firms that were undergoing restructurings in Germany, invariably maintained and sometimes increased their expenditures on R&D and employee training. The reason that German managers give for following this strategy is that their past policies have failed; they need to develop new markets and therefore must invest more in R&D and training. This is quite a logical response to past failure but it is not one that would be familiar to a UK manager under financial pressure.

To summarize: there is no evidence, from comparisons of either quoted and unquoted firms in the UK or large German and UK firms, that UK stock markets have acted to the financial disadvantage of large firms. On the contrary, quoted firms appear to outperform their unquoted counterparts on all counts. However, there are equally significant differences in the operation of corporate control between Germany and the UK. Here there is evidence that the German system may have acted to the advantage of its own firms.

Implications

This section draws together the implications of the above observations on financial systems for their performance in funding innovation for small to medium-sized and medium to large firms.

Small to medium-sized firms

It is clear from the above that small companies in all countries face difficulties in financing innovation. Equity finance in the form of venture capital is more readily available in the UK than in other European countries. In particular, UK firms have more opportunity to seek quotations on the stock market than firms elsewhere in Europe. The two observations are probably closely related in so far as venture capital finance is more likely to be provided where suppliers can see a simple exit route in the form of a flotation.

However, the form in which bank finance is provided in the UK may be less suitable than elsewhere. Start-ups everywhere have difficulty raising bank finance, but once German firms have grown beyond a certain size, they can more readily raise long term debt finance than UK firms. The UK capital market is therefore able to offer more equity finance than German markets but less long term debt finance.

The two observations may not be unrelated. The reason why German banks appear to be willing to loan more long term finance to medium sized German firms is that they expect to maintain long term relations with their borrowers. That is not true in the UK, partly because firms can seek alternative sources of long term finance from stock markets.

On this account, long term German bank lending is essentially substituting for the equity markets of the UK. From the point of view of innovation finance, there must be a preference for market equity over long term bank debt. Thus in terms of the financing of small and medium-sized firms, UK practices would appear to have distinct advantages over German-style systems.

Medium to large firms

Large companies in the UK have access to plentiful sources of finance. They can raise money from international bond markets, international bank syndicates and equity markets as well as the more conventional domestic bond markets. Large German firms continue to rely on their domestic banks and raise rather little from either bond or equity markets. UK firms appear to have more financing opportunities available to them than large German firms. However, these opportunities come at a price.

Associated with the sale of equity at the stage of becoming quoted, UK firms suffer a dilution of control, which is essentially transferred to outside shareholders. They exercise this control largely through the takeover market. This loss of control puts managers of UK firms under greater pressure than their German counterparts. This may act to the benefit of firms in terms of their corporate efficiency. The comparison of quoted and unquoted firms in the UK suggested that the former are indeed more profitable than the latter. But it may also put firms under more pressure in inappropriate ways.

The closely held group of owners of large German firms (primarily banks and other companies) displays a long term commitment to the activities of firms. This is shown by the ability of German firms to maintain long term investments in R&D and training during periods of poor financial performance. It is also shown by the ability of German firms to forego dividends during periods of financial distress. UK firms are not in that position. They feel compelled to maintain dividends and instead frequently forego investment expenditures. As a consequence, loss of control in the UK can manifest itself in the form of sacrifices of long term objectives.

The initial advantages of a UK equity market may disappear as firms grow: large firms may be unable to enjoy the advantages of closely held firms in Germany. The key difference between the German and the UK financial systems comes as firms develop from small, entrepreneurial activities into more mature entities. In the UK, they typically seek a stock market quotation; in Germany, they are funded by their banks. The central question is whether firms voluntarily move from unquoted to quoted status or whether they feel compelled to seek quotations for want of any other source of large scale development capital. If the decision is voluntary, taken in the full knowledge of the effects of future loss of control, then it is difficult to argue with the proposition that the UK financial system outperforms the German. However, if decisions to seek quotations are essentially involuntary, then the advantages of the UK system at the initial stages of corporate development may be outweighed by their later costs.

Conclusions for policies towards the financing of innovation

It is difficult to provide convincing evidence on the question of whether firms voluntarily become quoted or whether, if alternative sources of finance were available, they would choose them. There is almost certainly a trade-off — in some markets, the balance of advantages may go one way and in other markets it may go the other.

Policy should be adjusted with a view to making it as likely as possible that firms can select appropriately. A central feature of the German system is the ability of firms to retain control independent of pressures from outside shareholders. They can do this on account of a number of features of the German financial system: one of these is bank ownership of corporate equity; another is cross-shareholdings by two companies of each other's shares; a third is dual classes of shares that allow firms to issue shares with reduced or no voting rights.

Bank ownership allows German companies to raise long term debt and equity finance through banks at the stage at which UK companies are going to the stock market. It therefore avoids the necessity to dilute control at the crucial stage at which substantial outside financing is required. Cross-shareholdings allow related corporations to participate in each others' equity; if financing is no longer required, then the involvement of banks is no longer crucial. Instead, control is retained within the non-financial corporate sector. Dual classes of shares allow companies to access outside investors through equity markets as well as banks while avoiding dilution of control.

These features of financial markets are observed throughout Europe in varying degrees, not just in Germany. For example, in France, cross-shareholdings and share stakes are particularly important. They permit firms to develop what is probably the most significant difference between the UK and US financial systems on the one hand and most other countries' systems on the other: insider control. In insider systems, even quoted firms can retain control in a small group of closely involved investors. The advantage of this is that control is exerted by firms and institutions that have a direct interest in the success of the firm in question either through their other trading relations as suppliers or customers or through their substantial shareholdings. Control therefore resides where it can be best exercised.

The UK prides itself on its liberal policies towards corporate organisation. If one suggests that the corporate organisation of Germany or any other country may be superior to that of the UK, the immediate response that one draws from a UK government official is the assertion that there is nothing to stop a UK firm from organizing itself along German or any other lines;

there is nothing to prevent a company from introducing two tier boards or having close relations with banks. There is, in other words, no legislation that the UK government can introduce to improve the operation of the country's financial system.

This is too sanguine a view. Several features of both UK and US corporate law and regulation make retention of control in insider groups difficult. These arise from the overriding significance that is attached to the operation of stock markets in both countries. In particular, the wide involvement of a broad group of shareholders requires rules to protect minorities from exploitation by majorities. Laws or rules on insider trading, takeover procedures and dual classes of shares have protection of minorities as their prime objective. Insider trading rules are designed to avoid one group of investors being able to trade to the disadvantage of a larger group of relatively uninformed investors. Takeover codes are designed to ensure that minorities can benefit from the gains to takeovers to the same degree as other investors. Dual classes of shares are discouraged as a way of avoiding one class of shareholders acting to the detriment of others.

Of course, these are all important considerations. But their application may have come at a price. Insider trading rules discourage the close involvement of particular investors and impede the communication of information to a restricted group of investors. Takeover codes prevent the accumulation of share blocks as a means of exerting corporate control with less than 100 per cent ownership. Restrictions on dual classes of shares prevent outside investor participation while retaining internal control.

There is therefore much that can be done in terms of regulation and legislation to ensure that the UK enjoys the advantages of its well developed stock market economy without foregoing the advantages of insider control. However, there is also much that the corporate sector can do itself to improve its competitive position in corporate governance. Cross-shareholdings are an effective means of limiting outsider control and transferring ownership to a small group of investors which have a direct interest in corporate performance. Some UK companies are beginning to pursue this (for example, Guinness) but as yet it is still rare. Except where competition policy issues arise, it is not clear why this should be the case.

In conclusion, international comparisons of the performance of financial systems in funding innovation suggest that the criticisms that have been levelled against the UK system are too simplistic. In many respects, the UK system has advantages over its competitors, in particular in the funding of small, speculative firms. However, there are some advantages of other systems that supporters of the UK system have been slow to acknowledge. These are concerned with the control rather than the financing of corporations and they are particularly relevant to large enterprises. These advantages point to some policy changes that are needed to ensure that large UK corporations are able to compete on an equal footing with their overseas counterparts.

Notes

1   Small firms are defined over this period as having capital employed of less than £4.16 million. This corresponds with the cut-off used by the CSO.

Chapter bibliography

Blanchflower, D and Oswald, A (1990) 'What makes a young entrepreneur?', National Bureau of Economic Research, working paper no 3252

Blanchflower, D and Oswald, A (1991) 'What makes an entrepreneur?', mimeo

Cosh, A, Hughes, A, and Singh, A (1990) 'Takeovers and short termism in the UK', Institute for Public Policy Research, industrial policy paper no 3

Davis, P and Mayer, C (1991) 'Corporate finance in the Euromarkets and the economics of intermediation', Centre for Economic Policy Research, discussion paper no 570

Edwards, G (1987) *The role of banks in economic development*, London, Macmillan

Evans, D and Leighton, L (1989) 'Some empirical aspects of entrepreneurship', *American Economic Review*, vol 79, no 3, March, pp519–35

Evans, D and Jovanovic B (1989) 'An estimated model of entrepreneurial choice under liquidity constraints', *Journal of Political Economy*, vol 97, no 4, August, pp808–27

Francis, L (1990) 'The financing of German and UK pharmaceutical firms', National Economic Development Office, mimeo

Franks, J and Mayer, C (1990) 'Capital markets and corporate control: A study of France, Germany and the UK', *Economic Policy*, pp191–216

Garnsey, E and Fleck, V (1987) 'Acorn computers and technology policy', mimeo

Hay, D and Morris, D (1984) *Unquoted companies*, London, Macmillan

Hunsdiek, D and Albach, H (1988) *Financing the start-up and growth of new technology-based firms in Britain and Germany*, London, Anglo-German Foundation

Innovation Advisory Board (1990) 'Innovation: City attitudes and practices', June

Jenkinson, T and Mayer, C (1991) *Takeover defence strategies*, Oxford, Oxford Economic Research Associates

Mayer, C (1990) 'Financial systems, corporate finance and economic development', in G Hubbard (ed) *Information, capital markets and investment*, Chicago, National Bureau of Economic Research

Mayer, C and Alexander, I (1990) 'Banks and securities markets: corporate financing in Germany and the United Kingdom', *Journal of the Japanese and International Economies*, vol 1, no 4, pp450–75

Mayer, C and Alexander, I (1991) 'Stock markets and corporate performance: a comparison of quoted and unquoted companies', Centre for Economic Policy discussion paper no 571

Oakey, R (1984) *High technology small firms*, London, Frances Pinter

Organisation for Economic Co-operation and Development (1986) *Venture capital: context, development and policies*, Paris, OECD

US Office of Technology Assessment (1990) 'Making things better: competing in manufacturing', February

Yates, I (1989) *Innovation, investment and survival of the UK economy*, London, Institution of Mechanical Engineers

7

Innovations in Corporate Strategy

John Kay

Introduction

Business history is full of tales of firms which failed to establish competitive advantage from innovation. European business history seems to be particularly full of such stories: the UK company EMI was one of the most effectively innovative companies there has ever been; it was a pioneer in television and a leader in computers; in the 1960s its music business was at the centre of a revolution in popular culture, and its scanner technology transformed radiology. Today only its music business survives.

Philips was a pioneer in almost every major area of consumer electronics; it invented the compact cassette and the compact disc and led in the development and manufacture of video cassette recorders.

Europe has often enjoyed an innovative lead in aircraft manufacture. The jet engine was invented here, and first put into commercial production by de Havilland. The collaboration between Aerospatiale and British Aircraft Corporation produced the world's only supersonic passenger aircraft.

Sir Clive Sinclair created a reputation for innovation by bringing to market for the first time products as diverse as digital watches, personal computers and battery operated cars. Despite inspired publicity, commercial success has not always followed in his footsteps.

But it is not only in Europe that innovation is no assured route to success. Bowmar pioneered the hand-held calculator; and in the 1970s National Semiconductor and Texas Instruments seemed to lead the world electronics industry. That catalogue itself suggests that there is no single cause of failure to derive commercial success from innovation. The reasons why it is difficult to create competitive advantage through innovation fall into three broad categories.

1) Innovation is costly and uncertain: even an innovation which is technically successful may not be profitable.
2) The process of innovation is hard to manage: the direction of innovative companies requires special skills, as does the control of innovation in firms whose market position does not principally rest in their technology.
3) The rewards from innovation are difficult to appropriate: returns must be defended from competitors, from suppliers and customers, and the innovating company must also ensure that these returns do not accrue to groups within it rather than to the organisation itself.

Innovation as competitive advantage

A firm is, in essence, a set of contracts: it sells to customers, buys materials, hires labour and obtains capital from its banks and its shareholders. The contracts are both formal and informal in nature, and typically contain both formal and informal terms. In the language of economists, they are both explicit and implicit; in the language of legal theorists, they are both classical and relational.

Firms develop a distinctive capability when there is some feature of their group of contracts which distinguishes them from other firms, and they turn that distinctive capability into competitive advantage when they successfully identify a market to which it can be applied. In practice, these distinctive capabilities fall into four broad categories.

1) Some are the products of *innovation* — the existence of novelty, or other uniqueness, in the firms contract set, either (as with a product innovation) in relation to one specific output contract or (as with process innovation) in relation to the set of contracts taken as a whole.
2) Some are competitive advantages built on *reputation*. This happens in markets where the consumer is poorly equipped to monitor product quality, and is consequently willing to buy goods or services on terms on which he would not necessarily be willing to buy from other purchasers.
3) The third source of competitive advantage is *exclusivity*. This is the simplest: in one sense it is not a competitive advantage at all, but in another, the absence of competitors is the most potent of competitive advantages. Mostly, it arises through restricted access to scarce resources, such as broadcasting licences, mineral reserves, the public telecommunications network, or a German labour force with a highly developed mathematical and scientific education.

4) Finally the distinctive capability of the firm may lie in its *architecture*. Architecture is the most subtle and elusive source of competitive advantage. It is a feature of the set of contracts taken as a whole, and it emphasises the relational rather than the classical aspects of these contracts; by its nature, a classical contract can be written down, and what can be written down can be replicated.

Architecture is what Liverpool Football Club enjoys when it achieves results which are better than those which appear directly attributable to the quality of its players, where that quality is judged by their cost (including transfer fees and wages) or by their international appearances — while Manchester United, with broadly similar input quality, achieves broadly what players of that quality would imply. Manchester United is the sum of its parts; Liverpool rather more than that.

In a more commercial context, we recognise the same characteristics in Marks and Spencer, where the value added by the organisation as a whole is greater than the sum of the contributions of its individual members, and where different and quite ordinary individuals can be slotted into specific roles with little or no effect on the overall performance of the organisation. Marks and Spencer displays both internal and external architecture, in its relations with its employees and with its suppliers. A key feature of architecture — whether it is the product of firm specific know-how, implicit terms of individual relationships, or organisational routines — is that the returns to it are appropriable at the level of the organisation, rather than to the individuals within it, because they are largely independent of specific individuals within it. It is also, because of its informal and tacit nature, particularly difficult to replicate; you can read books about Marks and Spencer (and competitors have), you can hire Marks and Spencer employees (and competitors have), but you do not have Marks and Spencer in consequence.

What are often perceived as returns to innovation are in fact the returns to architecture associated with innovation — the creation of organisation routines conducive to either the generation, the application of innovation, or the development of organisation specific know-how. While innovation itself raises basic difficulties of appropriation, architecture, when successfully established, carries appropriability along with it immediately.

In some markets, innovation is central to competitive advantage, in that the firms with the strongest competitive advantage derive it fairly directly from their technology. For Cosworth Engineering — the UK's highly successful specialist high performance automobile engine manufacturer — technology is the business. In other markets, for example financial services, competitive advantage mainly accrues from other factors, such as reputation and architecture. In these, an innovative record comparable with that of good competitors will be necessary to success but the best record of innovation will not be sufficient for it. I distinguish these markets as those in which innovation and technology are, and are not, central to competitive advantage.

Contracts and games

If contracts can be seen as a means of defining the activities of the firm, contract forms are also a means of tackling the strategic problems which arise in the playing of non-cooperative games. There are two types of non-cooperative game which recur in the management of innovation which are known to have pathological outcomes. Some key issues in strategy for innovation rest on the development of solutions.

The Prisoner's Dilemma is probably the best known of all non-cooperative games, and need not be described in detail. The 'payoff' matrix is of the form shown in Figure 7.1. The key feature of this game is that 'cheat' is a dominant strategy for both players, and hence that 'cheat/cheat' appears an inevitable outcome even though 'don't cheat/don't cheat' is a clearly superior solution for both participants. The general lesson of the Prisoner's Dilemma is that the existence and recognition of general gains to cooperative behaviour is not sufficient to induce that behaviour.

		Player 2	
		Cheat	Don't cheat
Player 1	Cheat	(-7, -7)	(0, -10)
	Don't cheat	(-10, 0)	(-1, -1)

Figure 7.1 Innovation game — Prisoner's Dilemma

This problem emerges most clearly in the development of firm-specific know-how. The transformation of expertise held by individuals or outsiders into know-how is always critical in the effective application of technology, yet the individuals involved generally have an incentive to hold back. We can see this phenomenon clearly, for example, in the relationships between consultants and the Department of Social Security in the implementation of information technology. In a similar way, the transfer of knowledge by the firm to employees who are free to work for competitors is potentially costly; each of these factors limits the development of organisation capabilities of a kind which would be to the long-run benefit of all.

Of the two standard solutions to problems of the Prisoner's Dilemma — changes in pay-off structure or transformation into a repeated game, the first is not available here. The reason is that the transfer of skills and knowledge cannot, beyond a limited point, be effectively monitored. Williamson's distinction (1975) between perfunctory and consummate cooperation: the first, the level which can be imposed by the terms of a formal contract; the second, that which would be implied by maximisation of the joint gains from the relationship — is particularly relevant to this issue.

The second form of solution is the development of credible repeated game strategies which induce reiterated cooperative behaviour. It is important to note the principal conditions which are required for this to work, however: expectation by both parties of indefinite repetition; understanding by both parties of the 'rules' of the repeated game strategies; and the ability to identify and punish demand behaviour at least in the long run. Much of the naivety of the last few years about the prospects for skill transfer in joint ventures may have resulted from a failure to appreciate the significance of these conditions.

The second game type which recurs in the context of innovation is known as 'Chicken' (it is a simplified version of a game made famous in James Dean's cult movie *Rebel Without a Cause,* where the players drive at speed towards a cliff edge; the loser being the first to swerve away). The payoff matrix for this game is shown in Figure 7.2 and its essential feature is that a 'stick' strategy produces the best outcome for each player provided the other does not adopt it, but a disastrous one for each if both adopt it. This game has two Nash equilibria outcomes, but no basis for discriminating between them, and works out badly for everyone if they adopt what would be their optimal strategy in that outcome. In the context of innovation, Chicken games are most frequently found where strategies are profitable if adopted by any one firm but unprofitable for all if adopted by many.

		Player 2	
		Swerve	Don't swerve
Player 1	Swerve	$(0, 0)$	$(-1, 3)$
	Don't swerve	$(3, -1)$	$(-5, -5)$

Figure 7.2 Innovation game — Chicken

Chicken has no clear solution. It is widely thought that the most plausible outcome is one of mixed strategies, in which the players randomise their behaviour. It is not obvious that repetition helps, although it may enable one party to acquire a reputation as a tough player. The ability to precommit to a strategy certainly does help, but it is rarely available in practice. Often the best question to ask is whether you should be playing this game at all.

The process of innovation

Like games of cooperation, games of dis-coordination may have paradoxical outcomes. Sometimes there are no winners — profitable opportunities go unexploited because no one is willing to take the relevant risk. Sometimes everyone loses, as when everyone invests and no one gains advantage over others. Gains from innovation come to those who do what someone else fails to do. The process of innovation is a game of Chicken with the added spice that it is not always clear in advance whether the winner will be the one who sticks or the one who swerves.

The most common taxonomy of innovation distinguishes product innovation (which brings new goods or services to market) from process innovation (which brings established products to market in more economical ways). In looking at strategies which are based on innovation, however, it is often more important to see whether innovation is typically firm-specific, or not, and whether it is appropriable, or not.

The process of innovation is firm-specific if expenditure on innovation is related principally to the activities of a particular firm. The implementation of information technology in the financial services industry provides a good example. The general principles are well-known and well-established. The substantial investment required is in their development and implementation in the context of the particular firm. The use of robotics in the automobile industry has similar characteristics.

Firm-specific investment is necessarily appropriable, the benefits of it accrue to the firm which undertakes it. If innovation is not firm-specific, it may or may not be appropriable. Product innovations in fast moving consumer goods industries are rarely appropriable: once you have seen fromage frais in one supermarket, many producers can make it and everyone can stock it. Innovative software, such as Lotus 1-2-3, is more appropriable. Such appropriability may, as in this case, be the result of legal protection through the copyright or patent system, or it may be the product of strategy. I discuss these issues further below.

Firm specific innovation normally rests on the local application of generally available knowledge or technology. Success in this, although advantageous, is unlikely to create a sustainable competitive advantage unless the firm creates an architecture which enables it systematically to implement technology in advance of, or more cheaply than, its rivals: the Halifax Building Society has been able to take advantage of its dominance in a West Yorkshire local labour market to build up a staff which is experienced and sensitive to user needs; it has been able to introduce information technology cheaply and effectively in a way which other financial service firms have found hard to emulate.

The pursuit of firm specific innovation is, however, normally a low risk strategy. Innovation in other market or industry situations is not. If the innovation is appropriable, then the innovating firm is in a race in which the winner takes all. This is frequently the case in the pharmaceutical industry. This is a game with clear Chicken characteristics and, as with all such games, potential participants need to consider carefully whether they wish to play at all. If there are many players, then it is quite possible that their combined expenditures will exceed the value of the prize for which they compete. If there are few entrants, then large prizes may be available for low stakes.

	Firm specific	**Not firm specific**
Appropriable	Low risk, but rarely a source of sustained advantage	High risk, because losers get nothing
Not appropriable	—	High risk, because winner may not reap benefits

Figure 7.3 Innovation Strategies

Successful players of Chicken are those who benefit from at least one of three elements in their strategy. There is commitment (the strategy of pulling off the steering wheel and throwing it out of the window, so that rivals are certain of your intention to stay in the game). The problem of commitment, as the extravagance of the example illustrates, is achieving credibility. Preannouncement of innovative products which have certainly not yet been put in marketable form and may not have even reached a prototype stage has been a regular feature of the recent evolution of the computer industry. It has been such a regular feature, in fact, that such commitments have ceased to have much credibility and so have lost their strategic value. Short of legally contracting to supply a product which has not yet been developed, which is a decidedly risky strategy (although it is one adopted in the aircraft industry where uncertainties mostly relate to cost rather than product invention) it is difficult for business to make commitments sufficiently credible.

In its pure form, the game of Chicken suffers from the problem of symmetry and asymmetry. Someone needs to swerve, but there is nothing in the game to tell us who it should be. Sometimes in real life there is something to tell us who it should be. Costs may be lower or potential rewards higher for one of the participants. A new entrant is very unlikely to be the victor in a game of Chicken unless he/she brings some attribute that marks him/her out clearly from incumbents. So new entrants to the pharmaceutical industry, which has this strategic form particularly clearly, have rarely been successful. Ventures by Guinness and Distillers proved disastrous and ICI became an effective competitor only after a very extended period of losses. Boeing and Airbus will minimise the risk of mutually destructive competition if they focus, as to a degree they have done, on aircraft better designed to meet the needs of American and European markets respectively; head on competition is potentially enormously costly for both.

A reputation as a tough player is a powerful weapon in Chicken games, but it may be very costly to establish, since it militates against abandoning unprofitable lines of enquiry. It is not the strategy which successful long-term players in markets, where innovation is critical and R&D costs dominate total costs, have chosen to follow (for example, Hoffmann LaRoche, IBM, Boeing).

The management of innovation

Managing innovation is costly and risky. It is the nature of all product innovations, and many process innovations, that demand is uncertain. New products may fail because there is no demand, or insufficient demand. This is true of more fundamental innovations than the 'new' brands of confectionery or washing powder which fast moving consumer goods markets attract. Battery operated cars, three dimensional cameras, and holograms are more than the brainwaves of 'mad inventors' but less than commercial products. Uncertainties go in both directions. IBM's assessment that there was insufficient market to make the photocopier a commercial product is notorious. No market research, however sophisticated, can effectively measure wants which consumers have no opportunity to express in the market place.

Innovation also raises problems of integration into the remainder of the business. A common business mistake is to believe that innovation can compensate for competitive disadvantages in other areas. Such a strategy is almost never effective. Since innovations are rarely perfectly appropriable, a successful leap ahead is likely to be quickly imitated by stronger competitors. And since effective adoption of innovation is difficult, a successful outcome is less likely for the weak firm than for its competitors.

Midland Bank, the weakest of the four major clearing banks, was crippled by a disastrous US acquisition. It looked to technology to reduce the relatively high level of costs in its brand network and to achieve product innovation through a telephone banking system, First Direct. Neither of these appears to have been successful. Nor were they likely to have been; not only did they rely on the application of generally available technology but they both avoided using Midland's principal distinctive capabilities — its reputation and its branch network. These types of failure are widely repeated. Technology is particularly often seen as a response to low cost competition from lower wage countries. In industries as diverse as European cutlery and US automobiles, the belief that competitive disadvantage could be redressed through the achievement of technological advantage from non-appropriable innovation has been shown to be false.

The management of technology hinges on appropriability. The organisation must 'own' its innovation. In organisational terms, this requires the effective integration of technology into the firm. In economic terms, it requires that the added value created by innovation should accrue to the firm, rather than to a sub-group within it. The most effective mechanisms for doing this depend on whether innovation and technology are central to competitive advantage in the firm and the industry or not.

In many high tech industries, particularly those associated with electronics, pharmaceuticals or advanced transport equipment, technology is central to competitive advantage. This does not imply that innovation is the only source of competitive advantage; even in these industries the most successful firms are not necessarily the most innovative. It does, however, imply that a flow of innovative activity, or a quick response to innovative pressure, is an essential requirement. Successful high tech companies are generally characterised by extensive networks of relational contracts. Organisation structures are informal, while remuneration structures are flat and related to the performance of the organisation rather than to that of individuals within it. The shape of the firm is built around requirements for speed of response and the free sharing of information — the characteristics which technological adaptation require and which relational contracts facilitate.

Contrast this with organisations where technology is not central to competitive advantage. Take a financial services firm, where lack of innovation can destroy competitive advantage but innovation cannot create it. You can be the worst bank in the world if your technology is bad enough but no amount of technical innovation will make you the best bank in the world; that is simply not the nature of competitive advantage in this industry.

Here it is almost inevitable that the contract between those who manage the firm and those who manage its technology is essentially classical in nature. It is credible that the value system of a small producer of high performance engines revolves around success in technology — and that innovation will be recognised and rewarded. You will not become chief executive of a bank by making its computer system work; nor should you. You will look for a more explicit reward structure, and the management of the bank, unable easily to monitor your performance, will focus on those indicators it can control. Inevitably, the contract becomes more classical in form.

As generally with the choice between contract structures there are advantages and disadvantages to these different arrangements. Firms where technology is not central, which articulate the relationship between the innovator and the organisation within a more conventional framework of hierarchical control, minimise the risk that technological enthusiasm will run away with corporate resources. The cost of this is a much more limited capacity to integrate technology into the rest of the organisation.

Firms often look to innovation as a source of competitive advantage, or see the competitive advantage of other firms as based on innovation. Most often it is architecture that is crucial. The architecture that enables Sony to generate a seemingly endless series of innovations in consumer electronics supported by a reputation that ensures customers even for new and untried products, is a substantial competitive advantage. Imitators have the near impossible job of replicating that architecture, rather than the relatively simple one of reproducing the innovations.

Protecting and exploiting innovation

The issue of appropriability is fundamental. The central characteristic of a distinctive capability is that it cannot easily be replicated. A fundamental weakness of innovation as a source of competitive advantage is that it can be easily replicated. The result is that the innovators may expose themselves to the costs of innovation and the risks of development and introduction, only to see competitors share, or perhaps dominate, the fruits of their labour.

But it is also true that appropriation may be unexpectedly feasible. The Sony Walkman is an ingenious concept, but there is nothing about it that the innovator can protect. Once any electronics manufacturer in the world has seen it, they can make it. Yet Sony continues to be market leader. Marks and Spencer created a market for 'Cool Chill' foods, offering prepared meals of high quality and much higher price than had previously been available. The demonstration was immediately available to all food retailers and manufacturers; but Marks and Spencer continues to hold a prime position in the market. Although innovation is a primary source of competitive advantage, it is usually an effective source only if it can be deployed in concert with some other sources of competitive advantage, or if it is at least supported by other strategic weapons. Governments have long recognised that innovation generally suffers from a problem of appropriability. The results are potentially inefficient as well as unjust, since the prospect of replication reduces the incentive to innovate in the first place. Patent and copyright laws therefore protect innovators, and much innovation, including virtually all fundamental scientific research, is publicly funded.

Patent law has been unable to keep pace with the range and complexity of modern innovation, and it is almost a matter of accident whether or not a specific innovation can achieve effective patent protection. Such protection works reasonably well in pharmaceuticals, although even here there is a well known science of molecular manipulation, based on the attempt to invent round a patent by identifying a compound with essentially the same properties but distinct chemical composition. In other areas, patents may be used strategically — the innovation is surrounded with patents of doubtful value in the hope that legal costs will deter entrants. In many areas of innovation, such as product innovation in manufactured foodstuffs or in financial services, patents are generally useless. Most innovations (from calculus to junk bonds to flavoured yoghurt) are unpatentable.

If an innovation cannot be protected by law, it can sometimes be protected by commercial secrecy. This is almost never true of a product innovation. You cannot advertise new goods to your customers without at the same time advertising to your competitors. But for modest process innovations, secrecy may aid the innovator. Mostly, however, reverse engineering gives the imitator an equivalent opportunity.

If neither law nor secrecy is sufficient to allow an innovation to be turned into competitive advantage, then strategy must be used instead. This is most effective when innovation can be exploited in conjunction with a related competitive advantage. Innovation and reputation, or innovation and architecture, are often potent combinations.

There are few innovations in the financial services sector that cannot be copied rapidly by competitors. But a reputation for innovation attracts customers, who can gain access to the latest products without having to shop around. A good retailer need not even be the innovator if a reputation for being first with new products can be established. The reputation of the supplier may also induce customers to try innovations which they might otherwise view with reluctance. Coca Cola did not sell a low sugar product until the availability of aspartame enabled it to manufacture a good quality diet drink. Diet Coke then quickly gained an acceptability which drinks with other artificial sweeteners had not achieved, and established a new segment of the soft drink market in the process.

Architecture may be the source of a series of innovations, or it may provide the mechanisms by which innovation is disseminated within the organisation or is diffused to its customers. The success of classically innovative firms like Hewlett Packard rests less on any single innovation than on the architecture which enables them to derive a flow of innovative products. The continued lead enjoyed by Solid State Logic in the manufacture of synthesizers for recording studios rested not on the quality of its technology alone but on the combination of technology with a set of customer relationships which enabled it both to respond to customer needs and to secure product distribution.

Innovation is most effectively appropriated if it is associated with some other distinctive capability. Even if this is not possible, the combination with other strategic tools is generally necessary to enable innovation to be turned into sustained competitive advantage.

Standards

A particular type of complementary asset arises in markets where goods require the use of complementary equipment. Classic examples of this occur where hardware and software are associated: video cassette recorders with video tapes, computers with software and operating systems; satellite television programmes which require matching dishes. One of the most important standards issues of all will arise in the coming market for high definition television. Yet standards also arise where no particularly advanced technology is involved — the use of a credit card requires both cardholder and acceptor, and the Visa and Mastercard systems define the two dominant world standards.

In such markets it is rare for more than one standard to survive in the long run. More software will be developed for the leading standard which in turn leads new purchasers to prefer it, creating a cumulative process. Technical quality plays little part in the process: VHS is certainly no better than Sony's Betamax format; IBM's PC became the dominant standard although by common consent it offered little in the way of advanced or original design; Sky Television programmes have few critical admirers.

Two elements are critical in standards battles: the rapid achievement of an installed base and the credibility of the supplier — Sony wrongly believed that its dominance of the professional VCR market would be translated into equal dominance of the consumer market; JVC instead pursued an open licensing policy which ensured that there were soon more VHS than Betamax machines in operation in the major world markets and although the denouement was to take a decade, its outcome was by then inevitable; Sky Television's defeat of British Satellite Broadcasting (BSB) followed a similar pattern, and demonstrated that official sponsorship of a standard is no guarantee of success. By imposing delay and non-commercial obligations it may even prove disadvantageous. At the same time, Rupert Murdoch's commitment to the market was more credible than the fragmented and changing ownership of BSB. This credibility was the characteristic, above all, which IBM brought to the personal computer market.

Glaxo and EMI

In the 1970s, two UK firms, Glaxo and EMI, developed important innovations. Both depended critically on their sales in the US medical services market; Glaxo had founded an effective anti-ulcer drug, Zantac; EMI's scanner was the most important advance in radiology since the discovery of X-rays — Glaxo went on to become the most successful European company of the 1980s; EMI, crippled by losses on its scanner business, ceased to exist as an independent company and is no longer involved in medical electronics.

EMI's capability was much the more distinctive. The scanner won the Nobel Prize for Physics for its inventor, Geoffrey Houndsfield. The market for anti-ulcerants has long been recognised as a potentially lucrative target: ulcers are common, persistent and rarely fatal. While the first effective therapy was discovered by a UK scientist, Dr James Black, it was a US company, SmithKline, which developed Tagamet, the first commercial product. Zantac was discovered after Glaxo refocused its research programme following the publication of Dr Black's results.

The difference between the two companies lay in the effectiveness with which distinctive capabilities were developed into competitive advantage. EMI attempted to create its own US distribution network and to price at a level designed to recoup development costs. President Carter, concerned about spiralling medical bills, imposed a 'certificate of need' requirement on publicly funded hospitals. This delayed sales while General Electric developed its own version of the scanner. Although EMI had little experience of any manufacturing in this field, far less overseas, it established a US manufacturing plant, which ran into serious output and quality problems.

When GE entered the market, EMI was rapidly swept away and the rump of the business was sold to its larger competitor.

Patent protection — which had not proved sufficiently effective either for SmithKline or EMI — served Glaxo well, and helped ensure that its competitive advantage was sustainable. Glaxo marketed its drugs in the US through Hoffmann laRoche, whose sales of Librium and Valium had made it by far the most effective European pharmaceutical company in the US market. It entered Japan through a joint venture with a Japanese partner. In the UK and Italy where Glaxo had a strong established market reputation, it undertook distribution itself. Skilfully exploiting concern about possible Tagamet side effects, it priced Zantac at premia to Tagamet which reflected its own variable relative strength. By the mid 1980s, Zantac had become the world's best selling drug, and in the 1980s, Glaxo was by far the most successful of UK companies in innovative markets.

Conclusions — and some policy implications

The theme of this paper has been the difficulty of establishing competitive advantage from innovation. Success routinely has more to do with the quality of the supporting strategy, and with the possession of complementary competitive advantages, than with the underlying quality of the innovation itself.

It is difficult to overstate the role of innovation in establishing competitive advantage, but it is easy to misunderstand what that role is. Innovation may be the distinctive capability which gives rise to competitive advantage, but that outcome is actually quite rare. More often what appears to be the return to innovation is in fact a return to a combination of competitive advantages. The most powerful of these are those deployed by firms such as Sony or IBM, which marshal all three distinctive capabilities — architecture, reputation and innovation — and use each to reinforce the others. Firms less strongly placed may nevertheless give innovation a primary role in their competitive armoury; but unless they are favoured with regimes of high appropriability the translation of innovation to competitive advantage requires the strong support of associated elements of strategy.

It follows that general policies to stimulate innovative activity are unlikely to be effective means of improving industrial competitiveness. Indeed, the belief that innovation can compensate for other sources of competitive weakness has been a reiterated source of failure in both business and public policy; since innovation is generally imitable, success in implementing it is likely to be followed by the intervention of stronger competitors, while these other areas of weakness diminish the prospects that success will actually be achieved. The most relevant lesson from the innovative experience of other countries — or from successful companies here — is that if you get other aspects of management right, the capacity to handle innovation follows.

Chapter bibliography

Williamson, O E (1975) *Markets and Hierachies: Analysis and Antitrust Implications*, New York, Free Press

8

*Innovation of Processes: Success, Implementation and Practical Steps**

Christopher Voss

Discussion of innovation has tended to focus on products, despite the fact that in many cases one person's product is another person's process. It is an underlying proposition of this paper that management of process innovation is a major contributory factor to the competitiveness of firms and thus nations. For example, the received wisdom is that Japan may be relatively weak on product innovation and that its success is built around effective process innovation and implementation. As with all such received wisdom, there is overstatement on both sides of the argument, but there is much evidence on the importance of processes. A good example is to be found in the recent book, *The machine that changed the world* (Womack *et al*, 1990). The machine in question is process technology and the book's argument is that process innovations which the Japanese aggregate as 'lean production' are responsible for the level of performance of their car industry.

This paper will examine some of the factors concerned with process innovation, with a particular focus on manufacturing industry. A second underlying proposition is that consideration of process innovation must cover the whole life cycle of its innovation and adoption, and in particular should include implementation. The first three sections describe in more detail this view, as originally developed by Voss (1988a). Subsequent sections look at our knowledge of different parts of the innovation process.

Innovation, diffusion and implementation

The study and literature of innovation and the diffusion of technological innovation has generally split into two separate areas, one of which has been the study of the process of innovation. In the definition of innovation given

*The research reported in this paper was supported by the SERC and the ESRC/SERC joint committee.

by Utterback (1971), the innovation process is complete when the innovation has been successfully developed. The second area of study is that of the diffusion and adoption of innovations. The process of diffusion starts with the first adoption of an innovation, and it subsequently spreads. The reason for this difference in scope is that two different, sequential processes are being studied.

One area where there has been an overlap in research is the communication of ideas. Many innovations require a certain knowledge of the technical means necessary for the innovation. For an innovation to have taken place, the information must have diffused to the inventor and have been adopted. Both areas have examined the nature and source of communication, though diffusion researchers have focused on the speed of communication. This separation of research traditions naturally arises from the different processes being studied, but there are reasons for examining the interface further. If we examine the adoption of *process* innovations, we find that many issues fall between these two traditions.

The assumption of much of the innovation and engineering literature is that, once successfully developed, a new process innovation will work in all subsequent uses. Research on success and failure has been confined to the development and marketing of the innovation. The diffusion literature also assumes that the innovation works and hence that implementation is always successful. These assumptions break down when one considers complex innovations and particularly process innovations. There is much evidence that a process innovation can succeed in one attempt at adoption and fail in another. Once a new process technology has completed the innovation process (that is, first successful use), success or failure in subsequent applications can be considered as *implementation* success or failure.

Unlike innovation success, many of the activities and conditions that influence implementation success take place in the *adopting* organisation rather than the innovating organisation. Indeed, the study of implementation might more precisely be called the study of the process of adoption of innovations.

Defining success in implementation of innovations

A necessary precursor to discussion of implementation is the definition of what constitutes success (or failure). A study of the literature on process innovations and implementation will reveal that success, when not defined in purely subjective terms, is stated in technical terms. The following are typical examples:

Success = per cent uptime (Ettlie, 1984b)

       = use in actual production (Fleck, 1983)

       = has been in use for a year (Thurston, 1959)

Failure = limited per cent of parts actually made on the system
           (Ettlie, 1984b)

Where specific measures or indicators of success or failure have not been used, authors seem to see success in technical terms. Ettlie (1984a) asked practitioners what they thought were the most appropriate measures of success. His results indicated that the measures were predominantly technical.

Manufacturing organisations (and researchers) would seem to believe that they have successfully implemented new operating technology when two conditions are met: first, when all the bugs have been ironed out and it is working technically: second, when the operation is working reliably and there is little down time, and/or the new technology has a high utilisation rate. One can put forward the proposition that in getting the technology to work, only half the battle has been won. If we take the example of Advanced Manufacturing Technology (AMT), the prime motivation for installing AMT must be to increase the competitiveness of the organisation. The increasing importance of manufacturing-led competition is being stressed by many authors (eg Hayes *et al*, 1984 and Rosenbloom *et al*, 1983). The improvements in competitiveness promised by advanced manufacturing technology come not just from increased labour and machine productivity, but increased responsiveness, quality, flexibility and reduced inventories, lead time etc.

Full success is only realised if the benefits being looked for are realised, ideally in the market place through increased competitiveness. Technical success is a necessary but not sufficient condition for realising the full benefits of advanced manufacturing technology. We can propose two levels of success in implementation:

* technical success;
* realisation of benefits (business success).

The process of innovation implementation

The implementation of innovations can be defined as the process that leads to the successful adoption of an innovation of new technology.

A commonly held view of implementation is that it encompasses the actions from purchase and installation through to the successful use of the technology. This is a narrow view of the process of implementation. It can be argued that many important determinants of implementation success are actions and conditions prior to purchase or installation (Voss,1988b) eg strategic planning, technical planning, workforce consultation. In addition, one can postulate that antecedents such as the context of the firm, its skills, existing technology and managerial attitudes will have a significant impact on the process of implementation. This process has its roots in the firm's background and history, and embraces both pre-installation and post-installation factors.

It is possible to postulate a simple life cycle model of the process of implementation, in terms of a sequential process consisting of three phases. The first phase consists of those factors prior to installation that may have a positive or negative impact on the final outcome. This can be called the pre-installation phase. It finishes with the evaluations and go-ahead. (If there is no go-ahead, then there is no implementation.) The second phase is that of installation and commissioning. This is complete when the process is working successfully; when the technical and utilisation targets are being met consistently. The third phase is post-commissioning. In this phase, further technical improvement is likely to take place, as are the further activities needed to move beyond technical success to business success. The dividing line between phases two and three is diffuse, as is the end of phase three. It could be argued that phase three should not end, as an effective company should be continually seeking ways of improving its process. This model is represented diagrammatically in Figure 8.1. This figure includes some factors that Voss (1989) postulated as being important in each phase respectively.

Some evidence on process innovation and implementation

Success and failure

There is considerable empirical evidence that the innovation of processes does not necessarily lead to success. In a study of a sample of 17 identical innovations of computer application software, Voss (1984) found that 11 reached successful use, while 6 failed to do so. This pattern may seem obvious, though current innovation and diffusion theory implicitly assumes otherwise. Of greater importance are the findings of various studies that, although having achieved technical success, many process innovations fail to reach business success. In a further study of success and failure, this time focusing on advanced manufacturing technology, Voss (1988b) examined different definitions of success. He found the pattern shown in Table 8.1.

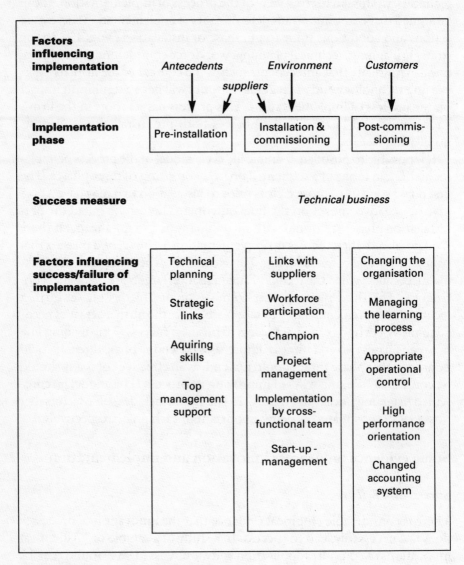

Figure 8.1 The process of implementation

Table 8 .1 Patterns of success

Measure of Success	Successful Firms (%)
Technical	
Technically successful	100
Business	
Productivity increases	86
Other benefits realised (eg flexibility, responsiveness, design-to-manufacture lead-time)	57
Competitiveness improved	14
	n = 14

Source: Voss (1988b)

Another example is a study of flexible manufacturing systems by Jaikumar (1986). He studied 35 systems in the US, and 60 in Japan. Flexible manufacturing systems are installed to deliver flexibility. He concluded that US systems 'show an astonishing lack of flexibility, and in may cases perform worse than the technology that they replace'. His indicators of flexibility included those shown in Table 8.2.

Table 8.2 Flexibility in Japan and US

	Japan	US
Number of parts produced per system	93	10
Number of new parts per year	22	1

Source: Jaikumar (1986)

A study by Tidd (1991) of robot assembly, comparing Japanese against UK practice, found a similar pattern to Jaikumar.

In conclusion, process innovations are not always successful in conventional, technical terms, and even when successful on this basis, often fail to achieve the capability and wider ranging benefits required of them, 'business' success. We will next examine some evidence of why this may occur. This will be done in the context of the implementation model proposed earlier.

Pre-installation

Strategy

Most writers on manufacturing strategy argue that choice of process and process technology should be consistent with both the characteristics of the products to be produced, and the competitive priorities of the firm eg Hill (1984), Hayes and Wheelwright (1985) and Voss (1986). The impact of this on process innovation can be illustrated by the work of Tidd (1991). He studied the adoption of assembly robots in Japan and the UK. He found, in contrast to prior expectations about Japan and technology, that the robots installed in the UK were more complex and technically sophisticated than those in Japan. However, despite this seeming technical advantage, the performance of robot assembly lines was far superior in Japan than in the UK. He proposes a number of explanations for this, some of which are at the pre-installation phase.

Table 8.3 Assembly robots in UK and Japan

	UK	Japan
Primary motives for development and adoption	To increase productivity and improve quality through the elimination of direct labour	To improve flexibility of production but continue to reduce costs through the elimination of waste
Technological trajectory pursued	Complex, sophisticated technology consistent with long-term goal of 'CIM', a computer systems approach	Relatively simple proven technology with continued reliance on operators, essentially a production engineering approach
Manufacturing	Reduction in diversity of production to facilitate further automation and computer integration	Flexible, but low cost production
Source of most significant developments	Specialist suppliers essentially 'technology push'	Major users essentially 'demand pull'

Source: Tidd (1991)

This is a remarkably similar set of conclusions to those of Jaikumar (1986) in his study of flexible manufacturing systems. He too found that the technology choice in the West was more sophisticated but less effective. US process innovations were highly sophisticated, but, because of their complexity, were very difficult to implement effectively. In addition, the pressure to start up the systems on time resulted in the systems in use not using their potential capability. In contrast, the Japanese systems were designed more simply and so were more reliable. Despite their relative simplicity, they were managed more flexibly. Their simplicity gave greater reliability, and enabled the maximum potential of the systems to be realised. As a result, the Japanese systems were both more flexible and achieved a higher utilisation than their US counterparts.

What can we learn from this research?

- Even within a single area of process innovation, technology choice is a vital decision. Technology-led approaches, as embodied in the robot and flexible manufacturing system examples, seem to run a number of risks. Technology can be adopted that requires greater knowledge and embodied learning to implement than many companies have.
- Objectives based on technical vision, such as 'achieving Computer Integrated Manufacture', are insufficient to guide innovation and may misdirect it, as they may force loss of sight of the business objectives and the fit with the product.
- Objectives such as getting rid of direct labour may not be consistent with business needs. It is interesting to note that, if this was the main objective in the UK, then simple robots rather than complex ones may have been the more appropriate response. In contrast, business led objectives would seem to lead to more effective choice of technology and innovation.

Evaluation

Much has been written on the way in which current financial evaluation systems hinder process innovation and the adoption of new process technologies. It is the opinion of the author that much of this effort has been focused in the wrong direction. That discounted cash flow techniques impede the adoption of new technologies is as much a function of the high cost of money leading to high discount rates, as the inability of the technique to take in all factors. In addition, there is no evidence to suggest that the Japanese investments do not have very high expectations of financial payback, and indeed do achieve·this. Conversations with Japanese managers indicate that they expect one to two year paybacks. Our problem may be that we cannot get as high a payback from the same investment.

A more fundamental problem is the complexity and systemic nature of many process innovations. This makes it difficult to evaluate an individual investment in isolation. For example Lindberg (1990), in studying manufacturing innovations in Sweden, concluded that 'in order to fully integrate the subsystems in manufacturing, a continuous and parallel development must take place'. To deal with this problem effectively in the evaluation stage, the full set of innovations and investments in a manufacturing system must be evaluated together, and investment appraisal must focus on alternative manufacturing systems.

Installation and commissioning

A wide range of factors has been found to be associated with effective installation and commissioning. For example, Horte (1991) identified 10 factors found through research in Sweden and from work elsewhere. These are:

- incremental stepwise installation;
- workforce engagement;
- relations to technology vendors;
- operator training;
- few technology vendors;
- project management;
- workforce participation;
- project champion;
- start-up management;
- cross-functional implementation teams.

These factors have been found in many studies of implementation, including those mentioned previously. For example, Tidd (1991) found these characteristics in the organisational context in UK companies: poorly trained, low-skilled operators; little communication between design, manufacturing and sales functions; distant relationships with suppliers and customers. On the other hand, the Japanese context was: highly skilled operators; good communication between design, manufacturing and sales; close relationships between suppliers and customers. Russell (1991), in studying implementation of CAD/CAM in UK companies, found many examples of poorly managed relationships with technology suppliers.

The use of cross-functional teams has been seen as a particular requirement for successful installation (and implementation in general). Many innovations involve a number of different technologies, have to be implemented in an existing production environment and draw on the expertise of various equipment suppliers.

Post installation

In characterising the implementation strategies of Japanese companies in comparison with US installers of Flexible Manufacturing Systems, Jaikumar

(1986) found many of the major differences took place at the post-installation phase. In US companies, once the system was up and running, the installation team was disbanded; in Japanese companies, it remained in place. Even after installation, it continually made changes and as result learning was maximised. This learning was translated into process mastery and productivity enhancement. The post-installation phase is often neglected, yet it is a vital part of the innovation and implementation process. This has been recognised by a number of authors, such as Ettlie (1984) who identified 'administrative innovations' required for successful implementation of process innovations, and Rogers, who uses (inappropriately) the term 're-invention' for the same phenomenon.

Leonard-Barton (1988) has developed a model that brings these together. She views implementation as a process of mutual adaptation of technology and organisation. When a process innovation is first used there are likely to be a number of misalignments. To overcome these, there should be a series of cycles of adaptation of both the technology and the user environment. Implementation thus becomes a continuous process of mutual adaptation. This process is illustrated in Figure 8.2. It is well supported by evidence from other studies. We can look at the adaptations in the post-installation phase in three main areas: organisation change, technology change and managerial control.

Organisation

In a study of implementation of process innovations, Voss (1988b) observed that those companies which had made some form of matching organisational change had achieved some element of business success, and those which had not done so had not moved beyond technical success.

The need to adapt organisations can be illustrated by the case of innovations of integrated processes in engineering and manufacturing.

The neglect of organisational issues in the implementation process has been identified as one of the reasons for underachievement of the anticipated benefits from such technologies. This finding is, perhaps, not surprising, given that managers are often faced with short deadlines in which to prove satisfactorily the investment in technology. However, unlike many technologies that are isolated in their operation (what Kaplinsky (1984) terms intra-activity technologies), the new integrating technologies are having a more widespread area of effect on the organisation and consideration is therefore warranted of parallel changes in the organisation and management of the technology, if benefits are to be realised. Figure 8.3 reflects

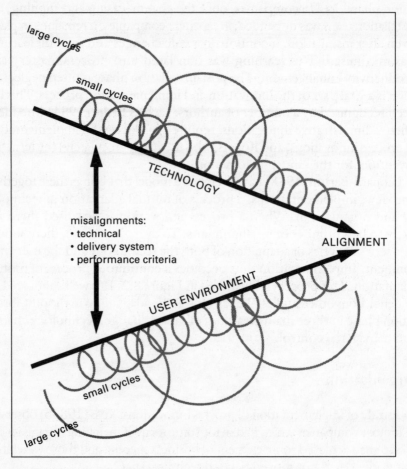

Figure 8.2 Mutual adaptation of technology and organisation

this need; typically, technologies are implemented with a disproportionate emphasis placed on technical integration (along line A–T); however, attention should now be directed towards organisational issues (a shift to the right).

In reflecting this need for improvement, Twigg *et al* (1991) have developed a framework to support the implementation of integrated process technologies through the consideration and integration of technical and organisation systems. The procedures have been developed to benefit both the company considering implementation for the first time and those that have already installed a system.

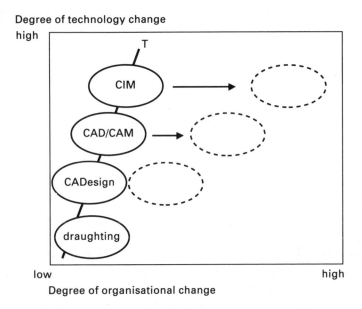

Degree of technology change

Figure 8.3 Aligning technology and organisation change

A framework for incorporating organisation issues
The framework aims to instil a procedure for continually assessing the extent and direction of implementation, that can be achieved internally to the company. It consists of the following steps:

- a review of the strategic context of the implementation;
- an audit of the existing system and its organisational context;
- the identification and choice of appropriate integration mechanisms.

The final element of the framework is concerned with providing support for the implementation of the methodology, giving guidance about managing the change.

A key element of integrated technology implementation is the need to improve integration between departments, functions and operations; the framework directs attention towards facilitating this through examination of and consideration for the linkages used.

The strategy stage involves the following steps:

- documentation of business strategy and product objectives;
- identification of the competitive criteria in key product lines;
- statement and evaluation of engineering and manufacturing strategies.

The first stage of implementation procedure is the identification and understanding of the overall business and relevant functional objectives: the market, product development, engineering and manufacturing strategies. These are important since they set out the agenda by which innovations can be implemented and assessed.

The audit stage consists of three steps:

- the identification of the innovation objectives;
- a review of the current and future situation of innovation usage;
- a review of the product development process.

The audit requires the company to consider the objectives to determine the key elements of its strategy, from which system requirements can be set and applications considered.

The audit begins with consideration of the objectives for adopting the innovation. These might typically include: reducing product development lead times; improving response to tender for contracts; improving design flexibility and complexity; and so on. These objectives are then reviewed against those stated in the strategy stage; if these are inconsistent, then a review should be made to realign the objectives more effectively. Having established these objectives, the performance of existing systems can be assessed. This data highlights key areas for managerial focus. Next, the technical system itself requires documenting.

Following this, the organisational context is considered. Since a key element of integrating technologies is the flow and use of information between engineering and manufacturing functions, a crucial consideration for successful organisational implementation is the mechanisms by which these functions are linked. The form of these links, and the links between all users, should be identified. Does this involve the transfer of detailed drawings, design analysis data, preliminary or finalised data? Is this data held on paper or transferred directly by computer interface? The key areas of organisation integration are likely to be those where there is very frequent and/or very intensive information flow, often accompanied by uncertainty; the next step identifies the frequency and intensity of information flows between different organisational units.

The change stage involves four steps:

- identification of the key linkages;
- identification of the current integration mechanisms;
- identification and evaluation of potential linkage mechanisms;
- assessment of priorities and choices between the alternatives.

In this stage, the linkages necessary to improve communication and integration are identified and highlighted. This stage provides an opportunity to consider organisation alternatives. There are a wide range of options for organising so as to facilitate integration. The most important options can be divided into two groups. The first is composed of those options that provide integration across the whole range of functions and is involved in taking new projects from market concept, through design and manufacturing and finally to the customer. The second group of options includes those that provide integration between individual functions.

These mechanisms are shown in Table 8.4 and are outlined in the appendix. Each group is ordered in approximate degree of difficulty. The earlier ones require little fundamental change and can usually be implemented easily; the later ones require more change and can consequently provide greater integration, which can be more difficult to implement. They are described in more detail in the appendix.

Table 8.4 *Ranked order of integration mechanisms used by companies to support computer integrated manufacture*

Integration across The whole organisation	Integration between functions
Direct Contact	—
—	Physical Proximity
—	Decision Rules in Software
—	Electronic Mail
—	Liaison Role
—	Secondment
—	Task Force
Project Team	—
—	Role Combination
Permanent Team or Cell	—
—	Integrator Function
—	Combined Department
Matrix Organisation	—

Note: Mechanisms are ranked in order of increasing difficulty. The ranking should not be seen to imply increasing integration effectiveness.

In the previous stage, a number of key linkages will have been identified; using this information, a review is made of those linkages needing improved integration. To make this assessment, a number of criteria are used:

- the extent of differentiation;
- cross-functional requirements;
- the level of uncertainty in the use, interpretation and content of data
- the intensity and frequency of two-way information flow;
- the complexity of product or task across these linkages.

All of these factors can lead to the need for integration mechanisms. If any of these criteria are met, then there is potential for managerial integration — the use of one or more of the integration mechanisms described above. On the other hand, simple routine communication, with a high degree of certainty, may not require sophisticated integration mechanisms or organisation change.

After an assessment of the extent of integration required for each key linkage, specific integration mechanisms are identified. This is done for both current and potential mechanisms, and then the available alternatives are evaluated. The appropriateness of any option may depend on a number of factors, such as its feasibility, its relevance to product development, the time span required, the cost and so forth.

Finally, the company needs to assess the priority of each option, and to determine which it will adopt. For this, the advantages and disadvantages must be considered, in order to identify the most attractive alternatives. The choice must be reviewed against a number of important criteria:

- Does it respond to the most important area(s) of need for integration?
- Does it match the current and future system configuration?
- Is it consistent with the organisation for product development?
- Will it enable the faster development and manufacture of products, more effectively and at lower cost?
- Is it a long term plan of change?

Technology change

The dynamic nature of technology change is found as much in process innovations as in product innovations. Leonard-Barton's framework indicates that we should expect to see both large cycles and small cycles of technology adaptation during implementation. The latter are consistent with incremental innovations, a phenomenon well documented in the innovation literature. Large cycles are less often considered as part of the innovation process, yet there is growing evidence of such cycles in the innovation and implementation process. In studying process innovation in Sweden, Lindberg (1990) identified both pro-active and re-active adaptation cycles. One of his cases, a flexible manufacturing system, was an initial failure. Technical tests showed that the process couldn't produce some products as designed after several months of delay and attempts to redesign them. Following this, it was necessary to redesign the production system. In studying CAD/CAM systems, Russell (1991) found that a significant percentage of companies had completely changed their software over the post-installation period.

Managerial control

Kaplan (1983) has argued strongly that management control systems no longer recognise the priorities and needs of manufacturing systems. This is particularly true as we move from innovations whose sole objectives are cost reduction and maximisation of output. Process innovation has led to the development of manufacturing systems whose objectives include flexibility, cycle time reduction and quality. These considerations are valid in the context of process innovation. In Jaikumar's (1984) research on flexible manufacturing systems, he identified a mismatch between the objectives of the technology and the managerial control systems as a major reason behind the problems with gaining effective innovation. In one case, studied separately by both Jaikumar and Voss (1986), a system installed to maximise medium term product change flexibility, had made no product changes whatsoever, and was also being managed to minimise short term flexibility. On close examination, this was found to be due to managerial control systems emphasising up-time and output. The only way up-time could be maximised was to minimise the flexibility of the flexible manufacturing system. Voss (1988b) identified a similar case in CAD/CAM, where a system had been installed to reduce design-to-delivery lead-times. The managerial control system emphasised return on investment. He found that:

> To maximise return on investment, the CAD system was run on two shifts with the third being used for overnight processing of data and drawings. To achieve high utilisation... large amounts of work were channelled through the CAD system. The results were two fold. First, because of the volume of work, a significant backlog of work developed, at one point there was a four month lead time. Second, there was little short term flexibility. As a result, emphasising getting maximum throughput and minimising costs led to failure to realise some of CAD's major advantages.

Although the evidence in this paper has been derived from technological innovation in processes, much process innovation is procedural and involves new management processes. A good example is the approach commonly called Just-In-Time (JIT) or 'Lean' production. It has been found that JIT implementation is as sensitive to performance measurement as the examples given above. In particular, individual incentive schemes put pressure on the workforce to do what is easiest and pays the biggest bonus. JIT approaches emphasise linked production and group production, where it is essential to produce in exact sequence.

Conclusions — some practical steps

This paper has set out to develop a framework for looking at innovation of processes. It has illustrated this with data from a wide variety of sources. Any such framework has limited use if it cannot be used to help companies manage new process technology. Part of the research described above is being adapted for use by practitioners through a workbook on managing organisational integration (Twigg and Voss, 1992). In reviewing the above a number of guidelines and practical steps emerge. These are listed in the sequence of the three-stage model used earlier.

Pre-installation
Important considerations at the installation phase include:

- Process innovation. To be effective, this should not be just technically led, but should support both the organisation's strategic direction and the characteristics of the products to be produced (detailed guidelines for doing this are in Twigg and Voss, 1992).
- The complexity, uncertainty and other characteristics of the technology should match the knowledge of the firm and its capability to handle it, as well as its business needs.
- Evaluation should be based on the full system to be developed, not parts of it.

Installation and commissioning
Installation requirements include:

- effective interaction with suppliers;
- the use of appropriately composed cross-functional teams;
- appropriate labour skills and availability.

Post-installation
Innovation and implementation does not stop at installation. Effective management of the post-installation phase can be crucial in obtaining success. Technical and user environment adaptations and modifications should be actively sought out.

- The implementation team should stay with the innovation until the main adaptations and learning have taken place.
- Appropriate organisational change should be actively sought out. Change should reflect the impact of the innovation on rules, communication flows and tasks.
- Performance measurement of those implementing and managing process innovation and implementation should match the objectives of the process innovation.

Appendix: organisation integration and process innovations

Options for integrating across a range of functions

Direct contact
Encouraging direct contact between people involved in the design process can be a simple way to promote integration. This can be accomplished in many ways, such as setting up patterns of meetings, design reviews, encouraging ad hoc meetings and informal contact in coffee lounges, lunch, etc.

The advantage of simple direct contact is that it is easy to set up and requires no special change. It is, however, a weak mechanism which is easy to let lapse, and can often be there in theory but not in practice.

Project team
This is probably the most widely used integration mechanism. A project team is normally cross-functional, involving a wide range of people skills and functions, meeting at regular intervals. Project teams come in a variety of types. They can be associated with the implementation project itself, or can be focused on the development of one or more new products. In an environment where projects are large and infrequent such as vehicle manufacture, project teams are normally set up around a single project. In companies where there are many small projects, project teams are more often set up to deal with a set of similar projects.

Permanent team or cell
Where a common data base in, for example, CAD/CAM is being used by a range of functions, then it may be possible to form a cell or team made up of people from different functions. This team can work closely together on a major project or a series of projects of similar characteristics. The key to the team's success would seem to be size; it must be large enough to contain the necessary functions for the design and manufacture of the task, but not so large that it becomes fragmented. Two examples illustrate: the first is a small Australian die manufacturer. It has a small permanent team made up of a draughtsman, a design engineer and a toolmaker. This team uses CAD/CAM to take customer orders from receipt of drawings, to preparation of an NC tape. The second example is a large vehicle manufacturer. There, a cell has been set up within the existing functional structure. It is composed of about 20

designers, analysts and engineers from four functions. They work as a team in an open plan office. The team members are responsible for the majority of the final stage of design and development of a vehicle. They all work using a unified CAD/CAE data base.

These cells are permanent project teams that provide a very high level of integration and can be configured around the system configurations. As with some previous options there are limitations. There are trade-offs between the functional expertise of a large function and spreading the expertise around different teams. A single cell or team within a strong set of functions can lead to tensions between the team and the others.

Matrix

In Matrix management, people working on a project or task will remain in their department reporting on technical matters but will report to a project manager for work on the project(s). This is particularly common in large organisations for major projects. A recent study of new vehicle development by Clark and Fujimoto found that most new projects used CAD together with Matrix management approaches. The successful projects were characterised by 'heavyweight' project management with involvement of all functions from marketing to manufacturing. The less effective projects were characterised by 'lightweight' project management and involved only functions in engineering.

Options for integrating individual functions

The following options are primarily for integrating the information requirements of individual functions, but can be used for integrating across a whole range of functions. They include both organisational and technical options.

Physical proximity

A very effective way to promote communication is to move groups or departments closer together, in the same building, in the same office or even across the same desk (sometimes called co-location). One example is the engineering department of a large manufacturer which moved to open plan offices in order to facilitate functional communication. Another example is a small company which arranged the desks of designers and manufacturing engineers who used the same CAD/CAM database, so that they faced each other in the same office.

Physical proximity can be achieved very simply and cheaply, sometimes by a moderate investment in office changes and layout. The feasibility is often dependant on the size of the group involved and its ties to physical equipment. Very large groups, physically distant R & D departments and factories in old buildings will all make this more difficult.

Decision rules

It is possible to build into the software in CAD/CAM systems decision rules, that reflect the considerations of downstream functions such as manufacture. A number of companies are now beginning to experiment with intelligent systems to support these efforts. Such rules, if effective, can reduce the uncertainty and hence the need for other integration mechanisms.

Electronic mail

There are a growing number of technical ways of supporting communication such as electronic mail and teleconferencing. These may be particularly important when there are large physical distances between functions, or there is involvement of suppliers. An example is the aerospace industry, where transnational projects are common. Teleconferencing is not without its problems; Zhuboff has described the difficulties in making teleconferencing effective.

Liaison role

A liaison person is one who is specifically charged with liaising between different functions to promote two way communication. The liaison role may be to do with systems. For example a number of companies who use CAD/CAM have a liaison person specifically to ensure that there are proper systems links between design, engineering and manufacture. In some companies there will be two liaison people, one in manufacturing and one in engineering. Similar considerations apply to the product development process.

Secondment

Secondment is the movement of a person from one department to another for a period of time, usually a fixed term. The benefit can be two way; first, to bring into one function, the considerations of another function. An example is secondment of manufacturing engineers into design which can be used to improve the quality of design for manufacture. A second benefit can be at the end of the secondment where the engineer can bring the consideration of the host function back to his or her own function.

Secondment can be appropriate where intensive interaction with another function such as manufacturing is necessary, and where there is a large number of projects requiring interaction. It is not always easy to implement; secondees can become professionally isolated from their home function and may not be accepted by their host. Uncertainty concerning the term of secondment can give rise to considerable anxiety regarding re-entry.

Role combination

New technology such as CAD, CAE and CAD/CAM often forces organisations to reconsider roles and task. In particular, access to a common data base provides the opportunity of taking tasks that were previously done by a number of people and bringing them together to be done by one group of people. For example, one company took the roles of analysis, design, drafting and NC programming and brought them together under a single engineer role. Each engineer now does all of these on a single project. Another company expanded the role of the tool room operators to include NC programming.

With role combination, other forms of integration become less necessary as a variety of skills are possessed in one individual. The limits to using role combination depend on the depth of skill needed. Where high levels of functional skills are needed, it may be difficult to create a 'super-engineer'.

Integration department

This fulfils the same needs as the liaison role, but on a larger scale. The integration department may be to do with projects. Many companies have project offices supporting project management across various functions. These may focus on systems, to manage CAD/CAM and to ensure that there are proper systems links between design, engineering and manufacture.

Combining departments

Sometimes the presence of a common data base raises questions as to the need for separate functions or organisations. A reorganisation in line with the system configuration may facilitate a more effective design process.

For example, one automotive company combined the manufacturing, engineering and design engineering functions into a single engineering organisation. On a smaller scale, another company, after installing CAE and CAD, combined the design and analysis department into a single department.

Chapter bibliography

Ettlie, J (1984) *The implementation of programmable manufacturing technology*, working paper, De Paul University, March

Ettlie, J (1984) 'The vendor user relationship in successful versus unsuccessful implementation of process innovations', paper presented to TIMS/ORSA meeting, San Francisco, 14–18 May

Fleck, J (1983) Robotics in manufacturing organisations, in G Winch (ed.) *Information technology in manufacturing processes*, London, Rossendale

Hayes, R and Wheelwright, S C (1984) *Restoring our competitive edge: competing through manufacturing*, Chichester, John Wiley

Horte, S A and Lindberg, P (1991) forthcoming, 'Implementation of advanced manufacturing technologies', Swedish FMS experience, *International Journal of Human Factors in Manufacturing*, vol 1, no 1

Hill, T (1985) *Manufacturing strategy*, London, Macmillan

Jaikumar, R (1984) 'Flexible manufacturing systems: a managerial perspective', working paper, Harvard Business School, January

Jaikumar, R (1986) 'Postindustrial Manufacturing', *Harvard Business Review*, vol 64, no 6, Nov–Dec, pp67–76

Kaplan, R S (1983) 'Measuring manufacturing performance: a new challenge for accounting research', *The Accounting Review*, vol XVIII, no 4, pp686–705

Kaplinsky, R (1984) *Automation*, Harlow, Longman

Lindberg, P (1990) 'Strategic manufacturing, a pro-active approach', *International Journal of Operations and Production Management*, vol 10, no 2, pp94–106

Leonard-Barton, D (1988) 'Implementation as mutual adaptation of technology and organisation', *Research Policy*, vol 17, pp251–67

Rogers, E M (1983) *Diffusion of Innovations*, New York, The Free Press

Rosenbloom, S R and Vossaghi, H (1983) 'Factory automation in the US', Research Report Series, Manufacturing Roundtable, Boston University School of Management, March

Russell, V (1991) unpublished research documents, London Business School

Tidd, J (1991) *Flexible manufacturing technologies and international competitiveness*, London, Pinter

Twigg, D and Voss, C A (1992) *Managing integration; a workbook*, London, Chapman and Hall

Thurston, P H (1959) *Systems procedures and responsibilities*, Division of Research, Harvard Business School

Utterback, J M (1971) 'The process of technological innovations within the firm', *Academy of Management Journal*, March, pp75–88

Voss, C A (1984) 'Multiple independent invention and the process of technological Innovations', *Technovation*, vol 2, pp169–84

Voss, C A (1986) 'Implementing manufacturing technology, a manufacturing strategy approach', *International Journal of Operations and Production Management*, vol 6, no 4, pp16–26

Voss, C A (1988a) 'Implementation, a key issue in manufacturing technology, the need for a field of study', *Research Policy*, vol 17, pp53–63

Voss, C A (1988b) 'Success and failure in advanced manufacturing technology', *International Journal of Technology Management*, vol 3 no 3, pp285–97

Womack, J P, Jones, D and Roos, D (1990) *The machine that changed the world*, New York, Macmillan

9

*The Innovation Management Tool Kit**

Norman Waterman and Mike Kirk

Innovation and its management have been the subject of countless books, most of which focus on case studies of successful companies. But what evidence is there that innovation can be managed successfully and how can a company set about improving its management of innovation? These questions were addressed by a Working Party of industrialists, trades union officials and civil servants, set up by the National Economic Development Council in the UK in 1988, and led by Sir Robin Nicholson FRS, Director of Pilkington, Rolls-Royce and British Petroleum, and chairman of the Advisory Committee on Science and Technology .

The answers have been provided by Quo-Tec Limited, a consultancy company appointed by NEDO to examine best practice in more than 50 UK-based companies. Innovation, the introduction of new ideas, is essential if a company is to survive and prosper. It can be managed, and a practical Tool Kit, developed to help manufacturing companies improve their management of innovation, is now available. This article describes the management of innovation as observed in more than 50 best practice companies operating in the UK and outlines the elements of the Tool Kit designed to help companies improve their innovation management.

---

*Dr N A Waterman is the founder and chief executive of Quo-Tec Limited, a consultancy company whose mission is to help its clients create new business from new and improved technologies.

Innovation and change

All manufacturing companies have to meet the challenge of rapid change:

- in the market place in terms of customers' needs and competitive pressures;
- in technology, which offers opportunities and also poses threats;
- in the attitudes and aspirations of its employees;
- in the expectations of investors.

If a company is to manage these changes successfully, it must itself change for the better by introducing new ideas, new products, new processes and procedures; in other words, it must innovate. Thus, 'successful innovation management' means 'change for the better'. Change is easier to measure and monitor than innovation: changes in products, processes and procedures are normally recorded. Changes in customer base, market share, numbers of competitors are also relatively easy to determine. Changes in the attitudes of people within a company are more difficult to measure objectively, but can certainly be detected by before-and-after contact with the company.

Hence, innovation management is concerned with much more than research and development and new products and processes. It concerns all aspects of company operation and is as important to day-to-day activities as it is to the longer term.

A major finding of the study referred to in the introduction is that best practice companies in the management of innovation are first and foremost well managed. If a company is not well managed, there is little or no chance that good new ideas will be exploited successfully.

Innovation is commonly perceived as being risky, especially technological innovation. Best practice companies are, in fact, averse to conventional risk taking and try to minimise uncertainty. However, they recognise that the greatest risk is to do nothing. A company must continually change for the better or risk extinction.

Most companies change because they are forced to, by external or internal pressures. The best of the best practice companies create a climate which anticipates change and they even foster it by continuously seeking out better products, processes and procedures. Companies which manage innovation or change for the better successfully, display a number of common characteristics almost irrespective of the nature of the business or size of the company. These companies are good at:

- promoting a positive culture and sense of mission;
- managing their people to realise their potential;
- communicating, both internally and externally;
- organising to suit the needs of their business;
- relating to their customers and identifying their customers' future needs;
- informing their investors of new developments and obtaining the necessary resources for new ventures;
- obtaining mutual benefits from their relationship with their most important suppliers;
- assessing their competitors' strengths and weaknesses;
- developing or acquiring unique, protectable technologies which form the basis of their business;
- nurturing successful new products, processes and procedures.

These ten areas of operation form the basis of the Innovation Management Tool Kit

Company culture and mission

The culture of a company may be difficult to put in words but it can certainly be experienced from the very first contact, by telephone or on a visit. Best practice companies emanate friendliness, efficiency and concern. If the person you want to contact is not there, everyone appears willing to answer the telephone, take a message, make sure the message is understood and acted upon, etc. When you visit, visitor parking is nearest to reception and there are no reserved places for management. The relationship between management and workforce is co-operative and mutually supportive.

The culture and associated atmosphere of a company may be easy to detect but its creation and maintenance requires hard work and dedication. Most best practice companies have explicit mission statements relating to product quality, customer service, employee welfare and profit.

While everyone in the company may not be able to quote the mission statement, the principles of the mission statement are believed and practised by most of the employees.

The people

All innovation management studies stress that people are the most valuable asset in any company and, like most clichés, this is true. People, not machines or buildings or profits, are responsible for innovation. Best practice companies attract very able employees, but there is little evidence from this investigation that they employ any special techniques to identify creative people, apart from situational interviewing (interviews which create imagined situations to simulate the working conditions and demands which the interviewee will face). There is no evidence that psychometric testing or other personality profiling techniques are used extensively by best practice companies in the UK for selection purposes, although these are more widely used for assisting decisions concerning career progression.

The stress laid on job descriptions has varied in the past decade. Most of the companies investigated have job descriptions for all of their employees and these are constructed to encourage innovation and change.

A common feature of best practice companies is the setting of clear targets, both for the company and individuals, and relating rewards to performance against those targets. Bonus schemes, based on company performance, are used extensively, especially for senior managers.

Training has a very high profile in the larger, best practice companies, with special emphasis being given to total quality management programmes. Small, fast-growing companies train fewer staff because limited resources and short-term business pressures often preclude the release of key individuals. This is one reason why some small innovative companies fail to manage growth successfully.

The most important innovation manager in any company is the chief executive. If he or she is not committed to innovation, then the company stands little chance of long term success. The study offers examples of companies which have turned their fortunes around, retaining the same workers, by appointing new chief executives with a commitment to innovation.

Sustaining the management of change for the better is possibly even more difficult than managing out of a crisis; examples are harder to find and less newsworthy.

Communications

Very good internal communications, upwards, downwards and sideways, are a strong characteristic of best practice companies. It is not so much that they all have formal briefing systems but that the information communicated through these systems is as important and interesting. Best practice companies also display a preference for face-to-face communication whenever possible and 'management by walking about' is seen as important for information gathering and transmission, and not primarily for public relations purposes.

Stimulating innovation in industry

In the words of Toshikata Amino, Executive Vice President of Honda US, quoted in *Fortune Magazine*, 30 January 1989: 'If you really want teamwork and good communications, it's time consuming'.

Organisation structure

Contrary to belief in some quarters, innovation appears to flourish best in organisations with a well defined organisation structure. Successful informality seems to require the framework of formality if it is not to become a recipe for chaos.

Best practice companies are adept at fitting the organisation structure to the needs of their business, rather than vice versa. A well-defined organisation structure does not have to be a rigid one.

Many of the more popular recommendations for changing the organisation structure to encourage innovation contain inherent contradictions:

- An open door policy may leave management with little time for other equally important aspects of creating a suitable atmosphere.
- Requiring all interested parties to be formally involved in decision making can cause damaging delays.
- Reducing the number of layers of management which have to vet new ideas may result in the approval of projects which fail and should have been weeded out at an earlier less expensive stage.

Best practice companies are good at reconciling these contradictions.

Customer relations

Customer concern is an obsession in best practice companies; it dominates their culture and is diffused throughout the organisation. The philosophy that the customer comes first starts in the car park where the visitors' parking spaces, rather than the directors', are nearest to the reception, and continues through to the monitoring of satisfied customers. The concept that the company has internal customers, ie one department's output is another's input, and that the same customer concern should apply, is also prevalent in best practice companies.

Resources and investor relations

Most significant innovations require resources which may be beyond the means of the company wishing to develop them. The ability to communicate well with investors and obtain the necessary resources is a characteristic of best practice companies.

Suppliers

In recent years, relationships with suppliers have been changing; more companies are following the Japanese lead and establishing close relationships with single suppliers. A textile machinery manufacturer provides a good example of this trend: a single supplier deal for a particular component was arranged, but only on condition that the supplier built a second factory to ensure continuity of the supply. This security-of-supply factor is the main argument against single supplier relationships put forward by other UK companies which prefer to rationalise sourcing, but only down to two or three suppliers. Supplier rationalisation will certainly continue but it is arguable whether or not single sources of supply will become the industrial norm.

Competitor analysis and market share

Companies which are successful at managing innovation have a strong preference for dominant market share. In fact many of these companies will not enter a new market unless they can see their way clear to achieving a dominant position, or at least to be in the top three of the market leaders. Best practice companies are very aware of the strengths and weaknesses of their competitors and many conduct regular formal reviews on each of their main competitors. They also monitor potential threats which are not associated with their direct competitors; that is products, processes or procedures which can fulfil the same function in a different way or by a different mechanism.

Technology

Best practice companies prefer unique, protectable technologies. Many will not invest any significant resources into new technology development unless it can be protected. This need not necessarily be through patents. A large know-how content may provide sufficient protection. These companies also have a clear vision of which technologies they must develop in-house to preserve the foundations of their business, and which they can afford to import from others under licence.

New products, processes and procedures

Best practice companies make continuous efforts to improve and try to make their own products, processes and procedures obsolete through the development of improved new ones. The onset of obsolescence is charted formally and used to remind staff of the need for regeneration.

Innovation Management Tool Kit

The Innovation Management Tool Kit produced from the observation and analysis of the characteristics of best practice companies is designed to:

- determine to what extent a company possesses these characteristics;
- identify the changes necessary to acquire and adopt the characteristics;
- instil a culture which sustains these characteristics.

The elements of the Tool Kit are listed below. Sample questions from the managers test are given on page 161.

The complete Tool Kit comprises the following:

The project leader's handbook
A user's guide for the person who will apply the Tool Kit. This person should know the company and understand the nature of its business, but ideally should not be directly affected by changes resulting from the implementation of changes resulting from the Tool Kit's application

The model innovative company
A set of characteristics displayed by best practice companies against which users of the Tool Kit can compare their own company

The tests
A series of diagnostic tests invite responses to a wide range of carefully presented statements on how the company operates.

The manager's test and the employee's test are a series of statements based on the key characteristics of a model company which will show how each perceive their own company.

The chief executive's assessment measures the chief executive's attitude to the management of change and innovation.

Significant divergence from the Model Company profile will immediately become apparent when the scores are plotted on the innovation wheel.

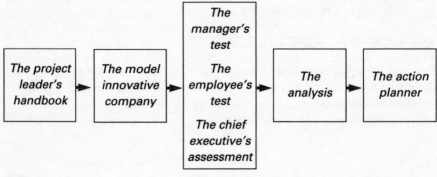

The analysis

The analysis can be used to compare differences of view and those areas shown to be furthest away from the Model Innovative Company. In addition, all ten characteristics can be examined to obtain a thorough and comprehensive view of all aspects of the company's management of innovation.

The action planner

The action planner is the practical conclusion of the exercise. It provides a list of techniques used by best practice companies. They may help to stimulate action where self-evident solutions have not already been identified. The chief executive plans the way forward and implements the findings of the Tool Kit within his/her company with the help of the project leader.

Sample questions from the manager's test

Respondents are invited to say whether they strongly agree, agree. slightly agree, neither agree nor disagree, slightly disagree, etc, that the answer applies to their company.

Company culture & mission people
The mission statement is known to the directors and senior staff only. Our training programme is prepared afresh each year in the light of identified needs.

Communications
The chief executive sets aside time for key personnel; receives feedback from them.

Organisation structure
We often form special teams to develop a new product, process or procedure from conception to completion.

Customer relations
We know exactly why customers buy our and not our competitors' products.

Investor relations
Funds are set aside for small speculative projects which do not have to justify the expenditure after the project has been approved.

Suppliers relations
We do not know which of our important suppliers also supply our competitors.

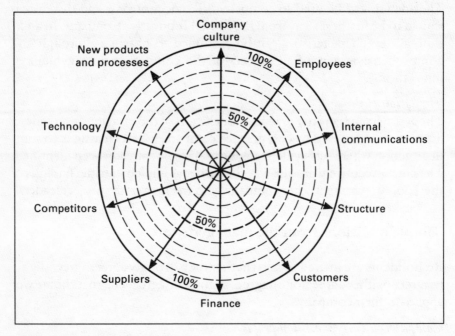

Figure 9.1 The innovation wheel

Competitor analysis
We always analyse our competitors' products to see what we can learn from
them.

Technology
We aim to develop unique technologies.

New products & processes
We regularly employ structured brain-storming and other techniques of this
kind to identify new product opportunities.

Reactions to the Tool Kit

The Tool Kit has proved to be very successful at identifying differences in
perception of how a company operates. Figure 9.2 shows the perceptions
of a managing director and his production director obtained by completing the manager's test and plotting the results on the 'innovation wheel'.
The results show very different views of the state of the company in many
areas of operation. The discussion which followed helped to clarify the

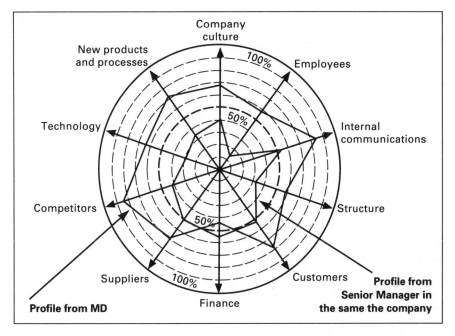

Figure 9.2 Innovation wheel profiles

reasons for the different perceptions and pointed the way towards improvements in the way the company should operate, particularly in how communication between the managing director and production director could be improved.

The differences in this case are extreme. In most cases innovation wheel scores are much closer and the most important differences relate to individual questions. Often simply highlighting these differences and discussing them is enough to resolve current problems. In the longer term, use of the complete Tool Kit will help a company to improve its management of innovation and change for the better.

Case study

The following case study of how one company has used the Innovation Management Tool Kit was given by Mr Mike Kirk, Managing Director of SPS Technologies Ltd.

The company is the UK subsidiary of an American supplier of fasteners to the aerospace industry. It is essentially a high technology sub-contractor in a highly competitive international business. There are over 1000 different parts in manufacture at any one time, requiring an average of about eight machine operations and four process operations. SPS's main requirement is for constant process innovation to improve performance, reduce costs and improve profit margins.

Mr Kirk attended a meeting of the East Midlands Engineering Association at which the Tool Kit was presented in June 1990. He was so impressed that he bought one on the spot, but the company was undergoing reorganisation and could not start to apply the process until October. The company had to decide whether to employ a consultant or to identify a project leader from its own ranks. In the event, it decided to employ a consultant because as a relatively small company it found that the existing management was fully stretched. The consultant conducted a series of workshops, two of which were aimed at managers, one at supervisors, and one at a mixture of shop floor and other staff. At each workshop there was a presentation of a scenario for the company in the 1990s and of the model innovative company from the Tool Kit. The participants then went on to complete the appropriate tests.

Predictably, the managing director's answers to his test led to a plot on the innovation wheel much nearer the model company than those from the shop floor. Other predictable biases emerged. But the more the company examined the responses, not just the plots on the wheel but also answers to some of the specific questions, the more certain critical underlying weaknesses emerged. SPS then appointed four working groups, each comprising a cross section of employees, to examine these weaknesses and recommend action. These selected eight topics for further work and the company decided initially to concentrate upon three:

- developing the company culture;
- improving performance in product introduction through tracking a specific new product just coming into the market;
- achieving improvement on yield and losses.

Working parties were set up in these three areas in March 1991 under the control of a steering committee.

The first output of the working parties was a new mission statement. The old one had been presented to the joint consultative committee, and circulated to staff and was on the notice boards, but nonetheless the employees knew nothing about it. The working party came up with a mission statement that made sense to its members and the managing and manufacturing directors spent two days talking to every employee in small groups, explaining exactly what it meant. That proved to be a very worthwhile exercise in developing the culture of the organisation.

The working party, looking at the introduction of a new product, found that the processes in the company did not enable new products to be introduced in a timely fashion. A project champion was not clearly identified or given sufficient authority. Changes have been made as a result of this which should have an impact in the future.

At the time of reporting the third working group was making a significant contribution to reducing process costs.

Innovation is a continuous process and receives continuing attention in SPS. The Innovation Tool Kit has been invaluable in helping SPS to focus upon those aspects of the innovation process where there was greatest potential for improvement.

The Innovation Management Tool Kit costs £250 and may be obtained from:

HMSO Publications Centre
P O Box 276
London SW8 5DT
Tel: 071 873 9090.

Part 3

Innovation in the Marketplace

10
Overview

Innovation in the marketplace

Marketing is not a timeless tool which can be reliably applied to the radical results of innovation in age-old ways. We must not assume that innovating and meeting customer demand are discrete activities that can be brought together after each has been planned in isolation; a successful marketing strategy inheres in the innovation process. In the previous section, Professor Kay described the concept of a firm's 'architecture' as its internal environment, a capacity to respond to changing circumstances by assessing innovations of all kinds and incorporating them into in the business structure. A static conception of how innovations should be brought to market is not what we should expect of a company with good architecture.

Ninean Eadie, President of ICL Europe, says that the key to success is the crossing of cultural boundaries between markets and technology. Describing the changing face of the computer business, he says that the lines of demarcation have broken down during the industry's development period to such an extent that it is now sometimes difficult to tell competitors and collaborators apart. Allies in a joint development project in one area may be vigorous competitors in another field. Competition used to be about managing a customer base, retaining customer loyalty and, since entry barriers were high, profiting from high margins. Now that switching costs for the customer have plummeted, the basis of competition in the computer market is very different. Customers can no longer be tied to product lines and the battle for success depends almost entirely on time to market. This has implications for both the process of innovation and the planning of market strategies—if, indeed, they can now be separated that starkly. The pace of change is so fast that new computers become obsolete within a year, and so competitors attempting to bootleg ideas are left trailing. In a marketplace characterised by its pace of change, success depends on understanding other companies, competitors, collaborators and suppliers and the changing relationships between competitors and collaborators. The premium on information and sophisticated lines of communication cannot be over estimated.

In such a context, the need for a framework for successful marketing is clear. Professor Cannon notes that there is a growing awareness of the difficulties involved in using marketing to direct innovatory activity and suggests that businesses pay particular attention to the interaction between internal management practices and wider market changes:

> There is a broad consensus on the importance of building a framework within which marketing can permeate the R&D process while shaping the relations between the firm, its internal stakeholders and its markets.

Acknowledging the importance of demand specification to innovatory success, he suggests that well managed marketing can enhance performance:

> The challenge for policy makers lies in creating ways in which the opportunities which emerge from R&D can be effectively exploited for the firm and the community.

One of the tools currently used in marketing analysis is the notion of technology push/marketing pull. The attention paid to the growth of new products reflects the strategic use of technology by firms, the level of R&D investment, the pace of innovation and the demands made by the marketplace, and can be measured in terms of these. We are warned, however, against placing too much stress on technological push measured in terms of its inputs. It is easy to assume that a high level of inputs will bring market success and to forget that innovation is actually about outputs. Indeed, Fraser and White argue that, at company level, dependence upon technology as the driving force for innovation is damaging to success. From a study of the performance of the top 250 companies in the UK they conclude that successful innovation must start in the marketplace and not in the laboratory. Successful marketing techniques are therefore crucial.

Eadie offers a redefinition of research, however, which implies the need for a review of the nature and status of marketing. He points out that the popular view of research is that it is a process of discovery through the application of pure intellect; scientists sit in splendid isolation seeking the solution to cosmic puzzles. He suggests that a more realistic view of the scientist is of someone who sits at the hub of a communication and information network, sifting through the work of others in the same or similar areas, looking for ideas to reinforce his own or spark off new lines of inquiry. The key to innovation is thus an efficient communication network.

This has important implications for marketing, and not merely to the obvious extent that market research to solicit customer desire is important. Fiona Gilmore, Managing Director of Springpoint Ltd, says that a fluid, customer-oriented approach is crucial, and that mixing technologists, designers and marketing specialists in teams from the outset of a project is the way to succeed. In this way, marketing can permeate the R&D framework in the manner Cannon suggests is critical.

Breaking down cultural boundaries and establishing sophisticated communications within a firm can foster success; collaboration with other firms can also enhance performance. Fraser and White find that companies aware that innovation should be driven by customer need rather than technological prowess are the most successful and that they are more likely to look externally for ideas and technology. Collaboration has traditionally been seen as a threat to competition and has been restrained by anti-trust legislation, but some kinds of collaboration can enhance competition.

Professor Metcalfe suggests that the apparent paradox—that competition and collaboration can be compatible—can be unravelled through recognising that competition is a two-level process. The market is the first level of competition, in which firms must establish a momentum of product and process innovation to maintain their positions. The second level is the creative competition to make better products and processes so as to ensure first level success in the market. This competition drives the first level:

> Competition at the two levels focuses on different dimensions of technology. At the first level, it is concerned with technology as artefact, products and the methods to produce them; at the second level it is concerned with knowledge and skills, the accumulation of which provides the basis for changing the artefacts.

The standard evolutionary process of the market is competition at level one: competitive pressure results in the elimination of variety and the concentration of market share. The maintenance of competitive pressure demands a continual supply of innovations.

Metcalfe directs our attention to a different kind of selection mechanism:

> Group selection provides advantages in the evolutionary process because the selective characteristics possessed by a unit of selection depend on the group it is in, *and would change* if it moved to a different group.

Collaborative research and design exemplifies 'group selection' at the second level of competition. In the UK, the first formal collaborative industrial research institutes were set up in 1917, with public grants and industry funds. Collaboration between private firms did not really emerge until the 1980s; the information technology and biotechnology sectors led the way. Eadie offers a positive account of the group selection mechanism. Citing Silicon Valley as an example, he says innovation is most effective where companies are close together. In such an environment, informal communication, active collaboration and competition provide a motivating atmosphere and the best context for the exchange of information. News about the activities of competitors passes freely when companies are close to each other, and provides both a benchmark against which current success can be measured and the stimulation to outstrip rivals.

No formal codification of collaboration arrangements has yet emerged. Reviewing the definitions in current use, Metcalfe notes that they all suggest that collaborations are never merely contractual:

> They involve interaction between the organisations to alter the behaviour of at least one of the parties.

Collaborations influence the boundaries of firms; a firm's knowledge base sets the outside limits of what it can do, and determines the scope and need for collaboration. This will vary from technology to technology. Metcalfe distinguishes between different knowledge base traditions, arguing that science and engineering collaboration prospects differ fundamentally because their differing theoretical bases push their research potentials in different directions.

Innovation has traditionally been seen as technology led, resulting from access to and investment in new ideas. Fraser and White warn of the dangers in this approach:

> A primary focus on technology as the driving force of innovation is not simply irrelevant but actually inimical to business success.

The evidence suggests that the firms which are first to market with technology-based products are rarely the main beneficiaries of the markets they create. The winners are the companies which innovate in developing the market. Fraser and White offer a number of case studies in support of this assertion, and identify three reasons why technology pioneers often stumble: the cost of exploitation and excessive commitment to a technology can hinder market success, but the most important distinction between technology-driven and more successful companies lies in their ability to define a clear market focus. For instance, IBM gained market ascendency with technologically undistinguished PCs because the company's emphasis was upon solving customers' problems.

Market focus is not simply a matter of researching markets and following through on survey results. Understanding customers sufficiently well to be able to predict and create demand is also important. White and Fraser note that:

> The critical difference between the company which is successful in the market and the typical technological innovator is that the former has gone to considerable lengths to understand its customers.

The research scientist abstracts the information he needs from the hub of a communications network. Technology clustering, the introduction of Marketing Information Systems (which Cannon notes are currently inadequately integrated into innovative activity) and the erosion of information boundaries all help to generate the free flow of information which is essential to market-led innovation. The days when technological novelties developed in conditions of secrecy could define and dominate markets are over. As Eadie notes: 'A strong competitor raises the game of all those who compete against him'.

11
Marketing and innovation

Tom Cannon

Context

Few commercial issues generate more interest and discussion in a modern industrial society than innovation. This is inevitable, as it is the process of innovation or society's willingness to harness technology which distinguishes industrial society from earlier eras. Deane (1969) puts the associated increase in the flow of inventions or of ideas for change suitable for incorporation into the productive process at the centre of the industrialisation process. The successful management of innovation has been associated ever since with corporate and national economic success.

A hundred years ago, during the 'second industrial revolution', which followed The Great Recession, Tom Vickers returned to this theme when he explained how:

> While most large metal and engineering producers rolled heavily in the doldrums of the 1870s and 1880s, Vickers' reaction to the Great Recession was to innovate a way through it, exploiting rather than mislaying their technical strengths... little wonder that Tom Vickers could agree with a somewhat bemused Royal Commission in the Depression of Trade that his firm has turned about to face the ill wind, and, to beat through them, has simply created a new business. (Trebilcock, 1977)

Vickers might not use the same language as the modern marketer but his underlying theme of using innovation to build business is the same.

His sentiments find many echoes today. The House of Lords Select Committee on Science and Technology (1991) recently commented that *innovation is crucial to the competitiveness of manufacturing industry*. Lord Weinstock put the situation in the most blunt terms: 'innovation is indispensable in maintaining a successful business. If you do not change as the times, the markets and the products require, you are dead'. Today, as during earlier times of rapid technological change, variations in the success with which firms and communities manage innovation are central to explanations of their different levels of competitive performance.

A marketing perspective

This paper develops this theme through an analysis of the distinctive role and contribution that modern marketing can make to successful innovation. This has been recognised by the UK's more successful firms.

> Top companies ... see innovation not as another overhead that the company needs to stay in business but as a flexible tool in the competitive game. (Goldsmith and Clutterbuck, 1984)

Despite this, there are barriers to the effective introduction of marketing. These exist at the strategic, tactical and operational level. Each of these issues will be explored in the course of the paper. Particular emphasis will be placed on the effect of this failure to use marketing effectively on the international competitiveness of specific firms and UK industry in general.

> The market share of British companies in many international markets (for example engineering products) has declined because of a failure to introduce new and better quality products to meet competition from overseas sources. (Baker, 1988)

Recognition of the importance of marketing has been matched by a growing awareness of the difficulties in using marketing to direct innovatory activity, improve its success rate and build a circle of market-based innovation leading to further progress. In part, this reflects the complexity of the underlying processes of invention, innovation, development and adaptation. Special attention will be paid to the interaction between internal management practices and wider market or environmental changes.

There is a broad consensus on the importance of building a framework within which marketing can permeate the R&D process while shaping the relations between the firm, its internal stakeholders and its markets. Rothwell (1986) points out that all modern studies of the technological innovation process emphasise the importance of demand specification to innovatory success. The attempt to understand the interaction between demand and the supply of new products and services has been a major preoccupation of modern marketing. This has to be set alongside the wider corporate concern with innovation and its effects on the enterprise. Research in marketing has emphasised the importance of human resources, finance, quality management and network on successful, marketing oriented innovation. Firms, industries and communities can and do use marketing to innovate more successfully. The challenge for policy makers lies in creating ways in which the opportunities which emerge from R&D can be effectively exploited for the firm and the community.

Technology push and marketing pull ?

The notion of 'push-pull' is important to all current marketing analysis of innovation. The special emphasis given to the growth of new products in modern markets reflects:

- the levels of R&D investment;
- the pace of innovation;
- the demands of the marketplace;
- the strategic use of technology by firms.

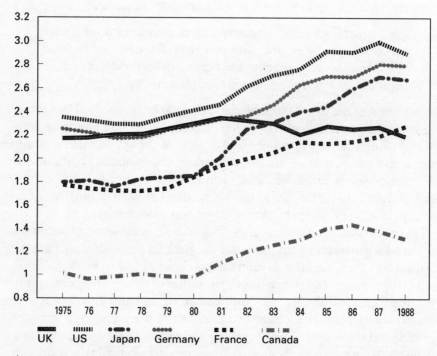

Figure 11.1 R&D as a percentage of GNP Source: Webster and Etzkowitz, (1990)

In part, this is driven by technological push. There is ample evidence in terms of the number of patent applications filed, scientists in employment and expenditure on R&D that this pressure to advance technologically is as strong as ever (see Figure 11.1).

The absolute number of patents applied for has increased dramatically over the last two decades, while their geographical dispersal reflects the increasing competition for access to new technologies (see Figure 11.2).

During the same period, the proportion of scientists and engineers in the workforce has doubled in virtually every developed economy. This has had a knock-on effect on the number of novel products and processes arriving on the market. Oakey (1991) has, however, warned against the 'misleading' impression that can be given by an emphasis on R&D inputs as a measure of innovation. The key measure is outputs.

At the same time, demand for new offerings, the speed with which technology transfer takes place and the blurring of the separation between product and process based innovation and manufacturing and services poses new challenges and opportunities. Markets are being shaped by products launched in the recent past (see Table 11.1).

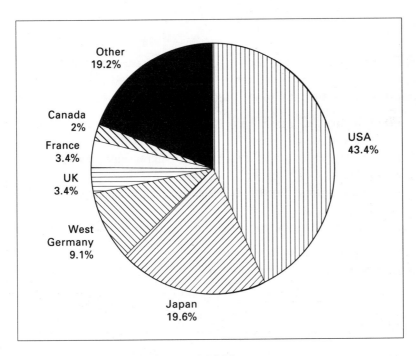

Figure 11.2 Patents applied for in US 1988 Source: Webster and Etzkowitz, (1990)

Table 11.1 Proportion of sales from recent introductions

Industry	Products less than five years old
Buildings & construction	45
Chemicals	29
Clothing	67
Elec.mach.	38
Gen. mac	41
Fabric metal	21
Food, drink & tobacco	11
Furniture	57
Iron & steel	21
Leather	54
Paper	24
Plastics	50
Print	38
Textiles	50
Misc	64
Stone, glass & clay	24
All	**38**

Source: Baker 1983

Evidence from the retail sector suggests that the rate of introduction of new products has increased since the survey described in Table 11.1 was undertaken. At the same time, it seems that:

- life cycles are getting shorter;
- ranging from core products or technologies is growing in importance;
- strategies for extending the life cycle are increasingly useful for improving returns;
- training and human resource issues are seen as intimately linked with marketing questions;
- Investment and funding strategies are centring on marketing questions.

Fuelling demand: the case of clothing

The recent evolution and current pattern of demand of the clothing industry illustrate how market pressures shape the process of innovation. It is a highly diverse industry; firms vary in size and nature from giant conglomerates such as Coats Viyella with its various specialist subsidiaries like Jaeger, to small specialist local retailers. Some, such as Benetton, are specialist, international firms. Others, like Dewhurst, are major suppliers of large, national retailers like Marks and Spencer. All have seen rapid change. The 1980s saw the rise and fall of niche retailers like Sock Shop. The same decade saw new technologies in production, processing, distribution and selling. The pattern of change and development seems certain to continue in the future. Many of these changes will reflect increasing competition. Firms are learning to use marketing techniques in increasingly innovative and sophisticated ways. New technologies and new ideas continue to enter the market. These create opportunities for those firms capable of exploiting them while posing challenges to all producers and middlemen. The effect of these developments will be powerfully influenced by the changes in market structure and competition prompted by the creation of the Single European Market.

Traditionally, the clothing industry has been shaped by a mixture of design push and retailer pull. The challenge will lie in pulling these and other aspects of marketing into an integrated approach to innovation. Success depends on:

> management skills, co-ordinating design activities with other tasks
> in the firm, particularly marketing, manufacturing and finance.
> (Walsh, Roy and Bruce 1988)

The clothing industry in the UK faces a marketing paradox. Some firms have tried to change, despite losing ground to rivals from overseas. At the same time, many customers criticise their approach to the market, especially their ability to innovate successfully. A recent study of the important and growing sports and leisure clothing sector (Dawson *et al*, 1987) found that retailers were critical of UK producers.

Table 11.2 Comments by retailers

- UK manufacturers have neither the low prices of the Far East nor the design skills of the continental Europeans
- UK manufacturers are slow to react to changes in the market
- UK manufacturers produce very few innovative ideas
- Some manufacturers are very poor at meeting delivery dates of respondents
- Labelling and packaging could be improved considerably
- Willingness to respond to requirements at a detailed level is low
- UK manufacturers are slow to produce samples of made-up garments for buyers to evaluate
- Quality controls are very variable between companies

Source: Dawson, Shaw, and Harris (1987)

Change has taken place but the rate, scale and impact of changes in approaches to marketing has not matched the expectations of clients or the levels of competitors. Many overseas competitors are increasing their investment in marketing and innovation even faster than UK firms. These affect every aspect of the marketing process, from the search for new ideas and the production of samples to the way they are shipped to and displayed in stores.

The influence of new technologies affects all aspects of a firm's marketing effort. Product developments will be shaped by new materials. These are emerging from research into new synthetics and the use of novel production processes with established materials. Superlightweight materials will compete with wool. New cutting machines used by workers with novel skills are needed. More immediately, CAD and CAM systems allow firms to turn concepts into finished garments at speeds undreamt of a decade ago. This is likely to produce twin pressures on manufacturers.

Some will be able to compete for new materials and processes. They will accept the high investment in R&D and seek technology driven routes into the market. Almost inevitably this will involve some degree of backwards integration with strong links with supplier industries. Other producers will cater to relatively volatile niche markets. The returns will be high but the risks considerable. Skills in innovation and marketing will be at premiums to get returns from high investment or to react fast enough to change in volatile markets.

The only real protection for a firm lies in close customer links and the skill to access and exploit the potential of new technologies. These are characterised by high availability, high customer specificity, speed of adaptation and scope for networking and increased scope for full supplier/customer interaction. Innovative, marketing orientated firms will be able to realise fully the benefits of incorporating marketing intelligence into marketing action to exploit new technologies for competitive advantage.

Over the last twenty years, changes in distribution systems and technologies have probably had more immediate and direct effects on clothing markets than any other factor. There is every indication that this pattern will continue. The Single European Market, with the direct challenge it poses to logistics and related systems, will act as a major spur to this. More obvious but equally dramatic developments such as the Channel Tunnel will have more immediate effects on the technologies of distribution.

New information technologies are eradicating the time lags that were once a barrier to entry to fast changing fashion markets. The full specifications for a range can be with a manufacturer in Hong Kong as quickly as with a firm in Huddersfield. Firms such as Federal Express have slashed the time taken to get samples to customers. The creation of the Single European Market will mean that firms across Europe will be seeking to use any edge they have to break into UK markets. These changes will affect home and international markets.

Simultaneously, the nature of retail demand is changing. The search for competitive advantage through successful innovation is shaping relationships up and down the market (see Tables 11.3 and 11.4).

Table 11.3 The changing nature of retail demand

- Far more precise views of needs
- Unwillingness to accept products and services which fall short of specification
- Greater professionalism in the buying function
- Greater willingness to undertake extensive search
- Specialisation with a willingness to employ and capitalise on technology, design, merchandising, promotion, advanced concepts in presentation and packaging
- Wider sourcing
- Investment in R&D. This, in turn, is prompting changes in retail buyer behaviour.

Table 11.4 Sports and leisure manufacturers: changes in buyer behaviour

	Yes	No	Don't know
Expecting shorter lead times	14	1	0
Planning order further ahead	5	10	0
More conscious of design	13	1	1
Less concerned about price	2	13	0
More concerned about price	12	3	0
Tighter delivery specs.	11	4	0
Expecting more Innovation	12	2	1
More Innovative	6	8	1

Source: Dawson, Shaw and Harris

The addition of these features to other changes in buying patterns are transforming the clothing sector (see Table 11.5).

This pattern of development is widespread. Technology push is creating the potential for change. Customers, at all levels, are seeing these innovations as important and are seeking out suppliers who can meet their needs. Observation of the changes in the clothing industry reinforces the emerging view that 'it is the interaction of product and process innovation' not product or process innovation on its own which determines market performance (see Kotabi, 1990).

Table 11.5 Changes in buying patterns

- Expectations of more frequent product changes
- Holding wider ranges
- More frequent but smaller orders
- Increased vertical integration
- Transfer of quality ownership
- Increased integration and sophistication of buying

The pattern of change and innovation

The life cycles of ideas, products and firms are shaped by these pressures. The notion of the Product Life Cycle has an important role in marketing thinking about innovation. It is a useful heuristic which suggests that individual products pass through a series of stages of development. These are commonly described in terms of introduction, growth, maturity and decline or renewal through innovation. This framework has been used as a basis for several related propositions about the process of technical change. Among the most popular are the notions that:

- life cycles are getting shorter;
- ranging from core products is the key to growth;
- strategies for extending the life cycle are dangerous or profitable (depending on perspective).

Underlying each of these concepts are valuable insights.

The proposition that life cycles are getting shorter highlights the rate of change and the extent to which discontinuous change is occurring. The emphasis on ranging is a useful antidote to the pre-occupation with single product/single market models prevalent in some disciplines. Together, they reaffirm and expand the assertion by Porter (1990) that: 'Competitive advantage is sustained by constant improvement and upgrading.'

Integrated marketing

The continuous nature of the process of innovation highlights the importance of close and enduring links with client groups. Research by Cunningham and others of the International Purchasing Group drew out important differences between UK practice and that seen in many other European countries. They explored the timing and extent of involvement

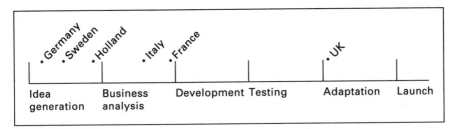

Figure 11.3 The timing of involvement

of customers by suppliers in industrial markets. A broad pattern emerged which indicated that UK firms were far less likely to involve their customers in the early stages of the development of a new product than their rivals from mainland Europe. Parkinson's research into the machine tool industry provided some confirmation of this. He noted that:

> In the West German companies in the sample, customer involvement in the product design and development process was seen as axiomatic if the company wanted to be successful. In contrast, in the British supplier companies, the prevailing attitude was not to involve the customer in the process until the product was put on the market.

These studies produce the overall pattern described in Figure 11.3, with UK firms involving their customers much later than firms from most European countries.

The nature and extent of involvement can be as important as the timing of involvement. Firms which involve a wide range of staff from their client companies, eg sales, production, design and engineering beside purchasing, are more likely to innovate successfully than those which restrict involvement (see Figure 11.4). Rothwell (1986) reinforces this view when he comments that: 'innovatory success is associated with active user involvement in product specification, design and development.' This means breaking the barriers which firms build up between themselves and their clients. It may mean eroding the internal obstacles to the movement of information, insight and creativity. At the same time, an integrated approach to marketing means adopting a process view of innovation. Many managers are reluctant to accept that the development of new products and services is not an instantaneous act 'but a series of activities that occurs over time' (Wheelwright and Sasser, 1989).

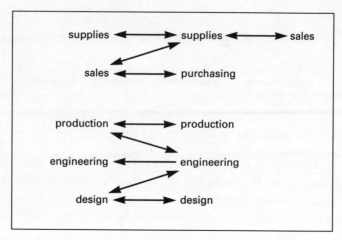

Figure 11.4 Intensive networks between firms

The roots and sources of marketing-led innovation

Successful products or services derive from a stock of ideas, concepts, research, development and projects. Firms can originate these themselves or obtain them from external sources. The fertility of a firm as a source of innovation is largely dependent on: the creative climate in the firm; its skill in seeking out innovation; the ability of its 'technological gatekeepers'; the priority given to innovation and the continuing commitment of top management. The potential sources of new products or services are unlimited. They can range from the 'Eureka' type invention to the systematic search for marginal improvements to existing products. All can play a part in sustaining the firm's competitive position. Success requires that innovations are managed with a clear view to meeting buyer needs, proper understanding of the market and awareness of the skills and resources required to build it.

Swintex: a case of road furniture to sports equipment

The opportunities and problems of successful innovation are well illustrated in the launch of a range of sports equipment by Swintex, a small plastics company based in the north-west. Until the launch of its new range, the company's business was largely based on the production of road cones; it was one of the leading UK producers of the familiar orange cone. The market, although large, was very competitive, with prices continually under pressure from low cost producers. In the recent past, Swintex had made two successful changes. The first was a product innovation: a range of cones to European size standards for export. The second was a process innovation which allowed much tighter product specifications with subsequent reductions in raw material specifications.

Despite these, the management felt it was locked into a highly competitive, low-margin business. The search for a new range of products was based on a wish to escape from this trap. After some searching and brainstorming, the firm identified the school sports equipment market as a target. In part, this reflected customer knowledge. The firm was regularly approached by teachers wanting cones to mark off race tracks or make cycle routes. There was also an element of serendipity—the sizes of the cones in their 'European' range matched the heights required for school hurdles. Other benefits were quickly identified: a hurdle made from two cones and an extruded plastic pipe was far cheaper than a traditional wood or metal hurdle; the firm's hurdles were lighter and easier to carry; other elements in its range of road furniture could be adapted for sports use; bases for warning lights made equally good bases for high jump, netball or basketball poles. A range soon took shape.

Swintex's problems started when it entered the market. The informal discussions with teachers had not brought out the complexity of local authority purchasing and the sales force had no experience of selling into the school supplies sector. The production of brochures and advertising was delayed until after the product was launched. There was reluctance to engage in the type of promotion or sponsorship activity which characterised this market. These and a host of other problems in the market eventually prompted Swintex to withdraw from any serious attempt to penetrate the sports furniture market.

The company did not lack creativity or an ability to innovate. It had shown some understanding of the four basic forms of innovation:

- improvement and development of existing forms;
- improvement and development of existing processes;
- introduction of novel production processes;
- introduction of novel products and services.

Swintex's problem lay, initially, in the low priority given to marketing analysis, research and development. In its existing markets, a mixture of experience and close customer links had reduced the firm's need for structure or formality in the examination of the market. Neither existed in the new market. The range of skills available to the company was not the key to success in the new context. It was, however, reluctant to buy in or acquire by other means the necessary skills. The new market called for higher expenditure in areas like advertising, merchandising, media relations and sponsorship was needed. Swintex lacked the will or the resources to undertake this spending. In part, these problems merely reflected a wider issue; at a more fundamental level, the company failed to appreciate the limitations on its capabilities—it was the victim of a more general error. Wheelwright has pointed out:

> New products often fail because companies misunderstand the most promising markets and channels of distribution and because they misapprehend their own technological strength or the product's technological challenges. (Wheelwright and Sasser, 1989)

For Swintex, the innovation was a one-off development with no basis in the strategic positioning of the firm.

Marketing, innovation and strategic positioning

The approach adopted by firms to the management of innovation shapes, and is in turn shaped by, the strategic positioning of the company overall. The strategic position of a company is the stance or combination of stances which it adopts to define its relationship with its market(s), customers and rivals.

Porter has suggested that there are four generic strategies. These are:

- broad cost leadership;
- broad differentiation;
- cost focus;
- differentiation focus.

Broad cost leadership means that the firm strives to be the lowest cost producer in the industry in which it operates. This will prompt the firm to seek out process innovations or product changes which allow it to reduce costs. The new range of cones produced by Swintex falls into this category.

Broad differentiation is based on an effort to be unique against one criterion seen as important to buyers across the industry. This will lead the company to seek innovations which refine or build on this distinctive strength. The American Airlines' emphasis on service is generally seen as an example of this strategy.

Cost focus is built on a concentrated effort to offer low costs to a target market. Innovations are driven by the desire to maintain this edge — Amstrad, Virgin Atlantic and the policy of vigorous price competition and inner city locations adopted by the retailer Kwik Save illustrate this approach — they gain competitive advantage by introducing innovations which reinforce the benefits offered to their core market.

Differentiation focus is based on determined efforts to deliver a particular benefit to a target market—customers will pay a higher price if they value this attribute. The mixture of image and engineering offered by BMW has protected it from price competition by its rivals. Innovations which reinforce these features will strengthen the firm's position in the market.

Aspects of the specific approach adopted by Porter have been criticised (Hendry, 1990). Despite this, there are tangible gains to be made from coherence in strategy and linking innovations with an integrated approach to market development. The recent ACARD study notes that:

> Of perhaps even greater importance (in assimilating and exploiting technology) is the ability of management to integrate technology into an overall business plan.(Rothwell & Beesley, 1989)

The differences in performance identified in Cooper's study (1985) of 122 industrial product firms highlighted the risks when policies for market development and new product development are poorly integrated. He identifies five basic strategies:

Table 11.6 Cooper's strategic positioning

- Technology driven with poor market focus
- Marketing dominant with weak R&D
- Cost control dominant with emphasis on adaptation and replication
- High budgets dominate but with weak controls and targeting
- Balanced marketing and technology

These policies produced different results: the 'cost control' and the 'balanced' approaches were linked with consistent success while the other policies performed less well. This work reinforces the need to link technology and marketing policies in an overall policy framework. This takes the firm up the learning curve while providing a basis for assessing proposals and making judgements.

These findings are consistent with Cooper's later study of industrial financial services (Cooper & Brentani, 1991). This places even greater emphasis on the effective management of marketing, especially during the launch or early introduction period. Table 11.7 shows that success in innovation is closely correlated with operational effectiveness.

Table 11.7 The keys to success

- Business synergy: the link between the innovation and the firm's current competences
- Product/market fit: the extent to which customer needs are identified, integrated and delivered
- Product introduction: the quality of the launch
- Superiority over rivals or uniqueness
- Quality of marketing from research through preparation of superior material to introduction.

Experience, learning and information increase in importance. Sunk investments in technology, skills and networks shape the strategic choices firms make:

> As product life cycles become much shorter than the life of production equipment, it becomes increasingly important to account for the characteristics of existing equipment in designing new products (Milgram and Roberts, 1990).

Information technologies are, themselves, increasingly important aspects of this equipment base.

Information and learning: the issues and technologies

The information and communications revolution of the 1980s had a profound effect on approaches to marketing and innovations. The information technology industries were a major source of innovation while the application of these technologies reshaped approaches to information management in companies. However, the recent downturn has cast some doubts over the more optimistic comments about the sector: that progress here has done much to 'cast a steady glow of light over the industrial nations' economic horizon' (*Time*, 26 November 1984). Information technology has provided the driving force for the growth of key firms, industry sectors and countries. Firms which have applied the new information technologies, effectively, investing to stay ahead rather than saving to survive, have prospered.

This prompted UK and European governments, often in collaboration with the European Commission, to embark on a range of initiatives to support the development and application of new information technologies during the 1980s. They ranged from the Alvey programme, designed to support research through assistance with applications projects such as CAD/CAM, to the Europe-wide programmes like ESPRIT (the European

Strategic Programme for Research and Development in Information Technology).

Table 11.8 Information technology initiatives sponsored by the EC

Euronet DIANE	Direct Information Access Network for Europe
INSIS	Community Inter-Institutional Information System
CADDIA	Cooperation in Automation of Data and Documentation for Exports, Imports and Agriculture
ESPRIT	European Strategic Programme for Research and Development in Information Technology
RACE	Research in Advanced Communications for Europe

Source: Budd (1987)

Marketing is central to the success of these developments in both the introduction of the technology and its use to assist change and improve operations. Change has occurred on two levels:

- in the nature of the goods and services sought by customers;
- in the ways companies organise themselves to produce, supply and distribute these goods.

The increased access to data provided by the new information technologies imposes extra responsibilities on management to use it effectively. This requires the construction of carefully planned and well organised marketing information systems (MIS).

A marketing information system is an organised arrangement of people, machines and procedures set up to ensure that all relevant and usable information required by marketing management reaches them at a time and in a form to help with effective decision making. Introducing such a system calls for a programme of planning, research, experimentation, introduction and feedback to ensure that the search for and development of innovations is intimately linked to marketing needs. Establishing these goals for the system is the first step. These should be clearly defined, linked to marketing strategies and their implications understood. Specific responsibility for managing and monitoring the system has to be clearly allocated to ensure continuing system efficiency as needs change and the range and variety of information on the innovation expand.

There has been surprisingly little research into the ways marketing intelligence systems are used to support innovation and new product development. Fletcher (1981) identifies eight common uses for information systems:

Figure 11.9 The uses of information systems

- Customer analysis
- Profit analysis
- Sales force control
- Competitor analysis
- Cost savings
- Improved data retrieval
- Sales forecasting
- Planning and decision making

These are listed in order of frequency. It is clear from this that Marketing Information Systems are not fully integrated into the process of innovation in a structured or central way. This is despite the gains that can be achieved through:

• the increased access to technology;
• the erosion on information boundaries.

The value is especially clear for the technology-based firm which 'more than ever needs to strive for synergy and the technology/marketing interface' (Bender, 1989).

The internationalisation of markets, especially through the integration of European markets, increases the importance of coherence in strategy, integration of technology and markets and high quality marketing information systems.

An international perspective

The adoption of the Single European Act by the members of the European Community marked the start of a crucial phase in the economic progress of Western Europe. It is a development which has provoked widespread discussion, comment and concern inside and outside the Community. This debate is inevitable—the Act seeks to create a Single Internal Market from some of the richest and most powerful economies in the world. The countries of the Community have a Gross National Product of $4 trillion and 330 million citizens. It is the single largest trading block in the world with a significantly larger population and only slightly small GNP than the US. The Community's share of world trade, excluding the Community itself, is virtually the same as the combined share of the US and Japan.

Much of the pressure for change and greater integration grows from the decline in the economic standing of Europe compared with the US and Japan for most of the early 1980s. From 1979 to 1985, the European Community's share of world trade (excluding intra-EC trade) declined by almost 1.5 per cent. The US share of world trade increased by roughly 0.75 per cent and that of Japan by over 5 per cent. This pattern of decline, and the underlying acceptance of failure, summarised in the term 'Euro-pessimism,' was seen as so well entrenched that only a major and dramatic initiative could reverse this process. A series of reports (Albert and Ball, 1984 and Dooge Committee, 1985) led eventually to the adoption of the Cockfield Report (1985).

The report's timetable spells out three basic stages towards the creation of a single European Market. These are:

1   The removal of physical barriers (frontier controls, transport quotas etc).
2   The abolition of technical barriers to trade and the prevention of new barriers arising. This is coupled with increased freedom of movement for workers, the creation of a common market in services, freer capital movement and greater industrial cooperation between members and across the community.
3   The removal of fiscal barriers, by bringing VAT rates into line and tackling the problem of excise duties.

There are potential gains from:

• lower costs from the elimination of frontier controls and simplification of administrative procedures;
• improved efficiency from increased competition;
• greater exploitation of economies of scale;
• reallocation of resources and greater comparative advantage;
• increased innovation, creating opportunities for successful innovators and threats to the less effective.

Hitherto, technology push has dominated thinking: new resources have been injected into R&D; supporting innovation is a priority and investment is concentrated in strategic areas. There is, however, evidence that many companies are failing to recognise or gear up to exploit the new market opportunities. This can be seen nationally and locally. Even Germany, the economic powerhouse of Europe, is described by Porter (1990)as having 'problems competing successfully in new industries ... (with) ... market positions gradually slipping in many sectors'.

A major effort is still needed to:

• increase real investment;

- reduce fragmentation and duplication;
- improve communication and collaboration;
- · build better links between research centres, notably universities and industry;
- improve R&D and access to a marketing intelligence infrastructure, especially in disadvantaged regions.

Information technology and telecommunications are especially sensitive given the rapid decline in the international competitiveness of European industry. The EC has moved from being a net exporter of IT into a major import market, especially for US and Japanese industry. Between 1978 and 1988, every major European country saw its share of world exports decline in computing, semiconductors, office equipment and telecommunications. The highly fragmented nature of European distribution and retailing is a constraint on the speed with which innovations can be disseminated. Innovators, early adopters, late adopters and laggards are local and the potential for rapid growth and the creation of a Europe-wide base for international growth is limited.

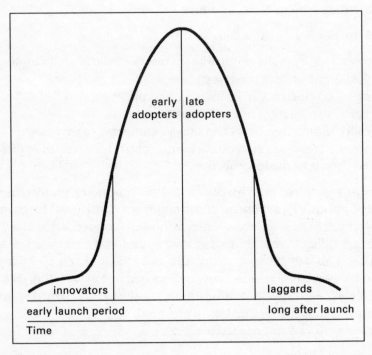

Figure 11.5 The diffusion of innovation

Some change can be seen. Some shifts will occur through competitive and organic growth but acquisition and merger will be even more important. The first signs of this can be seen in retailing. Major groups are seeking to establish themselves in other parts of the EC. Cultural and social diversity within the Community is a major barrier to change in local markets. Perhaps the greatest of these hurdles remains language: the countries of the Community speak 18 languages and numerous dialects—these act as a brake on the rapid integration of consumer markets. The gradual emergence of English as the trade language might affect this, but not in the short term.

The overall shape of the unified internal market can now be discerned. Figure 11.6 gives an indication of these shifts in the proportion of total external trade which is within the Community for some of the larger EC countries.

This process of convergence will accelerate as firms become more comfortable with intra-European trade and Europe-wide launches of new products become easier. Firms are preparing themselves for this through:

Percentage of total external trade within the EC

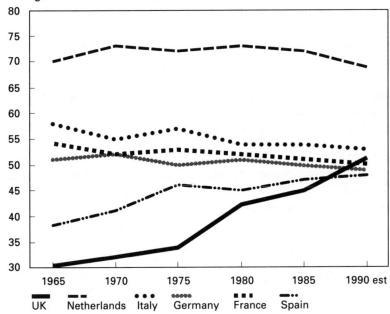

Figure 11.6 Patterns of intra-European trade
Source: Eurostat

- better integration of their business operations;
- diversification into related industries;
- strategic alliances;
- specialisation.

The increase in the scale of European operations places a premium on operational effectiveness in managing innovation and on effective integration of the technology/marketing interface. The costs of failure increase with distance. These are heightened by the shorter product life cycles of new products and higher costs of R&D.

Diversification into related industries has increased in most European markets. In part, this is a reaction to the high risks associated with non-related diversification. The notion of 'sticking to their knitting' has widespread currency among European industrialists. Companies relieve their need to expand into new areas through 'strategic alliances' to exploit particular opportunities (eg central or eastern Europe) or to manage resource intensive projects such as the European Airbus project. Initially, these links were largely 'horizontal'—between firms in complementary sectors. The buyback agreement between Siemens and Philips illustrates this. More recently, vertical alliances involving companies at different stages of developing marketing systems are growing in importance in Europe. The link between National Freight Company and Christian Salvesen gives some indication of the potential for this type of organisational innovation-based collaboration to exploit marketing opportunities.

These developments will improve the competitiveness of innovations by European firms if a strongly internationalist perspective is built into the process. Cooper & Kleinschmidt's research (1988) indicates that when compared to failures, successful products:

- were designed for world use;
- included foreign markets to a greater extent as part of their total market;
- featured foreign market research;
- had more trail selling or test markets in foreign markets;
- included much stronger foreign launch efforts.

This has been recognised by those non-European firms which have sought access to European markets through acquisition or other market entry policies. In 1988, almost 300 European companies were acquired by non-EC companies. Their combined value was $19,718 million. This greatly exceeds the value of acquisitions by EC companies of companies in other EC countries. These purchases were largely concentrated in the UK. Access to technologies and markets for innovations is central to these entry strategies.

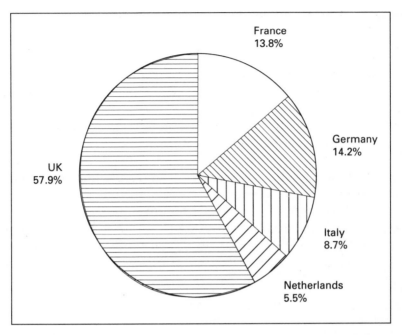

Figure 11.7 Acquisition by non-EC companies of EC companies (1988)

Conclusion

Innovations in products, processes and services have shaped the commercial environment of today. Effective innovation separates the successful community and enterprise from the less successful. Traditionally, this success has been equated with access to sources of new ideas, investments in technologies and the 'push' of research and development. It is now clear that really successful firms have combined skills in accessing new ideas with a determined effort to understand the needs of markets and deliver new products and services based on customer benefits.

This is not achieved through a series of isolated or lucky actions. The more successful firms view innovation as a continuing process in which marketing skills are wedded to systematic attempts to access new technologies. This process calls for a fully integrated approach to innovation which combines business strategies, management skills and the effective deployment of adequate resources.

Stimulating innovation in industry

In the marketplace, it is important to break down the barriers between suppliers and customers. Research suggests that many UK firms involve the customers much later and in a more restricted way than their more successful rivals at home and overseas. A strategy for successful innovation is at the heart of effectiveness. Policy makers need to highlight the opportunities which can emerge from this approach while widening access to international market opportunities.

Chapter bibliography

Albert, M and Ball, R J (1984) 'Towards European economic recovery', European Parliament Working Document

Baker, M (1983) *Market development*, Harmondsworth, Penguin Books

Baker, M (1988) *Marketing: theory and practice*, London, Macmillan

Bender, H O (1989) 'Marketing technologically advanced products', *European Management Journal*, vol 7, no 2, pp. 159–65

Budd, S A (1987) *The EEC: a guide to the maze*, London, Kogan Page

Cooper, R G (1985) 'Overall corporate strategies for new product programmes', *Industrial Marketing Management*, vol 14, no3, August

Cooper, R G and Brentani, U de (1991) 'New industrial services: what distinguishes the winners', *Journal of Product Innovation Management*, vol 8, no 2, June, pp75–90

Cockfield Report (1985) 'The White Paper on completing the internal market', Commission Document

Dawson, J, Shaw, S and Harris, D (1987) *Impact of changes in retailing and wholesaling on Scottish manufacturers*, Stirling, Stirling University

Deane, P (1969) *The first industrial revolution*, Cambridge, The University Press

Dooge Committee (1985) Ad hoc committee for institutional affairs,Council Document SN/1187/85

Goldsmith, W and Clutterbuck, D (1984) *The winning streak*, London, Penguin

Hendry, J (1990) 'The problem with Porter's generic strategies', *European Management Journal*, vol 6, no 4, Dec, pp443–50

House of Lords Select Committee on Science and Technology (1991) *Innovation in manufacturing industry*, London, HMSO

Johne, A (1986) 'Substance versus trappings in new product development', *Journal of Marketing Management*, vol 1, no 3, pp291–301

Kleinschmidt, E J and Cooper, R G (1988) 'The performance impact of an international orientation on product innovation', *European Journal of Marketing*, vol 22, no 10, pp. 56–71

Kotabi, M (1990) 'Corporate product policy and innovative behaviour in European and Japanese multinationals: an empirical investigation', *Journal of Marketing*, vol 54, April, pp31–33

KPMG (1989) *Deal watch*, London, March

Milgram, P and Roberts, J (1990) 'The economics of modern manufacturing: technology, strategy and organisation', *American Economic Review*, vol 80, no 3, June, pp511–28

Oakey, R P and Cooper, S Y (1991) 'The relationship between product technology and innovation performance in high technology small firms', *Technovation*, vol 11, no 2 , March, pp79–92

Porter, M E (1990) *The competitive advantage of nations*, London, Macmillan

Porter, ME (1985) *Competitive advantage: creating and sustaining superior performance*, New York, Free Press

Rothwell, R (1986) 'Innovation and re-innovation: a role for the user', *Journal of Marketing Management*, vol 2, no 2, Winter, pp109–23

Rothwell, R and Beesley, M (1989) *The importance of technology transfer*, London, Advisory Council on Applied Research and Development

Trebilcock, C (1977) *The Vickers brothers*, London, Europa Publications

Walsh, V, Roy, R and Bruce, M (1988) 'Competitive by design', *Journal of Marketing Management*, vol 4, no 2, pp201–16

Webster, A and Etzkowitz, H (1990) *Academic-industry relations: the second academic revolution*, London, Science Policy Support Group

Wheelwright, S C and Sasser, W E (1989) 'The new product development map', *Harvard Business Review*, May–June, pp112–25

12

*Innovation and the Marketplace**

Douglas Fraser and Howard White

Introduction—the nature of innovation

Innovation is about outputs. It is manifested in new products and services, new processes and new means of marketing and distribution. Successful innovation should lead to improved market share and profits.

Yet much of the discussion of innovation is in terms of technological inputs. In part this is because R&D, numbers of scientific personnel, and patenting activity are measurable and have clear links to the innovation process.

It is also because of an assumption that a high level of technological input will lead to a high level of output, that companies which invest heavily in R&D are necessarily the most successful innovators.

In this paper we seek to demonstrate that this assumption is invalid, and that the converse may sometimes be true. At the level of the company, dependence upon technology as the main driving force for innovation is, in general, damaging to the success of an enterprise. We document a number of examples and then present an analysis of the top 250 companies in the UK. The reasons for technological innovation being harmful to company performance are discussed and the conclusion is drawn that successful innovation must start in the marketplace.

Technology in context

No matter how good a company's technology, it has to be embodied in products or services, efficiently produced and effectively marketed. A number of authors focus upon the need to incorporate technology properly

*Thanks are due to many colleagues in the National Economic Development Office who contributed to this paper. The views expressed are those of the authors and should not be attributed to NEDO

into business strategies and to develop organisations capable of exploiting it commercially (eg Grindley, 1991).

It is important to establish whether the company which produces technically leading edge products which it then fails to exploit in the marketplace is merely deficient in the above respects or is in a more profound sense different from the successful innovator.

This would be less important if the benefits of early technological innovation could be appropriated through licensing or monopoly profits. However, with the possible exception of the pharmaceutical industry, this does not appear to happen. Competitors respond quickly and often adapt technology to invalidate patent protection. Smaller companies are especially vulnerable because of the cost of protecting their intellectual property.

Evidence from companies—not just UK ones—suggests that those which are first to market with original technology-based products are rarely, if ever, the main beneficiaries of the market they have created. The beneficiaries are companies which have the capability of seizing and adapting the technology, but which are also able to produce economically and, in particular, innovate in developing the market.

Reconciling the paradox

On the face of it, this does not appear to be consistent with the argument for which considerable empirical evidence exists, that a high level of R&D expenditure in an economy as a whole is associated with industrial success. We shall argue from examples that the most successful enterprises are those which innovate by looking for new and better means of satisfying the needs of their customers. One way of satisfying such needs is through the application of new and improved technology: in pharmaceuticals and electronics this is the principal route to innovation. However, even the largest company can only hope to have a fully competitive capability in a small range of technologies. In very many cases the technology needs to be brought in from outside. This can be achieved through formal technology transfer, through poaching skilled staff or through arrangements with suppliers.

All of these routes work more effectively where an enterprise is physically located near centres of excellence in a broad range of technologies and has frequent and early contact with leaders in the field. This is why nations which generate a strong indigenous technological capability, also tend to generate successful companies exploiting that technology, themselves often spending significant sums on development in order to do so.

The existence of such clusters may explain why countries succeed where companies fail. Furthermore, it is not part of our argument that companies should not spend on R&D—on the contrary, this is often a necessary part of meeting customer expectations. We are rather concerned with companies which are primarily technologically driven: those which see their technology as providing a comparative advantage against competition and take pride in the advanced products produced from internal resources. Such companies are often very capable, and responsible for technological innovation disproportionate to the resources that they employ. These are often the companies that we speak of with pride and respect.

This paper argues that such companies are not successful if they focus on technology rather than customers and restrict themselves unduly to the limited resources at their own direct command. They are frequently the first into a new market—indeed they create it—but they are overtaken by companies which focus more effectively on their customers.

Some case studies

A good example can be found in the case of video magnetic recording. Although many companies experimented with recording television images on magnetic tape, the first successful product was developed by the US company, Ampex. The Ampex quad system based on two-inch tape became the broadcast standard. Ampex established and dominated the world market, producing a range of recorders and diversifying into other studio equipment. Sony of Japan realised that this technology had much greater application than in the relatively small broadcast market. In particular it looked at educational applications (in the early 1950s Sony had established itself in audio tape recording by targeting the educational market—which is quite significant in Japan with its strong ethos of self-improvement). However, the product needed to be cheapened and made simple to use, hence the development of one-inch helical scan recording systems in the 1960s. The new standards were at first totally unacceptable to broadcasters, but Sony worked on improving performance and introduced professional-quality one-inch machines in the 1970s. Initially, these were only used in broadcasting where space was at a premium and two-inch was retained for high quality applications, but one-inch progressively took over. Ampex introduced its own one-inch standard and licensed it to other companies such as Bosch-Fernseh in Germany to retain its position in the market. However, Sony became the dominant supplier in the broadcast as well as the educational and security fields.

It might be expected that this success would be translated by Sony into the biggest market of all, the consumer market—but it was not. There was no great insight needed to see that when video recording systems could be produced which were sufficiently cheap and robust, demand from consumers would be enormous. Many companies in the United States, Europe and Japan experimented with systems in the 1960s and 1970s—not all magnetic medium based. The non-Japanese company which came nearest to succeeding was probably Philips which developed a standard for video cassette recording which almost became established. However, the most significant loser was Sony which fought hard for its Betamax system and lost in the marketplace to the arguably inferior VHS created by Matsushita, owner of the National Panasonic brand. Matsushita's strength was market based, originating primarily from a deal with CBS which put a great deal of VHS software into the US market.

EMI was a leading UK company in electronics, recording and entertainment from its formation in 1931 to its merger with Thorn in 1979 as the very much weaker partner. It brought a series of fundamentally new products in computing, marine radar, automation and components to market over a lengthy period, but never established itself as a force in any of those markets. EMI's invention of computerised axial tomography revolutionised medical radiography but it brought the company to its knees as competition developed from firms better established in the medical imaging market.

In automotives, BMC with the Austin Mini pioneered the transverse engine, front wheel drive package which is now standard in small cars. Rover introduced the four wheel drive utility vehicle. Lotus (now part of General Motors) introduced multivalve technology.

IBM grew to dominate the mainframe computer market by looking after its customers and solving their applications problems, whilst RCA, Honeywell and others produced computers of greater technical sophistication. Apple and Commodore created the microcomputer market, but it was the entry of IBM which widened that market beyond specialists and enthusiasts. Key to this enlargement was the increased availability of software.

The link between technological innovation and success is probably stronger in pharmaceuticals than in other businesses because the benefits can more readily be appropriated. Specific chemical compounds can be patented unambiguously and such patents are not easy to circumvent. However, the same general arguments apply. Tagamet, a fundamentally new approach to ulcer treatment, was produced and marketed by Smithkline. Glaxo very quickly followed with a slightly improved product, Zantac, and an aggressive marketing and production campaign which took it into the lead position.

There are many other cases that could be quoted, in integrated circuits, machine tools and numerical control. In the great majority, the pioneer is rapidly overtaken by later entrants to the market. These are often more innovative in adapting the products to meet customer requirements and in marketing them.

Top UK companies

Are the above cases merely a series of anecdotes or is it possible to find a systematic link between innovation and company performance? We analysed the 250 largest public companies registered in the UK by asking colleagues in NEDO, who had frequent and often confidential contact with many of those companies, to score them according to their innovative ability. Having looked at different aspects of innovation in a pilot survey, we came to focus upon two:

- **Technological innovation**—is the company known as a technological leader, bringing a stream of new products to market, often based upon new and innovative technology?
- **Marketing innovation**—is the company known as an innovator in the marketplace, finding new means of distributing, presenting or supporting its products?

These ratings were compared with the compound annual earnings per share growth of the same companies, adjusted for inflation (wholesale price index), over the period 1980 to 1989 (taken from Beresford, 1990). A number of other possible measures including the added value concept advanced by Davis and Kay (1990) were considered. The variable used was selected largely on grounds of data availability. However, earnings per share embraces both growth and profitability and the use of a nine year span should iron out random fluctuations and financial engineering. More details of the analysis, including alternative variables, are given in the appendix.

Figure 12.1 shows the correlation between company performance and technological innovation. A negative relationship (correlation coefficient −0.26) may be seen, as also indicated by the least squares line shown in the figure. By contrast, Figure 12.2 shows a slight positive relationship (correlation coefficient 0.21) between innovation in marketing and growth in earnings per share.

Two further conclusions emerged from the correlation analysis:

- Innovators in marketing are not strongly identified with technological innovators (though there is some correlation between the two).

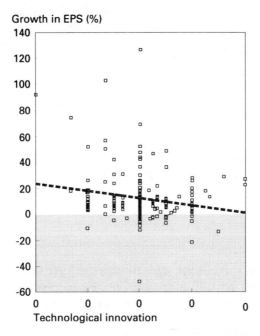

Figure 12.1 Company performance and technological innovation

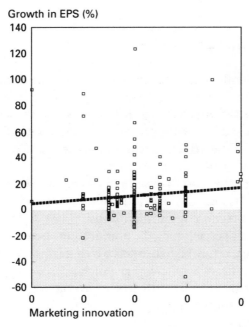

Figure 12.2 Company performance and marketing innovation

- Companies perceived as technological innovators retain that characteristic through time, whereas market innovators are less likely to do so.

Correlation analysis is crude since it does not take into account the impact of other variables on the dependent variable (in this case performance) or relationships between the different explanatory variables. However, as reported in the appendix, multiple regression techniques not only support but in fact strengthen the findings reported above as regards company performance. The results found these relationships to be robust to various specifications, including allowing for sectoral effects; we are not simply seeing, for example, the contrast of the UK's weak electronics industry with its successful retailing one.

Lessons

A primary focus on technology as the driving force of innovation is not simply irrelevant but actually inimical to business success. Drawing on the above case studies we can identify three reasons why this might be so:

- the cost of exploitation;
- excessive commitment to a technology;
- the lack of market focus.

Cost of exploitation

It is a rule of thumb in manufacturing industry that each stage of the product inception process costs ten times that preceding it. For every £1 spent on research it is necessary to spend £10 on product development, and £100 to manufacture and launch the product. Companies which pride themselves on the fertility of their R&D may not have the resources to back all of the products which result.

It was certainly the cost of developing its medical imaging business that damaged EMI. Indeed, EMI entered many markets as a consequence of having developed a technologically innovative product. In each case, it faced not only the cost of establishing the product, but also the cost of establishing itself in a new market. Even in markets which it largely created and in which it remained significant for many years, such as broadcast equipment, EMI was not able to invest sufficiently to remain competitive. In all cases it was compelled to withdraw, selling its remaining interests to better established competitors.

Cost also has implications for timescales: one way of making a new product introduction affordable is to extend its timescale and fund later stages from the cash flow earned at the beginning. Yet in short lifetime products, a delay of six months in introduction to market can cut profits by one third (Reinertsen, 1991). To generate funds from the new product itself, in order to achieve volume production, demands monopoly profits on initial low volume production; yet this is the formula which gives the greatest incentive for competitors to enter the market.

Implicit in the recent review of the Alvey programme (Guy & Georghiou, 1991), a joint government, university and industry programme to develop advanced information technology products in the UK, is the recognition that the resources required to exploit the technology developed at great expense were never forthcoming and that this is an important part of the explanation for the disappointments of the programme.

Excessive commitment to a technology

One of the reasons for a shortage of funds to exploit products is that many of the 'technology innovators' are not sufficiently ruthless in cutting out their less promising products. Glaxo, an outstandingly successful company, has a reputation for taking a very hard look at its new product development programmes, cutting most and concentrating resources on those which appear to be most promising while its competitors still pursue several in parallel.

Even a successful product can be enhanced and kept in the market for too long, as Ampex found with its quad machines. In principle, the technology innovator should be better placed to develop the next generation than its rivals—it understands its products and has a lead in their technology. In practice this rarely happens. Later entrants leapfrog the pioneer, usually—as in the cases of Sony and Glaxo—offering improvements which are of particular value to the customer.

Another way in which technology innovators become dangerously enthused with their own creation, is when they seek to extend the technology unrealistically. An example of that is the use by BMC of the transverse engine/front wheel drive package pioneered in the Mini, in the 1300, 1500 and 1800 series of models. The advantages diminished with increasing vehicle size; the application of those resources to improving the Mini and reducing its production costs would have led to a much stronger position in the small car market.

One common characteristic of technology innovators is the 'not-invented-here' attitude. Their pride in their technology will often lead to a preference for inventing their own solutions rather than obtaining the best from elsewhere.

An important distinction has to be made between products which are seen by their creators as the manifestation of an original and ingenious technical solution and those which are seen as embodying a series of services to customers. It is commonplace in discussions of innovation to say that successful innovators need to be committed to their own products. We accept that that is probably true, but companies which are committed to specific technological implementations will almost always be out-manoeuvred by those which find better solutions to the same customer needs.

Lack of market focus

The most important distinction of all between technology-driven and more successful companies is the former's lack of a clear market focus.

In the case studies quoted, IBM gained advantage in both mainframe and micro computers because the emphasis of the business was on solving its customers' problems. The first IBM PC was criticised in the industry as being technically unambitious, but it was capable of offering the great bulk of non-specialist customers a very useful business tool. This, coupled with the backing of a large company and the rapid development of software, gave customers greater confidence than additional technical features would have done. Today it is IBM that is under pressure: in mainframes the pressure comes from Japanese companies and their affiliates which are also well tuned to the market; in micro computers, the pressure comes from a host of manufacturers, mainly in the Far East, offering what has become a commodity product at very low prices. The pressure does not come from technology-led companies, since these mainly occupy specialist niches such as advanced engineering workstations, and IBM is now putting pressure on them.

Market focus does not simply mean researching markets and producing what the research indicates. In the case of technology products, it often means empathising with customers sufficiently to be able to create a market on the basis of latent need or demand. Sony has been outstandingly successful in this respect. One technology in which that company invested 13 years of effort was the charge coupled device, because it realised that this offered the potential of 'electronic film'—photography with instant access. The critical difference between the company which is successful in the market and the typical technological innovator, is that the former has gone to considerable lengths to understand its customers. In one Japanese company senior technical officers spend up to 30 days each year getting close to customers while in another, the chief engineer of a new development went to live with a US family typical of the customers for that development (Hamel and Prahalad, 1991).

Links between technological and marketing innovation

The above observations do not imply that technology is unimportant. On the contrary, IBM, Matsushita, Glaxo and the other winners quoted all have technological capability of a very high order. It is, however, firmly subordinated to the needs of satisfying market demands. This is achieved through the value system and organisation of the company itself. An important part of this value system is a willingness to look outside the company for technology and ideas. It is well known that Japanese companies are avid searchers of the world's technologies, but the most successful western companies exhibit similar characteristics.

This may be why the survey of top companies in the UK found a low correlation between technological and marketing innovation. Companies which search externally for the best technology are likely to use technology pioneered by others, perhaps more so than that originating in-house.

It is in smaller companies that technological and marketing innovation are most likely to come together, and this paper is mainly based upon the experience of large companies. However small companies rarely have the resources to invent a technology; they often develop when an entrepreneur with a clear view of a market opportunity takes a technology from a larger company, a university or a research establishment. In many cases, the entrepreneur has previously been employed by the larger organisation which developed that technology.

Renishaw is a small UK enterprise which has some 40 per cent of the world market for the high precision contact probes used in advanced machine tools and measuring equipment. It was started by an inventor who had developed the probe whilst working for Rolls Royce to meet a specific need of that company and was in that sense market driven. Rolls Royce wisely recognised that it could not distract itself from its main business by developing a business in contact probes, but it wanted the product. Rolls helped and encouraged the founder of Renishaw to establish his own company.

Fairchild developed silicon integrated circuits but became an 'also-ran' in the business. The most successful companies of the first generation, including Intel, which provided the microprocessor for the IBM PC, were set up by what became known as the 'Fairchildren' who left their parent company. Today the industry leaders are large vertically integrated Japanese companies. These are willing to invest in what has become in part a commodity business, the tradition of manufacturing excellence and process improvement in an industry where costs are vitally dependent upon process yield, and substantial internal markets which know what they want.

Intel, although now a substantial company, remains the principal source of microprocessor designs for personal computers and many other products. It is perhaps one of the exceptions, a technology company which has sustained success over a period. This is because Intel has remained close to its market, has continued to innovate at a pace which challenges its rivals and has stuck to the markets it knows best.

But behind Intel and the other offshoots of Fairchild was the extraordinary phenomenon of 'Silicon Valley'. In a small area near San Francisco there is a concentration of leading edge technology companies around the Berkeley campus of the University of California. The first major company to arise from this complex was Hewlett Packard in the 1950s and since then many component companies have been founded, together with others which depend upon leading edge component designs. It was here that IBM sited its own PC developments.

Technology clustering and technology transfer

Successful innovators look for and use the most appropriate technology rather than that which they happen to possess. However, the act of identifying the right technology to satisfy a market need and transferring it into the company is complex and demanding. Even the largest companies have difficulty reviewing technologies which might be available, not least because the more widely known an innovative technology is, the less likely it is that any one user can employ it to create a competitive advantage. A number of schemes have been developed in various countries to promote technology awareness and technology transfer (NEDO, 1987).

As the Silicon Valley example illustrates, one very successful approach is the co-location of university, technology leaders and technology exploiters. This is because a high level of informal contact can lead to those involved knowing of new developments before the outside world. The act of technology transfer can thus be effected through formal licensing, through buying in advanced technology incorporated into devices or, more often, by simply poaching the key person.

In Japan, government-organised industry research programmes in fields such as supercomputing, VLSI components and advanced information technology have been very effective. The input has been partly home-grown, partly based on systematic technology audits of international competitors and largely obtained from visiting overseas researchers. The output has been in the researchers returning to the participating companies which initially seconded them. Major electronics companies have reported that 20 to 30 per cent of their researchers are involved in such programmes (NEDO, 1991). As Japanese technology becomes more advanced, it becomes more difficult to obtain the initial input. Japanese companies are increasingly investing in 'technology listening posts' wherever world class research takes place.

A further method found in Japan, especially in the automotive industry, is collaborative development between companies and their suppliers. In the UK the food processing industry works closely with its suppliers of plant and machinery; both are relatively strong internationally. Technology transfer is effected where technology developed in one product area is applied in another through the medium of a supplier of common equipment.

All of the above depend upon close personal contact between those who understand and those who need a technology. By the time a technology is fully understood, documented and generally available, it is too late to gain any advantage from its use. Personal contact can more readily be achieved where there is a very local concentration of technology providers and exploiters. This is why there is a strong relationship between the level of R&D which takes place in an economy, and industrial success. The total level of technological innovation achieved in an industrial society, whether manifested in specialist supply companies, universities and polytechnics, research establishments or producers of end products, represents an important national resource which can be tapped by enterprises needing technology to satisfy customer demands. For the most part these will be local. Paradoxically, companies such as EMI, Ampex, Fairchild, Plessey and RCA have contributed much more than they have received in benefit.

Marketing innovation

Given the negative correlation between technology innovation and the success of large UK companies in the 1980s, the question on market innovation was included to test whether the relationship observed had simply to do with excessive concentration on technical novelty—as suspected—or with innovation generally. Examples of marketing innovation from the most successful UK companies include Body Shop International, which made a business out of marketing environmentally benign products—previously an eccentric niche. Albert Fisher, another high performer, developed a pan-European distribution system for fruit and vegetables. BPB Industries established manufacturing and distribution facilities throughout Europe and adapted its marketing to local practices—even persuading the Italians to consider plasterboard instead of tiles. Dunhill developed an exclusive brand to cover a range of luxury goods sold into wealthy markets such as Japan and the US. Hillsdown operates through decentralised, sharply focused, value-added food marketing operations. All of these companies have one thing in common: they are led by an intimate knowledge of their market and a determination to succeed in it. Products and technology are a means to an end and never the end itself.

Amongst high technology UK owned companies, Racal contrasted with Plessey and EMI, neither of which now exist as independent companies, in the extent to which it had a clear understanding of a limited number of markets including tactical radio communications and data communications. Racal's most successful commercial success has been in cellular radio, Vodaphone. The company probably had much of the technology needed to develop its own system but instead it entered into a joint venture with the US company, Millicom. Racal realised that the benefits of reliability that come from using proven technology are critical in building confidence in a new market, and the benefits of speed from not having to develop a new technology are critical in establishing market share.

Japanese companies appear to be highly effective in marketing innovation. Sony, for example, has been responsible for a series of innovative products in the audio and video field which start from a perception of what customers would like (personal radios in the 1950s and personal stereos in the 1970s). The Chairman of the company carries prototype products around with him, uses them and shows them to others. The Chief Executive was not a technologist but an opera singer at the beginning of his career. When Sony strayed from the personal entertainment market, which it knows so well, into micro computers, the results were much less successful. The technology behind Sony's successes is formidable but the company's work on thin-film video recording heads, for example, was undertaken not because this was an interesting technology capable of extension but because Sony believed that customers wanted smaller, cheaper, lighter video recorders.

Technology and industrial structure

A more radical explanation for the negative correlation between technological innovation and success at the level of the company than those as yet
put forward here is that at this stage of the development of the UK, technology is less important. Newly industrialising countries adopt technology from overseas—as Japan did up to the 1970s and as South Korea does
today. It is only at a late stage of industrial development that indigenous
R&D effort becomes an important part of industrial success. What should
happen in economies that have been, but are no longer, at the forefront of
technological advance?

Countries such as the UK and US are failing in their attempts to match
their technological progress with that of their new competitors. It may be
argued that they should not be striving to do this. Just as a newly industrialising country cannot expect high returns from R&D, the same may be
true for countries that have fallen back from world leader status. Industrial
growth through learning from others has delivered high growth rates for
many countries, and there is no reasons why it should not do so for those
that have previously grown through their own innovative efforts.

If this argument were to be entirely correct, we would expect investment
in R&D (or at least in research) not to show such a high return in the US
and UK. At the company level it may damage performance because of the
opportunity cost of not undertaking a more worthwhile investment. Conversely, in Japan a positive relationship between company performance and
technological innovation may be expected.

This argument could be consistent with the maintenance of wealth if the
industrial structures of the mature economies had changed to move
emphasis from high value added activities based on technology to those based
upon other attributes. The most likely contenders would be tradeable
services—in the UK the reduced importance of the UK-owned electronics industry and the increased role of financial services could be quoted in
support of this view.

If this were so, the case for further improvements in education and
training would be overwhelming. High value-added tradeable services
depend primarily upon the skills of those delivering them. In manufacturing, a skilled workforce is necessary both to incorporate technology from
overseas and to attract overseas investment.

Conclusions and implications

In the UK during the 1980s, the financial performance of the larger companies which excelled at technological innovation was significantly poorer than the generality. Although circumstances in the UK may be different from those in the rest of the world, we have sought to show that this relationship is probably general. We have argued that there are plausible reasons why a concentration on technology as the vehicle for achieving innovation can be damaging to a business.

Companies which drive their innovation process through looking for new and better ways of satisfying customer needs succeed financially. These companies know their markets well and go to great lengths to understand each market's likely response to new products. They are often themselves technologically very capable but also look externally for ideas and technology. The technology operations within such companies assimilate and exploit technology from outside rapidly and effectively.

These conclusions have two implications for public policy. The first concerns the nature of any public support for innovation—whether by grant or through taxation. It is counterproductive to frame, present or assess such support in ways which encourage innovation through a primary focus on technology. A related consideration is whether the supported company has, or is likely to obtain, the resources necessary to exploit whatever capability it develops. It could be argued that the additionality rule which confines support to those projects which would not otherwise go ahead is especially perverse, since companies which cannot afford to invest in the early stages of product inception are unlikely to be capable of investing in the latter. There appear to be important contrasts with the systems of support in Germany, which are more even-handed, and those in Japan, which have been used to encourage the strongest companies to be more adventurous.

The second set of implications concerns the science base in the UK and the manner of its funding. In so far as technology is locked into companies, either in their own facilities or through exclusive contracts with universities, polytechnics and other centres of research, it is not available to those companies' competitors. This leads to the technology-driven as opposed to the market-driven model of innovation. If UK companies are to be able to draw upon the best technology to satisfy the perceived needs of their customers, that technology needs to be readily available to them. Since technology awareness and transfer are best achieved at the national if not the local level, public sector supported research in the UK needs to be of sufficient quantity, high quality and accessible to locally based companies. This is not to say that investment cannot be recouped by appropriate licensing when technology has been transferred to the exploiter, but that funding arrangements should not lock technology into specific companies at too early a stage.

The most important conclusions of our study are for companies. Successful companies are those which take pains to understand their markets and look for new and better means of satisfying the needs of their customers. They develop a competitive capability in technology because they recognise that technology is an important tool for satisfying those needs, but they also look for the best technology outside the company. Companies which become imprisoned by their technology fail.

Appendix: statistical analysis

The data set for the quantitative analysis presented in the paper was calculated from two sources: assessments of company innovation were based on a NEDO survey and company performance was measured by growth of earnings per share during the 1980s, as listed in *Management Today*. For the survey, a questionnaire was sent to staff of NEDO, who have a long and intimate knowledge of UK industry. Respondents were asked to mark the top 250 UK companies, on a scale of 0–4, for their innovative performance in the areas of technology and marketing for both 1981 and 1991. They were also asked to assign each company to one of 12 sectors. Fourteen responses were received, which allowed 188 companies to be included in the sample. In addition to the ratings calculated from the questionnaires, the changes in score for the two types of innovation were also calculated.

Company performance was measured by the compound growth in earnings per share (EPS) over the period 1980–9 (adjusted for inflation). Davis and Kay (1990) discuss a variety of measures of corporate performance. As they show, not all such measures are particularly highly correlated, so that the choice of dependent variable could have an important impact on our results. Their main criticism of the measure we have used, growth in EPS, is that it tells us nothing about the *level* of corporate performance. This is correct, but it is not clear that we are concerned about the level of performance. One might suspect that innovation leads to *improved* performance (or conversely that lack of innovation results in declining performance). On the other hand, a consistent innovator over the sample period might well be marked by a constant level of performance. This issue requires further investigation in a more detailed study of corporate performance. We hope this study will contribute to the conduct of such work.

We accept that our independent variables are also less than perfect. The subjective nature of variables means there might be a lot of noise (equivalent to measurement error) which would lead to a downward bias in the estimates. This criticism may be made of much economic work and we will follow the practice of noting it, making the case for more work with better data. A further problem with our regressors is that people's perceptions might be influenced by their actual performance, as measured by EPS growth. We think this unlikely, since it would require a very detailed knowledge of the EPS of a large number of companies over a long period. Such a problem would have been identifiable by very high correlation coefficients with the dependent variable—they are low enough to suggest that the problem is not present. Companies are now required to publish R&D data. This is, however, not a suitable proxy for technical innovation for two reasons. First, a sufficiently long time series is not yet available. Second, expenditure on development may be consistent with the type of market orientation we argue breeds success. Separate data on research are not available. The above arguments, together with data availability, led us to choose the variables used.

Looking at the data set suggests some of the relationships confirmed by the subsequent analysis: with one exception, companies in the top ten for one innovation category are not among the top performers in the other category: indeed, some appear at the opposite end of the spectrum. None of the companies that rank high for technological innovation come near the top of the list for company performance, whereas this is not the case for marketing innovation.

These impressions are supported by the data in Table 12.1, which shows the correlation matrix between the variables in the data set. The following points may be seen from this table:

Table 12.1 Correlation coefficients

	EPS	M81	T81	M91	T91	DM
EPS	1.00					
M81	.21	1.00				
T81	-.17	.21	1.00			
M91	.16	.27	.21	1.00		
T91	-.26	.05	.73	.24	1.00	
DM	-.08	-.59	-.01	.62	.24	1.00
DT	-.14	.36	-.31	.06	.42	.34

Note: Critical value, for Ho, of zero correlation coefficient is 0.12 at 10 per cent and 0.14 at 5 per cent

Key: EPS — compound growth in earnings per share 1980–9, inflation adjusted
      M81 — rating for market innovation in 1981
      T81 — rating for technological innovation in 1981
      M91 — rating for market innovation in 1991
      T81 — rating for technological innovation in 1991
      DM — change in market innovation rating
      DT — change in technological innovation rating

Source: NEDO survey data

- There is only a weak correlation (0.27) between innovativeness in marketing in 1981 (M81) and 1991 (M91), whereas that between technological innovation in the two periods is high (T81 and T91 respectively) (0.73)—this is also shown by the correlations of the levels and difference variables.
- There is only a low correlation between market and technological innovation in either period.
- Using this crude indicator, there appears to be a negative relationship between technological innovation and performance (EPS) and a positive one with market innovation.

The correlation coefficients only provide a crude estimation since they take no account of other factors that affect company performance. Since marketing and technological innovation are slightly positively related but their relationship with performance is in opposite directions, we would expect the strength of the innovation performance to be weakened by not excluding the effect of the other variable. In the analysis that follows some allowance is also made for other factors by using dummy variables for each sector. Table 12.2 lists the (unweighted) average EPS growth by sector: the differences are sufficient to suggest that such sectoral dummies are probably desirable.

Table 12.2 Company performance by sector

Sector	Average EPS growth (% pa unweighted)
Engineering (mechanical, electrical and automotive)	9.2
Electronics and IT	11.8
Chemicals	8.8
Pharmaceutical and healthcare	19.4
Building, construction and allied products	14.0
Retailing and distribution	18.8
Financial services	14.3
Travel, hotels and leisure	15.5
Other services	16.3
Drink and food processing	11.8
Garments and textiles	4.1
Music records and entertainment	4.2

Source: Calculated from *Management Today*, June 1990

An unrestricted equation, with EPS on the left hand side and on the right the four levels of variables (M81, T81, M91 and T91), a constant and eleven sector dummies, was used as the general equation. This is Equation 1 in Table 12.3 (the coefficients on the dummies are not shown). Significant relationships in this equation are a positive impact on performance from marketing innovation in 1981 and a negative one from technological innovation in 1991. However, this is an unnecessarily complicated equation. It is most likely legitimate to restrict some of the independent variables to get a more parsimonious equation.

The first restriction that was tried was to use the difference, rather than levels, terms (eg DM = M91—M81). This equation (not reported here) performed very poorly: only the constant term was significant, the $\bar{R}^2$ was only 5 per cent and the residual sum of squares 66168 (compared with 59146 in the unrestricted equation—the F-statistic testing the validity of the restrictions is 10.21 compared to a critical value of less than 3.0). A far better equation is obtained by dropping the technological innovation term for 1981 and retaining the other three levels terms. This is Equation 2 in Table 3.3,and it performs considerably better than either equations 4 or 5, which include the levels variables from only one of the years (1981 and 1991 respectively). This result is not surprising.Technological innovation is a 'lasting characteristic' so that T81 and T91 are highly correlated. Little explanatory power may therefore be expected to be gained by including both variables in the equation. The better performance of the later variable may be due to technological innovativeness in 1991 being judged on the activities of the preceding years. By contrast, firms are seen as not typically retaining their high standing as market innovators. It is therefore quite likely that the period over which performance is being judged (1980–9) is too long to be captured by a single estimation of innovation in the marketplace. It is possible that M91 is helping to capture good performers towards the end of the decade and M81 those from earlier on. Whether this hypothesis is true must await further investigation.

Table 12.3 Regression results

Eqn	M81	T81	M91	T91	Const	Dums	F	RSS	$\bar{R}^2$
1	6.23	-3.52	3.90	-7.00	12.71	All	2.10	59146	0.15
	2.78	3.82	2.19	3.69	7.19				
2	5.15	-	3.99	-10.34	13.07	All	2.19	59436	0.15
	2.52	-	2.49	2.60	9.60				
3	8.74	-8.94	-	-	10.77	All	1.91	61238	0.13
	2.61	2.70	-	-	8.57				
4	-	-	5.27	-10.48	22.96	All	2.00	60880	0.13
	-	-	2.43	2.62	8.38				
5	5.00	-	4.23	-8.38	9.08	D1&D2	5.49	60818	0.13
	2.43	-	2.41	2.24	7.84				
6	5.14	-	4.21	-8.86	10.46	None	8.56	61416	0.13
	2.42	-	2.38	2.20					

Note Top line for each equation reports estimated coefficients and the lower line the standard
error. The Dums column lists the dummy variables included in that equation.

The equation may also be simplified by reducing the number of dummy variables. Two different sets of dummies were tried in addition to the sector specific variables. The first was a set of six dummies based on a functional classification. These did not perform well and are not reported here. Second, two variables (D1 and D2) were defined for the four sectors with the lowest average growth in EPS. An equation using these is reported as Equation 5 in Table 12.3. This may be compared with Equation 6, which contains no dummies. The absence of the dummies does not make as large an impact as one might suspect as both equations 5 and 6 easily pass an F-test as valid restrictions of the unrestricted Equation 1.[2] The estimates of the coefficients are robust between these different specifications. In both equations, the positive relationship between marketing and performance and the negative one with technological innovation are significant at the 5 per cent level.

All specifications were tested for heteroscedasticity, which was found not to be present in any case. However, in all equations the low $\bar{R}^2$ should be noted. Further work including more determinants of performance would be desirable.

Notes

1　A pilot survey had asked about four areas: technology, marketing, management and product, but these two emerged as the most significant.

2　The F-statistics for testing Equation 5 against Equation 1 is 0.49 and that for Equation 6 is 0.55, compared to a critical value of about 1.9 in both cases.

Chapter bibliography

Beresford, P (1990) 'Winners and losers', *Management Today*, June

Davis, E and Kay, J (1990) 'Assessing company performance', *Business Strategy Review*, vol 1, no 2, Summer, pp1–16

Grindley, P (1991) 'Turning technology into competitive advantage', *Business Strategy Review*, Spring

Guy, K, Georghiou, L and others (1991) *Evaluation of the Alvey programme for advanced information technology*, London, HMSO

Hamel, G and Prahalad, C (1991) 'Corporate imagination and expeditionary marketing', *Harvard Business Review*, July/August, pp81–92

NEDO (1987) *Technology transfer mechanisms in the UK and leading competitor nations*

NEDO (1991) *Partners for the long term: lessons from the success of Germany and Japan*

Reinertsen, D G and Smith, P G (1991) *Developing products in half the time*, London, Chapman and Hall

13

*Competition and Collaboration in the Innovation Process**

Stan Metcalfe

Introduction

To anyone benefiting from a traditional schooling in economic principles the juxtaposition of competition with collaboration is paradoxical. Generations of students have absorbed the doctrine that collaboration always limits competition and should be restrained, if necessary by anti-trust legislation. The central thesis of this paper is to the contrary. Some kinds of collaboration, in particular collaboration in the development of technology, enhance the operation of the competitive process, constituting examples of what we shall call group selection.

Few issues have engaged more official attention and public comment in the last decade than competitiveness, and it remains the constant concern of commentators on the industrial and management scene in all the advanced nations. Discussion of 'technology gaps', of 'catching up' and 'falling behind' has been commonplace, yet no clear agreement has been reached other than that the issues are somehow dynamic and that technology is important to the competitive advantage of nations. Three reasons can be put forward to explain our still fragile understanding of these issues. First and foremost, the relation between technology and competition reaches to the core of a capitalist market economy, and this core is inevitably complex. Even the concepts of technology and competition admit diverse and often incompatible interpretations. Secondly, however important it is as a contributory factor, technology is only one element in a web of influences which

---

*I am grateful to colleagues Hugh Cameron, Luke Georghiou and Martin Currie and to participants in the NEDO seminar, for helpful discussion on the topic of this paper. Financial support from the ESRC is also gratefully acknowledged.

determines patterns of competitive behaviour, and there are no simple ways to separate the technological from other important elements of performance. This is particularly true of the relation between technology and organisation. Indeed, it is an open question whether technological change or organisational change has contributed more to recent industrial growth—granted that the two can be separated. This second reason must be born in mind continually in what follows, for I shall not have the space to qualify the alleged importance of technology at each step of the argument. Finally, and perhaps most significant of all, technology itself is complex. It has many dimensions, it is located in different institutions, and its mechanisms of accumulation differ considerably across its different parts (Pavitt and Patel, 1988).

Other chapters in this book explore the role of innovation in the growth process and the ways in which broad trends in technology might be measured. This chapter explores why collaboration is an increasingly important route to technological development in some circumstances. The structure of the paper is as follows: discussion of competition and its various meanings is followed by a selective survey of recent examples of collaborative research activities. This is followed by an outline of the arguments for collaboration in general, and collaboration in technology in particular. Central to this is a clear understanding of the multidimensional nature of technology. The incentives for collaboration are then pursued, drawing the conclusion that the principle reason why collaboration takes place is that it raises the efficiency and creativity of the research process. The chapter concludes with some remarks on recent UK policy in this area.

Competition: equilibrium versus process

I referred in the opening paragraph to the paradox that collaboration may be a prerequisite to greater competition. To understand this more clearly it is necessary to dwell at some length on the nature of competition. A central thesis in modern economic theory views competition as a state of equilibrium, the chief determinant of which is the structure of the market, as typically represented by the number of competing firms. This is true for the traditional thesis of perfect and imperfect competition and for the modern variants of strategic competition between small numbers of firms. In all cases the purpose of the theory is to characterise equilibrium (Tirole, 1989). The strengths of this approach cannot be dismissed lightly. Modern theory has broken from the emphasis on price competition: product differentiation and investment in new technology are central elements in the new industrial economics (Jacquemin, 1985; Laffont *et al*, 1991) and the systematic application and development of game theory has brought about an ever-expanding refinement of the analysis. Yet it is not obvious that the equilibrium paradigm is the only way to proceed, even discounting the fact that many game theoretic results are extremely sensitive to underlying specifications. The modern equilibrium view suffers from exactly the same deficiency as the traditional view: namely that it has lost sight of the notion of competition as rivalry, and with it a process perspective on competition. Hayek put it forcefully when he chastised economic theory: 'If the state of affairs assumed by the theory of perfect competition ever existed, it would not only deprive of their scope all the activities which the verb 'to compete' describes, but would make them virtually impossible' (1948, p92).

To modern students of strategic management the process view is crucial (Hamel and Prahalad, 1989). A long-standing tradition in industrial economics, exemplified by the writings of Marshall, J.M. Clark, Downie, Penrose, and more recently Porter, emphasises competition as the outcome of differential behaviour. In its essentials, a firm competes by serving customers better and at a lower cost than its rivals.

Naturally, the differential command of technology has always played a central role in the process view of competition, a theme articulated most effectively by Schumpeter in his theory of creative destruction. Among recent management scholars, Itami (1987) has stressed that the essence of competition is the creation of differences, and that the process of differentiation raises three strategic problems for a business:

- knowing which differences give competition advantage;
- knowing how to limit the ability of rivals to erode these differences;
- knowing how to limit direct competitive confrontations.

In pursuit of these objectives, a company's key assets are the invisible assets associated with knowledge and its accumulation. Similar views are expressed by many others, eg Clark (1989) and Georghiou *et al* (1985); they emphasise the temporary nature of knowledge-based advantages, and the corresponding need to maintain a momentum of competitive innovative behaviour.

At this point it is worth noting that the process view provides a quite different perspective on the role of profits in the competitive process. In the equilibrium view, excess profits (above the normal level to keep capital in a line of activity) are the result of undue market power and are to be deplored. By contrast, in the process view 'excess profits' come not from the exercise of market power but from differential competitive advantage; they are rents based upon superior ability, and technology is one of the key routes to superiority. As Fisher *et al* (1983) emphasise in their penetrating analysis of why the IBM anti-trust case failed, a successful competitor 'must not be turned upon when he wins', nor 'can a dynamic competitive market whose basic feature is technological change be analysed in terms of theoretical long-run equilibrium' (p344).

Increasingly the link between technological differentiation and the competitive process is informing public debate. A recent report from the Office of Technology Assessment (1990) provides a clear statement of the issues. US manufacturing firms, it is argued, face unprecedented competitive threats from overseas rivals, and their increasing lack of competitive advantage is reflected in a continued deterioration in the US external trade performance. No single solution can reverse this situation but the basis for recovery is to be found in improved technology in terms of product design and manufacturing process. Intellectual capital will play a central part in achieving this improvement, and its generation will depend in part on more collaborative R&D. In support of this view, the report advocates the foundation of a Civilian Technology Agency to establish priorities and support collaborative ventures in industry. Expressions of concern such as this are commonplace wherever technology and industrial policy are discussed, in the UK no less than in the US. The links between technology, collaboration, and competition should therefore be explored in more depth.

The two levels of competition

We can cut to the core of the apparent paradox of competition in the presence of collaboration by recognising that competition is itself a two-level process. Every business unit employs technology to produce products and survives and competes with other business units for its share of the relevant product and factor markets. Higher quality products, embodying more of the characteristics consumers are willing to pay for, and more efficient production methods, which permit prices but not profit margins to be reduced, are the dominant routes to competitive advantage. Every business stands in a chain relationship with its competitors, being superior to some and inferior to others, with its overall competitive position measured by its distance from the average performance of the competing group. A particular combination of product quality and unit cost defines average performance at any point in time. Businesses which are better than average are more profitable and have the potential to expand their market share; those which are inferior are less profitable and stand to lose market share. How rapidly these changes in relative position take place depends on the properties of the selection environment and the propensity to expand in the different businesses. Working out the mechanisms which underpin this process is the task of the rapidly developing evolutionary tradition of economic analysis (Nelson and Winter, 1984; Eliasson, 1985; Carlsson and Stankiewicz, 1991; Metcalfe and Gibbons, 1988). In this evolutionary framework, the market is the first level of competition. But firms with a static technology do not hold their market position for long, and unless their market is peculiarly sheltered or stagnant they do not long survive. The reign of the mass-producers of thermionic valves, for example, was scarcely three decades and examples like this can be multiplied at will (Braun and MacDonald, 1978).

To maintain competitive advantage and prevent the erosion of its market share, a business must establish a momentum of product and process innovation. This brings us directly to the second level of competition: competition of creativity to enhance product and process characteristics. Resources to innovate are important but so is resourcefulness. Creativity depends on their interaction, otherwise established large business units would dominate the innovation process, which they manifestly do not (Hamel and Prahalad, 1989). By improving its technology, a firm seeks to change its relative position in the competitive chain. If it is to maintain its market share, it must at least keep step with changes in average practice among its competitors. Competition is a race, but one in which the finishing line is ever receding into the distance. The ability to innovate is thus crucial to long term competitive performance. It is competition at this second level which drives the changes in competitive differentiation at the first level. As we shall suggest below, competition at the two levels focuses on different dimensions of technology. At the first level, it is concerned with technology as artefact—products and the methods of producing them; at the second level it is concerned with knowledge and skills—the accumulation of which provides the basis for changing the artefacts.

Our knowledge of evolutionary processes sheds useful light on the different levels of competition. The standard evolutionary process is one in which a selection environment (market) applies selective pressure to entities which differ in certain dimensions (artefacts and their performance characteristics) and changes the relative weight of the different entities in a population (share of a given market). This is a process of individual selection or first level competition. In a market economy it results directly in selection for products and their methods of production and, indirectly, in selection of the business units to which they are attached. It is a process, the unfettered action of which results in the elimination of variety and the concentration of market share. Competition, like evolution, consumes its own fuel. To maintain competitive pressures it is necessary to have a continual source of new product and process variety which innovation mechanisms supply.

In the past decade, evolutionary theorists have recognised, and fiercely debated, cf. Sober (1985), a different kind of selection mechanism: group selection. It is not necessary to explain the deeper aspects of this concept such as its relation with altruistic behaviour. For our purposes the central point is clear; group selection provides advantages in the evolutionary process because the selective characteristics possessed by a unit of selection depend on the group it is in, *and would change* if it moved to a different group. Students of cartels and other market-rigging arrangements will find nothing new in this. Students of technical change might, for collaborative R&D is a prime example of group selection at the second level of competition. This theme will be central to what follows and to the appraisal of collaborative arrangements. It will be obvious to anyone who has studied the trend of events in the world microelectronics industry where the national pursuit of group advantage is an ever-present theme (Malerba, 1985; Dosi, 1984).

Technological collaboration: some examples

Rather than delve immediately into the reasons and incentives for collaboration, some remarks on recent history are in order. It seems likely that informal arrangements to share technology are as old as industry itself; indeed, Marshall made the sharing of technology among geographically concentrated firms one of his primary external economies. In the UK, formal, collaborative, industrial research institutes were established in 1917 with a combination of public grants and industry subscriptions. In the early 1970s some forty such research associations were in operation. Of negligible significance for the national R&D effort, they nevertheless provided an important focus of research in several highly fragmented industries (Johnson, 1975). The modern form of collaborative R&D venture between private firms emerged in the early 1980s and grew rapidly in importance, particularly in the information technology and biotechnology sectors (Hagedoorn and Schackenrad, 1990). The general strength of Japanese competition and the rapid ascendancy of Japanese firms up the international competitive ladder provided one stimulus, but so did the development in Japan of successful collaborations such as that in VLSI technology between 1975 and 1979.

The US response to this competitive threat is instructive. In 1983, 19 firms jointly formed the Microelectronics Computer Corporation (MCC) and successfully lobbied Congress for a relaxation of the anti-trust laws which did not permit such ventures (Peck, 1984). Up to this time collaboration in the US had been limited to the joint industrial funding of university research, although regulated industries had from the 1970s developed several joint research centres (Evans and Olk, 1990). In 1984, the National Cooperative Research Act exempted joint research ventures from the provisions of the Sherman Act, and limited the damages which could be levied if any successful anti-trust case were to be brought by injured third parties. Between 1984 and 1989, some 140 ventures were registered with the Federal Government. Forty of these were limited to two partners (Evans and Olk, 1990) and were concentrated primarily in the chemicals, machinery and electronics industries (Link and Bauer, 1987). Broadly speaking, these collaborations are of two limiting kinds: where an administrative body is established to co-ordinate research activity carried out in the distributed facilities of the participants; and where a central research institution is established under the participants' control. The MCC is an example of the latter kind. While the nineteen founding members of the MCC could not be considered small, neither were they large relative to their major competitors, IBM, ATT, and the larger Japanese producers. Eight of the members are large scale users of IT products, including the Boeing and Xerox Corporations. The focus of research is on the development of generic technological knowledge in four main research areas. Members buy into these areas, sharing all costs, and are free to turn the results into proprietary technology by expenditure of their own additional R&D funds. Hence the concept of pre-competitive or enabling R&D. Any exploitation leads to payment of royalties to MCC, and the members of a programme are given a three year lead time after which results may be licensed to other MCC members and firms outside MCC. The advantages to the participants are obvious. They buy into the results of a $35–$50 million annual research programme at a fraction of this cost.

Similar in broad outline to the MCC is its European equivalent, the European Computer Research Centre, founded in 1984 by Bull (France) Siemens (Germany) and ICL (UK). The members share all costs and results, while the research is carried out at a centre in Munich. Roughly one third of the programme is linked into the EC funded European Declarative Systems project. The takeover of ICL by Fujitsu in 1989 threatened the survival of the collaboration and although it continues this has been at the expense of changes in research focuses and an agreement to open membership to Japanese and US firms (Georghiou and Barker, 1991).

A characteristic of both MCC and ECRC is that they are primarily private sector collaborations. In stark contrast is the Alvey programme introduced in the UK with substantial government funding and involvement in priority setting (Oakley, 1990; Guy and Georghiou *et al*, 1991). This was established in 1984 to fund pre-competitive work in information technology, primarily centred around projects in IT process technology. It brought together companies, universities, and government research laboratories in a programme funded with approximately £200m of public money and £150m of private funding. The programme terminated in 1989 after a total of 192 collaborative industrial projects had been funded with an additional 117 university based projects. By UK standards the main participants were large firms, and the top ten absorbed 80 per cent of the public funding. Unlike MCC, the Alvey programme operated with a central directorate, staffed by government officials as well as industry secondees, the research being distributed among the laboratories of the participants. The principal aims of the programme were to strengthen the UK industrial and academic IT research basis, to develop four specific areas of enabling technology, and to strengthen the competitiveness of UK firms. The research carried out in Alvey was similar in area to that carried out in MCC and in the European Strategic Programme of Research in IT (ESPRIT). The Alvey Programme was unquestionably a response to the Japanese IT challenge, at a time when the UK industry was losing ground rapidly in international IT markets and when other national governments were introducing research support initiatives in their own IT industries.

With these examples in mind we can turn to the arguments in favour of collaboration in general and technological collaboration in particular.

Collaboration in general

It has long been recognised that collaborative arrangements are commonplace in industry, arranged along a spectrum which has as its two limits complete internal administrative co-ordination and the anonymous market transaction. Since this spectrum is so broad, it is not surprising that a clear taxonomy of collaborative arrangements has yet to emerge. The following three definitions are representative of current understanding.

- Mariti and Smiley (1983) have defined a co-operative agreement as any long-term explicit agreement between contracting parties.
- Pisano and Teece (1989) are more explicit; they define collaboration in terms of inter-organisational agreements to contribute or exchange assets or their services for a jointly agreed purpose. Such arrangements may or may not involve shared equity participation.

- Harrigan (1987) defines joint ventures as strategic alliances whereby two or more parties create a separate venture to combine skills and share equity.

In each of these definitions the idea of a more or less durable commitment between parties known to each other is important. Contractual elements are involved but collaborations involve more than contracts; they involve interaction between the organisations to alter the behaviour of at least one of the parties.

As Richardson (1972) persuades us, it is the boundaries of the firm which are at issue when any form of collaboration is undertaken, since external parties are being granted influence over administrative decisions in the firm. Any business is a constellation of many different activities, each one performing a transformation on materials, energy and information, and each activity requiring a capability or competence defined in terms of a knowledge base and relevant skills. Whenever these capabilities set the limits to the firm, they define its boundary in terms of the markets it can serve at a profit. Over time the set of capabilities can be developed and this possibility is essential to the notion of the second level of competition outlined above. The need to augment existing capabilities can be particularly acute in the presence of rapid changes in the selection environment or when distinctive new capabilities give a competitive advantage to rivals. The firm must then decide on the most economic way to augment its capabilities either through internal accumulation or external sourcing (Langlois, 1990). As we shall argue below, the most economic way depends on the kind of knowledge which underpins a new capability. In many situations, external sources have clear advantages in provision based on economies of scale and economies of experience and learning, the traditional sources of the division of labour. Specialisation augments efficiency but it equally results in limits to creativity.

However, reliance on external sources does not imply reliance on the anonymous market transaction in a clearly specified artefact for which the question of the identity of who one buys from or sells to is irrelevant. For many kinds of anonymous transaction the required futures markets and insurance markets do not exist. Such market failures are likely whenever a transaction is complex and multi-dimensional so that agreement on what is being transacted is not reached readily. Transactions in information and technology are particularly prone to this difficulty, the solution to which is bilateral or multilateral negotiation and interaction (Silver, 1984). Moreover, because of the uncertainties inherent in this situation, efforts must be made to limit capricious, opportunistic behaviour (Williamson, 1986). These difficulties are further exacerbated when the parties to the transaction must make irreversible investments in physical, organisational or knowledge capital, investments which have limited and inferior alternative uses. Joint commitments are then required to reduce the prospects of avoidable capital loss, to avoid so-called gunpoint or hold-up costs. When these transaction costs become particularly acute the solution is full internal administrative control by a single organisation, but in many other cases this is not necessary and the potential gains from external sourcing can be achieved more effectively by one or other form of collaboration.

To understand the relation of these arguments to technological collaborations we must first dwell in some detail on technology and its constituent elements. Before doing so one final observation is in order, namely the danger of overdrawing the distinction between collaboration and the market. Both involve selection in so far as there is a market in collaborative arrangements. The point here is akin to Demsetz's distinction between competition-in and competition-for markets. Firms compete for collaboration throughout the spectrum; it is just the nature of the competition which requires careful specification (Demsetz, 1968).

Technology and forms of collaboration

Our starting point for this discussion is the notion of technology as a range of entities with artefacts at one limit and abstract knowledge at the other (Layton, 1974). Any business activity can be defined either in terms of a set of artefacts or in terms of the underlying knowledge base, those concepts, facts, theories and actions which constitute the relevant capabilities and enable the artefacts to be produced. Division of labour applies to knowledge as much as it does to artefacts and each business is typically specialised and organised around a narrowly defined or bounded knowledge base. But any technology can also be defined in terms of a broader community of practitioners (Constant, 1980) carrying out their activities within traditions of practice which focus problem solving, suggest solutions to emerging puzzles and provide methods for the appraisal of competing solutions (Laudan, 1984). A firm typically embodies a number of different traditions which it must implement to be effective. Members of a firm also belong to wider scientific and technological communities beyond the boundaries of the firm; they share educational backgrounds and can communicate readily with other members of the tradition. However, their knowledge is also focused more precisely by the particular transformation process in which they claim expertise. Specialists in automotive technology may understand little of the detail of aircraft technology though the broad disciplinary training of the individual engineers and technologists may be similar. These considerations have particular significance when a firm judges that it must acquire technology from external sources.

For an existing technology a number of transfer routes are available. When technology is embodied in clearly defined artefacts an obvious route to acquisition is via a market transaction. For process technology a licence may be obtained and in some cases the purchase of the supplying firm may be an appropriate method. For example, ICI in establishing its genetics-based seeds business had the core bio-technological capability in- house but lacked the technology to produce and market seeds. Consequently it has acquired a number of established seeds producers, each with a specialised crop and international market focus. To have built these capabilities internally would have taken ICI well beyond its established comparative advantage in research and technology development. On a much smaller scale, knowledge can be purchased via a contract to report on the state of the art in a particular area, a favoured route with universities, or obtained through informal knowledge trading by practitioners in different firms (von Hippel, 1990).

It is when we turn to the generation of new technological knowledge that collaboration issues become more complicated, with the preferred routes depending on the kind of knowledge to be acquired, its institutional location and its natural mode of accumulation.

A number of distinctions are worth making at this point, each related to the fact that any knowledge base is structured according to its underlying traditions. In any line of production rival firms will hold much knowledge in common, the generic knowledge of facts and principles and the infra-technology of metrology and operational standards. Knowledge of this kind is in the public domain. However, the differentiation which makes competition possible depends on firms developing distinctive capabilities based on proprietary knowledge which must necessarily be accumulated internally. This familiar division between public and private knowledge is further clarified by a number of overlapping distinctions. Some knowledge is codifiable and communicable in words, symbols or drawings. For other important classes of knowledge this is not possible. Every technology contains more than is describable, and individuals express this tacit component in levels of skill. Secondly, the familiar distinction between knowing how and knowing that (Ryle, 1949) has been usefully elaborated by Vincenti (1990) into a distinction between explicit knowledge and procedural knowledge. Explicit knowledge is codifiable and consists of descriptive knowledge, facts and their interrelation, and prescriptive knowledge of the ways to achieve particular ends. Descriptive knowledge is judged by its veracity whereas prescriptive knowledge is judged by its effectiveness. Prescriptive knowledge and tacit knowledge combined form procedural knowledge, the strongly focused knowledge which underpins any productive activity. Now this is not epistemological hairsplitting but a serious recognition of the diversity of kinds of knowledge which define any one technology, a diversity which maps into the institutional location of knowledge and its manner of accumulation. Both are crucial factors in determining the scope and content of technological collaboration.

The principal route to acquiring procedural knowledge is experience in production and use; the principal route to acquiring descriptive knowledge is a research programme. In this regard science and engineering differ fundamentally. Scientific research is not only codifiable, it is also theory dependent. Engineering research, by contrast, often operates beyond the bounds illuminated by prevailing theory and the accumulation of understanding takes place in localised experiments of a trial and error kind. Managing a scientific collaboration is quite different from managing an engineering one. Since science and engineering knowledge of a descriptive kind can be acquired independently of production activity, and since much of this knowledge is difficult if not impossible to make proprietary, it is primarily accumulated in specialised institutions, universities and public research laboratories.

By contrast, procedural knowledge cannot be advanced independently of production and use; it builds from experience and because of the significant tacit component the process cannot be shortcircuited. One cannot gain this knowledge without participating in its acquisition. Correspondingly, this is the kind of knowledge which contributes significantly to proprietary competitive advantages.

The lesson to be drawn from this is that the variety of routes to acquire knowledge by external means reflects the variety of forms that knowledge can take. There is an appropriate acquisition route for each kind. Generic descriptive knowledge is typically sourced from public research institutions via the medium of a research project. In many cases firms have joined together to fund jointly he production of public generic knowledge. When the knowledge is closely linked to a firm's proprietary advantages a research contract will be preferred to a research grant. Both grants and contracts are near to the market transaction end of the spectrum. It is when we turn to the acquisition of procedural knowledge that we find the typical collaborative research ventures between a limited number of firms. Even though the knowledge may be generic, it is strongly focused to support the development of particular artefacts and is more often engineering than science in terms of its mode of accumulation. The member firms participate directly in the research work to minimise problems of the transfer of tacit knowledge components.

It naturally follows from the considerations above that the scope and need for collaborative ventures will vary enormously across different technologies. All the available evidence suggests that collaboration is more likely in emerging technologies in which clear lines of advance have yet to be established, and in technologies threatened by a major qualitative shift in the underlying knowledge base. Biotechnology and microelectronics are the classic examples. The pace of change makes it expensive to keep up with the frontier of knowledge, and the emergence of new technological traditions forces established firms to find complementary partners. Not all firms respond to technological threats in this way. Some respond by accelerated development of existing technology or attempt to develop new knowledge bases alongside their existing activities (Cooper and Schendal, 1976). However, collaboration is gaining ground as a recognised pattern of response. In this view, collaboration is also a device to keep a window on technological possibilities which are young and of uncertain significance (Hamilton, 1986).

Incentives to collaborate: cost sharing, profit dissipation and profit enhancement

We now turn to a more formal discussion of the incentives for firms to engage in technological collaborations. A small but technical literature has emerged to address this issue, although at this stage no strong conclusions have emerged and results are particularly sensitive to the underlying assumptions (Grossman and Shapiro, 1986; Tirole, 1989; Katz, 1984). However, one point is clear; incentives to collaborate are considerably influenced by the underlying appropriability regimes for a firm's capabilities, that is, the effectiveness with which knowledge may be kept proprietary (Nelson, 1990; Jorde and Teece, 1989; Pisano and Teece, 1984).

We begin with a highly simplified argument under conditions of strong appropriability of technology. Firm A can undertake a research project at a cost X_0 which it evaluates will enhance its future profit stream by a present value sum of B_0 with probability h. There is no threat from rivals. The increment in expected value this brings to the firm is $V_0 = hB_0 - X_0$, and the expected rate of return on this investment is V_0/X_0. Suppose now that firm A can also collaborate with another firm to share the costs of R&D in a joint venture. Imagine to begin with that the collaboration generates exactly the same technology with exactly the same probability of success. The incentive to collaborate is that the R&D costs are shared. The corresponding disincentive is that a potential competitor has been created with whom the market value of the new technology must also be shared. This is the profit dissipation effect. To fix ideas further, imagine that profits are dissipated equally and costs are shared equally so that the expected value of the technology to A with collaboration is $V_1 = hB_1 - X_1 = V_0/2$. Clearly the expected rate of return on R&D is the same in the two cases. Collaboration is neutral in its effects, costs are halved and profits are halved. If capital markets were perfect that would be the end of the matter but, wherever there are limitations on the ability of firms to raise finance for R&D, even a neutral collaboration has further consequences. In particular, collaboration releases resources to devote to other projects, projects which at current rates of interest add to the wealth of the firm but which cannot be carried out because of the lack of resources. This perhaps suggests why more creative firms (large firms with R&D laboratories) are favourably disposed towards collaboration simply because they have a wider range of profitable options in which to invest. Now this is, to repeat, a stylised example. It is impossible to imagine that technology collaboration would have achieved its current state if this neutral model were realistic. It is not, and the purpose of its lack of realism is to indicate where a positive case for collaboration may lie.

The first assumption to be questioned is that of strong profit dissipation. Firms may consider that while they share costs on an equal basis they will individually retain a competitive advantage when it comes to exploitation so that profits from the technology are not shared equally. Obviously, not all of the partners to such a collaboration can have their expectations fulfilled. More substantially, the obvious way to avoid profit dissipation is to collaborate with firms which are not direct competitors. Even if they are in the same line of activity, they serve different niches or geographically distinct markets. Costs are shared while profits are not, although there is always the danger here of creating future competitors. Collaborations between users and suppliers are a particular case of the general phenomenon; costs are shared and the development of the technology is co-ordinated more closely with the development of users' needs. Similarly, universities make particularly good collaborators from this viewpoint, as there is no question of profit dissipation and university research is inexpensive.

The case for collaboration is further strengthened when we recognise the potential for profit enhancement, a phenomenon which is at the core of the group selection argument. By collaborating, superior technology can be generated, more quickly and with a greater probability of success than could be individually achieved by the partners working alone. The group develops better technology than firms outside the group, and with it a collectively shared competitive advantage. In a fundamental sense the group effect increases the productivity of the R&D process.

The sources of this enhanced efficiency are well identified in the literature. It is thought that collaboration:

- eliminates wasteful duplication of effort when firms cluster too much around similar R&D options (Dasgupta and Maskin, 1987);
- permits the pursuit of a broad programme, with longer time horizons, and multiple projects performed in parallel to explore a greater technological space;
- permits the construction of larger scale facilities to exploit economies of scale and scope; superior facilities in turn attract higher quality researchers;
- may permit better management of research and in particular facilitates management of the transition to exploitation, so reducing risks of project failure;
- brings together firms with complementary knowledge bases and the corresponding 'clash of ideas' stimulates creativity in research—avenues open up which are hidden to non-collaborators.

We can connect the argument at this point with the concept of a trade-off between the timing of a given discovery and the cumulative cost of carrying out the necessary research (Mansfield, 1971). Figure 13.1 illustrates this argument, as cumulative R&D expenditure increases, so the time to make a given advance is reduced. There is a cost threshold or critical minimum expenditure, C_0, below which no advance can be made and there is a time threshold, T_0, before which the given advance cannot be achieved, however much is spent on the R&D programme. Greater advances in technology relative to current practice and knowledge define successively higher trade-offs each with its own time and cost thresholds.[1]

To summarise, the case for collaboration falls into two parts. Pooling resources to accelerate the expected discovery times enables a move along the trade-off R_0R_0, say from a to b. This is often the rationale for collaboration in a fragmented industry where individual firms may not be able to command the critical minimum expenditure to advance the technology. More substantially, the group consequences of collaboration shift the time cost trade-off in a productivity enhancing fashion to R_1R_1. With the cumulative expenditure of C_a, the time of discovery is brought forward from T_a to T_c giving the group a competitive lead time to exploitation. Alternatively, by the time T_a, an even better technology could be developed with expen-

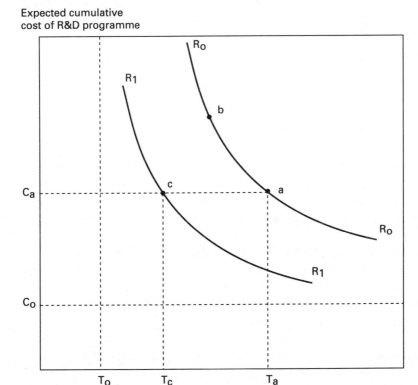

Figure 13.1 Trade-offs between time and cost needed to make a discovery

diture of C_a. It is this possibility of shifting the time cost trade-off which appears to be the crucial motive in collaboration.

Relaxing the strong appropriability assumption brings us to a final argument in favour of collaborative research. One of the central arguments in the economics of R&D is that weak appropriability is a strong disincentive to invest in research. In the presence of knowledge spillovers, firms which do not carry out research can make competitive use of ideas which they have not paid for. Collaboration, it is argued, internalises these spillovers and restores the incentive to conduct research (D'Aspremont and Jacquemin, 1988; Katz, 1986). Correct in its own terms, the relevance of this argument is not obvious. The crucial point which destroys research incentives is not spillovers per se but asymmetry in spillovers. If spillovers are equalised, firms stand to gain on the swings as much as they lose on the roundabouts. Often a strong research effort is now needed to be able to understand the research

233

advances of rivals (Rosenberg, 1990). Apart from a limited number of sectors where patent protection is strong, it is not normally possible to curb technology spillovers. However, appropriability can be strong if a firm can maintain a rapid rate of innovation and exploit learning economies more quickly than rivals (Nelson, 1987). Collaboration facilitates this by enabling the group to keep ahead of outside firms with a faster momentum of technical change.

Management issues

The productivity gains from shifting time cost trade-offs are only potential gains; it is not automatic that they will be realised. The design of the collaboration and the management of its resources become the crucial issues in achieving group selection effects (Georghiou and Barker, 1991). The administrative costs of the collaboration may be substantial, as may the persuasion costs of reaching agreement on objectives. Agreement also has to be reached on intellectual property rights and the valuation of anterior knowledge transferred to the collaboration as well as the content of the programme of work. Firms which come to a collaboration from different but complementary backgrounds may find these communication issues particularly taxing (Arrow, 1978). Organisations as different as firms and universities are bound to experience problems in achieving an effective collaboration. Other dangers also lie in wait: partners who fail to deliver quality research and development; and partners who change strategies and withdraw in mid-programme. It is apparent that the choice of partners becomes the principle issue in establishing a collaboration. Not only is their knowledge base important, but so is their ability to manage complex research programmes. These considerations are particularly relevant to collaboration with smaller firms. The management overheads bear unevenly on them. They may be unduly constrained in the management resource they can devote to the collaboration and particularly exposed to the risks of a project failing or changing direction.

The evaluation of the Alvey programme throws interesting light on these important management questions (Guy and Georghiou, 1991). In terms of promoting collaboration between universities and industry it has been judged a considerable success, strengthening industry's knowledge and skill base in the process. Over half the project managers reported that academic contributions were critical to success. Many collaborations have continued beyond the termination of the programmes. Most of the technological targets were also achieved, and the productivity of research generally enhanced. Nevertheless, many participants reported difficulties managing the overheads of collaboration with their partners; difficulties occurred when partners changed objectives or withdrew, and there were difficulties in agreeing intellectual property issues. Half of the projects were adversely affected by organisational, strategic and personnel changes in partners. Saving R&D costs was not a dominant motive for industrial collaborators, gaining access to complementary knowledge bases was. Like MCC, Alvey was predominantly concerned with generic enabling technology and primarily directed its attention to the generation of software rather than hardware. At this point in time the jury remains out on whether the competitiveness of UK firms has been enhanced and there are grounds for questioning the lack of user industry involvement in the programme. Initial exploitation is considered to be disappointing, with hardware exploitation particularly limited. All this indicates that collaboration is not a panacea; it has to be designed and managed appropriately. Whether a central research institute along MCC lines would have generated a superior management model is doubtful but is obviously an issue which cannot be resolved, other than in a hypothetical sense. However, it is clear that several of the organisational innovations in the programme proved to be very successful in communicating results to participants (Ray, 1990).

National policy and strategic arguments

We draw our discussion to a close with reflections on innovation policy in the UK. Economic arguments have long supported a view that markets will not allocate resources to technical development at an optimal rate. But whether private firms do too much or too little, do it too early or too late, or do projects which are too similar or too different, remains unresolved. Policy making necessarily proceeds on more *ad hoc* grounds only generally justified by market failure considerations. However, it is important to locate the market failure argument more precisely. On the one hand, it can concern the markets for knowledge outputs, the familiar disincentive to the production of knowledge of a public and codifiable kind. On the other hand, it can concern the methods for producing knowledge, when uninsurable risks and imperfect markets to supply knowledge-generating inputs (skills, funds, etc) limit the efficiency of the innovative process. Collaboration has emerged as a central policy response to this second category of market failure. In this respect, the 1980s was a period of considerable change in UK policy-making, with the demise of single company support schemes aimed at developing specific innovations (artefacts) and their replacement by collaborative schemes to develop knowledge bases. A key aspect of this policy shift was the elimination of near-to-market support for development in favour of support for pre-competitive generic research. All the major UK technology support schemes currently emphasise collaboration either between companies (the advanced technology programme) or between industry and higher education institutions (LINK scheme). In this they are a generalization of the Alvey philosophy, without the overlay of a co-ordinating management structure, although the continuation of the Alvey programme, the Information Engineering Advanced Technology Programme, maintains a central directorate.

The arguments outlined above give strong support to several aspects of the change in policy. By promoting collaboration with universities, a stronger integration of the national knowledge base is obtained. By eliminating unnecessary duplication of effort, a greater variety of technological options can be explored and the general rate of innovative experimentation increased. On the negative side, the two limitations of the emphasis on far- from-market collaboration are lack of support for smaller firms which are unlikely to find collaboration congenial, for reasons outlined above (ACOST, 1990), and the failure to encourage strong user-supplier interaction in the innovative process. Both are serious deficiencies, although some attempts have recently been made to support small firms with separate schemes. Nor is the far-from-market criterion particularly enlightening given that the risks of innovation are greater the closer a project is to market exploitation. The inability of market institutions to shift innovation risks is a central limitation in a capitalist economy, and it is this rather than distance from market which should guide policy.

The rationale for collaborative research policies can be looked at from a different perspective, namely that of strategic group selection. The emphasis here is on the dynamic interaction between the two levels of competition, an interaction which supports cumulative processes of growth and decline. Superior artefact technology gives competitive advantage in market competition and with this go higher profit margins, increasing market share, and correspondingly, proportionately more of the resources to further advance technology. Success builds on success while failure encourages further failure. Group selection is one way in which firms that have fallen behind in the competitive race can attempt to recover their position. The enhanced generation of technology made possible by collaborative research provides a base for better market performance. As we have argued above, public policy can make an important contribution to the success of these ventures; not simply by subsidizing research but more crucially by the effective design and management of collaboration programmes. In short public policy can produce strong group selection effects at a national level.

Notes

1) The downward slope of the trade-off depends on diminishing returns to research. To see this, consider the following simple model: if research is undertaken at rate x the probability of discovery is h(x) with $h'(x) > 0$ and $h''(x) < 0$. Let h(x) be independent of past research efforts, the expected time to discovery then has a geometric distribution with mean $E(T) = 1/h(x)$ and variance $v(T) = [1-h(x)]/h(x)^2$. Both mean and variance decline with increases in x so that bigger programmes are less risky. If r is the given invariant rate of interest the expected cumulative cost of making the discovery is $E(c) = X/[r+h(x)]$. A sufficient condition for $E(c)$ to increase as x increases is that the elasticity of h(x) with respect to x is less than unity. Diminishing returns in the sense that more haste means proportionately less speed! In this case $E(c)$ and $E(T)$ are inversely related, although without further assumptions the precise shape of the trade-off is unknown. The argument is readily extended to probability processes which possess memory, cf. Nelson, 1982.

Chapter bibliography

ACOST (1990) *The enterprise challenge: overcoming barriers to growth in small firms*, London, HMSO, 1990

Arrow, K (1978) *The limits of organisation*, New York, Norton

d'Aspremont, C and Jacquemin, A (1988) 'Cooperative and non-cooperative R&D in duopoly with spillovers', *American Economic Review*, vol 78, pp1133–54

Braun, E and McDonald, S (1978) *Revolution in miniature*, Cambridge, Cambridge University Press

Carlsson, B and Stankiewicz, R (1991) 'On the nature, function, and composition of technological systems', *Journal of Evolutionary Economics*, vol 1

Clark, J M (1961) *Competition as a dynamic process*, Washington DC, Brookings Institution

Clark, K B (1989) 'What strategy can do for technology', *Harvard Business Review*, Nov—Dec

Constant, E W (1980) *The origin of the turbo jet revolution*, Johns Hopkins University Press

Cooper, A C and Schendal, D (1976) 'Strategic response to competitive threats', *Business Horizons*

Dasgupta, P and Maskin, E (1987) 'The simple economics of research portfolios', *Economic Journal*, vol 97, no 387, pp581–95

Demsetz, H (1968) 'Why regulate utilities?', *Journal of Law and Economics*, vol 11, pp55–65

Dosi, G (1984) *Technical change and industrial transformation*, London, Macmillan

Downie, J (1955) *The competitive process*, London, Duckworth

Eliasson, G (1985) *The firm and financial markets*, Stockholm, Almqvist and Wiksell

Evans, W M and Olk, D (1990) 'R&D consortia: a new US organisational form', *Sloan Management Review*, vol 31, no 3, pp37–46

Fisher, F M *et al* (1983) *Folded, spindled and mutilated*, London, MIT Press

Georghiou, L and Barker, K (1991) 'Growing together or growing apart: managing collaboration under conditions of change', *PREST*, University of Manchester

Georghiou, L, Metcalfe, S, Evans, J, Ray, T and Gibbons, M (1986) *Post innovation performance*, Basingstoke, Macmillan

Grossman, G M and Shapiro, C (1987) 'Dynamic R&D competition', *Economic Journal*, vol 97, no 386, pp372–87

Guy, K and Georghiou, L *et al* (1991) *Evaluation of the Alvey programme for Advanced Information Technology*, London, HMSO

Hagedoorn, J and Schakenrad, J (1990) *Alliances and partnerships in biotechnology and information technologies*, Limburg, MERIT

Hamel, G and Prahalad, C (1989) 'Strategic intent', *Harvard Business Review*, May—June

Hamilton, W F (1986) 'Corporate strategies for managing emerging technologies', in Horwich, M (ed) *Technology in the modern corporation*

Harrigan, K (1987) 'Joint ventures: a mechanism for creating strategic change', in Pettigrew, A (ed) (1987) *The management of strategic change*, Oxford, Blackwell

Hayek, F (1948) *Individualism and economic order*, Chicago, University of Chicago Press

Itami, H (1987) *Mobilizing invisible assets*, Cambridge, Mass., Harvard University Press

Jacquemin, A (1987) *The new industrial organisation*, Oxford, Oxford Clarendon Press

Jacquemin, A (1988) 'Cooperative agreements in R&D and European anti-trust policy', *European Economic Review*, vol 32

Johnson, P (1975) *The economics of invention and innovation*, London, Martin Robertson

Jorde, T M and Teece, D J (1989) 'Competition and cooperation: striking the right balance', *California Management Review*, vol 31, no 3, pp25–37

Katz, M (1986) 'An Analysis of cooperative R&D', *Rand Journal of Economics*, Winter, vol 17, no 4, pp527–43

Laffont, J J and Moreaux, M (1991) *Dynamics, incomplete information and industrial economics*, Oxford, Blackwell

Langlois, R (1990) *Transactions cost economics in real time*, mimeo, University of Connecticut

Laudan, R (1984) 'Cognitive changes in science and technology', in ibid., *The nature of technical knowledge. Are models of science relevant?*, Dordrecht, D Reidel

Layton, E T (1974), 'Technology as knowledge', *Technology and Culture*, vol 15, no 1, pp31–42

Link, A N and Bauer, L L (1987) 'An economic analysis of cooperative research', *Technovation*, vol 6

Malerba, F (1985) *The semi conductor business*, London, Francis Pinter

Mansfield, E (1971) *Research and innovation in the modern corporation*, London, Macmillan

Marshall, A (1920) *Principles of economics*, 8th ed. (Variorium), London, Macmillan

Mariti, P and Smiley, R H (1983) 'Cooperative agreements and the organisation of industry', *Journal of Industrial Economics*, vol 13, no 4, pp437–82

Metcalfe, J S and Gibbons, M (1984) 'Technology, variety and organisation', in Rosenbloom, R and Burgleman, R (eds) *Research in technological innovation, management and policy*, vol 4

Nelson, R (1982) 'The role of knowledge in R&D efficiency', *Quarterly Journal of Economics*, vol 97, no 3, pp453–470

Nelson, R and Winter, S (1984) *An evolutionary theory of economic change*, Cambridge Mass., Harvard University Press

Nelson, R (1987) *Understanding technological change as an evolutionary process*, North Holland

Nelson, R (1990) 'The capitalist engine of economic progress', *Research Policy*, vol 19

Oakley, B (1990) *Alvey*, Cambridge Mass., MIT Press

Office of Technology Assessment (1990) *Making things better; competing in manufacturing*, US Congress

Pavitt, K and Patel, P (1988) 'The international distribution and determinants of technological activities', *Oxford Review of Economic Policy*, vol 4, no 4, pp35–55

Peck, M (1989) 'Joint R&D: the case of the microelectronics computer corporation', *Research Policy*, vol 18

Pisano, G and Teece, D (1984) 'Collaborative arrangements and global technology strategy: some evidence from the telecommunications equipment industry', in Rosenbloom, R and Burgleman, R (eds) *Research in Technological Innovation Management and Policy*, vol 4

Ray, T (1990) 'Transferring expert systems technology to potential users: a case study of Alvey awareness clubs', *Journal of Computer Applications in Technology*, vol 3

Richardson, G B (1972) 'The organisation of industry', *Economic Journal*, vol 82, no 327, pp883–98

Rosenberg, N (1990) 'Why do firms do basic research (with their own money)?', *Research Policy*, vol 19

Ryle, G (1949) *The concept of mind*, London, Hutchinson

Silver, M (1984) *Enterprise and the scope of the firm*, Oxford, Martin Robertson

Sober, E (1985) *The nature of selection*, Cambridge Mass., MIT Press

Tirole, J (1989) *The theory of industrial organisation*, Cambridge Mass., MIT Press

Von Hippel, E (1988) *The sources of innovation*, New York, Oxford University Press

Vincenti, W G (1990) *What engineers know and how they know it*, Baltimore, Johns Hopkins University Press

Williamson, O E (1986) *Economic organisation*, Brighton, Wheatsheaf

Part 4

Conclusions and the way forward

14

The Process of Innovation

With one conclusion, at least, all the contributors to this volume would agree. Innovation is a complex and varied process which requires a range of supporting institutions. There is no 'quick fix' to the problem of poor innovatory performance in the form of some simple new policy departure by government, or the introduction of some management technique that has unaccountably been overlooked. Rather there seems to be a skein of related factors which influence the ability of firms to innovate profitably. Innovation requires not merely a supply of new ideas (Part 1) but the managerial capacity to utilise and develop them effectively (Part 2) and the marketing expertise to ensure that they are embodied in goods and services which consumers want (Part 3).

Any organisation can be seen as a set of 'capabilities'. In a manufacturing company these may constitute research, engineering, production, marketing, distribution and so forth. The successful innovator is the organisation which is capable of articulating these capabilities in a way that moves it from its existing position to a new one. The process of articulation may be compared with that of the human skeleton—when a person walks it is not possible to ascribe movement to any specific bone, but rather to the way in which all parts work together. The stimulus for progress may come from any of a number of sources, what the eye has seen, the body has experienced, or the brain has determined. Just as in a company the stimulus for innovation may come from research laboratories, an insight into customer demands or the entrepreneurial spirit of management. The achievement of progress depends upon the ability of the organisation to articulate all of its parts in harmony.

The effectiveness of the human body is largely determined by the effectiveness of its nervous system which enables the brain instantaneously to monitor the position of each limb and to send motor instructions. The successful innovator similarly needs to have institutional arrangements for communication and co-ordination which enable its parts to work together effectively. The cause of the apparent inability of the UK to innovate as effectively as some leading competitors is therefore likely to be found in a set of institutional arrangements which are not so well adapted to these requirements. Most observers of the Japanese scene note that the research and development capabilities of companies have not until recent years been strong; similarly, it would be difficult to ascribe the success of the Japanese in world markets to their marketing competence. It would appear that the success of the Japanese in product innovation is primarily associated with their ability to articulate the whole of their organisations and to ensure that the operation of each part complements that of the others.

Horizontal co-ordination

If successful innovation depends upon an organisation's ability to articulate the whole of its capabilities, there must be occasions when those capabilities are found lacking. For example, when Glaxo wished to exploit Zantac in world markets, it found that its marketing capability in the dominant US market was inadequate. Under these circumstances the successful innovators either acquire the necessary capabilities or enter into joint arrangements with those who already possess them. Glaxo arranged for Hoffmann LaRoche, which had an extensive sales team under-employed since the demise of Valium, to sell Zantac in the US. Japanese firms have become noted for their ability to acquire technology they need from external sources and then to incorporate it into their own operations. Horizontal co-ordination of this kind appears to work well where the organisations concerned have complementary capabilities and a clearly understood goal.

Where firms find it costly to maintain control over valuable research results and expect them to leak away rapidly to competitors, research activities will be discouraged. An obvious solution to this problem would be for groups of firms to get together to share the costs and the benefits of such research. By forming a research club, the firms would expect the gain from the joint benefits accruing to their research efforts. There would always be an incentive for firms to remain outside the club if they could thereby receive the benefits without paying. But if results only filtered through to such firms with a lag, or if lack of participation made the use of the results more difficult, membership of the club might be preferred to 'free riding'. There is scope for action by public bodies to encourage the formation of such clubs.

Even where maintaining control over research results is not a problem there are advantages to collaboration as described by Metcalfe in Chapter 13. Technology cartels might benefit their members through cost sharing, avoidance of duplication, the spreading of risks, and faster diffusion of results. As Baumol (1992) points out, if ten independent firms pursue different research programmes which reduce their costs by 0.5 per cent per year, the sharing of results would imply that all ten firms might reduce their costs by 5 per cent per year. Sharing results in this way need not give particular members of the cartel a differential advantage over others, but it will give the group as a whole an advantage over those outside. This is the group selection process emphasised by Metcalfe.

Japan appears to have been the most successful country in making 'research clubs' work effectively. It appears that they have concentrated on the development of underlying capabilities that can be picked up and refined further by individual companies, rather than the development of particular products. For example collaborative work on the manufacture of integrated circuits did not involve the design and production of specialised goods incorporating the new technology. The Japanese fifth generation project which might be seen as a departure from this tradition, in that it aimed to produce a family of products, has not in practice worked that way. Participating companies have, instead, used the project to improve the performance of their own operations in respect of a number of 'enabling technologies' which they have gone on to apply to a wide range of different innovations.

Vertical co-ordination

A relatively low propensity to innovate may be associated less with a restricted ability to produce innovations than with an unhelpful environment for exploiting them. To innovate successfully will often require suppliers of complementary inputs to adjust their production processes, or buyers to change their ways of doing things in significant ways. Making the best use of an innovation may require 'tacit' or 'procedural' knowledge which can be acquired only by experience of dealing with the same customers and suppliers over time. These considerations suggest that it is in the area of vertical relations between firms that opportunities exist to improve the UK's innovatory performance.

Recent work by Geroski (1991) charts the large flows of innovations between sectors and finds that productivity growth is related to innovations used rather than innovations produced. Mechanisms for ensuring the diffusion of innovations may therefore be of central importance in raising productivity growth. The diffusion process is heavily dependent upon establishing close relations between upstream and downstream firms. An innovation producer has to convince the suppliers of inputs that their co-operation will be profitable, and downstream buyers that the disruption entailed in adjusting to the innovations will be worthwhile. Full vertical integration may, on occasion, be resorted to if the requisite co-ordination cannot be achieved by other means, although the Japanese have shown that relationships short of full vertical integration may offer more flexible and effective alternatives. As Geroski (1992, p143) puts it:

> One of the issues facing those concerned with industrial policy is whether the right kinds of vertical relations are formed between innovation producers, innovation users and suppliers.

The danger of vertical integration is the extent to which it introduces rigidities; companies are often reluctant to pursue innovations which could render large parts of their existing investment obsolete. It is not coincidental that in electronics, for example, market leadership in the production of each generation of active device has passed from an established company to a new one — RCA, Fairchild, Intel. It is the Japanese companies which have gone furthest in finding an effective compromise in that their close and co-operative supply relationships bring many of the benefits of vertical integration but few of the disadvantages.

Competition policy

Encouraging 'technology cartels' and improving vertical links to aid diffusion are inevitably associated with the dangers of creating dominant market positions. A technology cartel might conspire to reduce the rate of innovation if it became insulated from outside pressure. There is a further danger that discussions might extend from pre-competitive research and the design of research programmes of joint interest to methods of fixing prices and restraining competition. One of the advantages of the encouragement of closer vertical relationships is that it is less vulnerable to the objection that monopoly power might thereby be encouraged.

Where arrangements between companies exist in order either to enhance their capabilities (as in the case of the Japanese collaborative research projects directed at enabling technologies) or to give companies access to capabilities that they need in order to exploit innovation (as in the case of the partnership sourcing) there appears to be little harm and could be a great deal of good. Arrangements between companies with dominant market positions to determine the specification of products entering that market may have a superficial attractiveness because they reduce development costs and risk, but they would also, almost certainly, suppress innovation. Under such circumstances companies are likely to compete in terms of second order characteristics, such as the way in which the product is marketed, rather than through disturbing the comfortable consensus. There are voices within the EC which argue that Europe can only compete in some of the most expensive areas of product development through major, publicly supported, collaborative development programmes aimed at end products. One of the few cases where this argument can be sustained is that of Airbus Industrie and here the intense international competition between Boeing, McDonnell Douglas and Airbus must be at the root of the apparent success of this project.

Policy to ensure a vigorous competitive environment is, therefore, a necessary complement to the closer business relationships required for effective innovation. There will always be a tension between the advantages of co-operation and the importance of maintaining competition, but cosy and protected relationships are not associated with a good innovative record. Work by Patel and Pavitt (1991, p32), which analyses the sectoral patterns of patenting activity in the United States by 19 countries and by the top 20 firms in each technological area, indicates that pure size of firms is not a good indicator of technological strength.

> Our clear statistical conclusion that rivalry amongst the big — rather than gigantism and monopoly — is the characteristic of national technological strength, is a clear pointer towards the vigorous enforcement of a strong European competition policy.

Government research spending

As was seen in the chapter by Bowen, Buxton and Ricketts, governments finance a significant fraction of total R&D spending in most major countries. In the case of the UK this has declined from 55 per cent in 1975 to under 40 per cent in 1989. Historically, the ratio of defence R&D expenditure by government to civil expenditure has been much higher in countries such as the United Kingdom, the US and France, compared with Germany, Italy and Japan (see Table 2.4). The countries with large defence commitments in research and development have been those whose technology policy has been characterised as 'mission orientated' (Ergas, 1987). This contrasts with countries such as Germany or Switzerland where policy is 'diffusion orientated'.

'Mission orientated' policy is associated with the concentration of resources on a limited number of specific projects. These projects are typically undertaken by a small number of large firms who have an interest in restricting access to research results and minimising 'spillovers' to other companies. Apart, therefore, from the criticism that emphasis on defence related research may divert scientific resources from other productive lines of enquiry in the civil field, the institutional arrangements used to conduct the research may inhibit the transfer of technical advances to other areas of the economy. Indeed, mission orientated support is by no means confined to military projects. In the UK, civil projects such as the development of the Magnox nuclear reactors and the Concorde have been clearly 'mission orientated'. These projects always involve a 'national champion' or consortium of firms, a structure which discourages the growth of outsiders or newcomers. Further, these projects tend to become enmeshed in a public purchasing process which is bureaucratic and inflexible.

'Diffusion orientated' policy, in contrast, concentrates on facilitating change by spreading funds more widely across firms and industries and by using industry associations or other co-operative organisations to determine research priorities. Technology policy can be seen not as a way of achieving particular 'missions' or objectives, but 'as an intrinsic part of the provision of innovation related public goods: notably education, product standardisation, and co-operative research' (Ergas, 1987). By attempting to encourage co-operative effort which is of joint benefit to a range of firms, the diffusion orientated policy gives no special advantage to very large firms. Indeed, Germany, the country most often used as a case study of the diffusion approach, is characterised by a large sector of small and medium sized companies.

Encouraging diffusion and transfer

There is a common argument that companies are unlikely to invest in exploiting a technology unless they have exclusive ownership of that technology. There are circumstances in which this is true, but there may be greater danger in excluding other companies from access to the same useful technology. The other companies may be able to exploit that technology in other and non-competitive markets, some of which may be more important, or may be able to provide competition and thus stimulate the process of innovation. There is probably a great deal more to be gained by government policies promoting the openness of the technology diffusion process than in permitting its exclusiveness for short term benefit. This has an influence, for example, upon the kinds of arrangements between companies and universities and the point at which, under such arrangements, intellectual property rights transfer from one party to the other. The exclusive ownership of technology can be pernicious in another way in that it encourages the company to focus upon the exploitation of this unique asset. A number of papers argue that successful innovation is more likely to come from seeking to satisfy a perceived need in the market place than from seeking to exploit a proprietary technology. Where a company's innovation is market based, it needs access to any technology which can help it realise that innovation, and in so far as it is not able to protect that technology, it has an incentive to exploit it rapidly in the market place.

Stimulating the use of innovations requires channels of communication to be established from market to laboratory and through the entire supply chain. Government actions can influence the speed of diffusion in several ways:

- Public procurement policies affect the incentive to innovate directly, and may be used to influence matters such as the establishment of technical standards that may then be adopted elsewhere.
- Direct efforts to encourage contact between universities, research institutes and business firms help to create the kind of environment more common in the US where there has been a tradition of more mobility of scientists and engineers between university and industry than has been the case in the UK.
- Geographical proximity of firms may be important to establishing the relationships required to encourage the diffusion of innovation. Clusters of firms in a limited geographical area engaged in related activities are more likely to establish institutions for their mutual benefit than if they are widely dispersed. This clearly has implications for the conduct of regional or land use planning policy and of urban renewal schemes.

Thus there are important elements of government policy towards innovation that do not concern the traditional issue of direct spending on research and development. The influence of government in framing the right environment in which individual firms make decisions about innovation is also significant, and is particularly relevant to encouraging the diffusion of innovation. This indirect influence of government policy is most significant in education and training.

Education and training

The use of innovation requires a flexible and skilled workforce. As was pointed out in the chapter by Bowen, Buxton and Ricketts, the UK has a lower proportion of its workforce with intermediate level vocational qualifications than other leading competitor countries (Table 2.6), although at graduate level the proportion of the workforce qualified is very similar to that in Germany and elsewhere. If the diffusion and use of innovations are the important determinants of productivity growth, it is the supply of educated and skilled people able to adjust to new ideas and procedures that will produce long term success. An elite core of scientists and engineers may simply produce innovations which will be taken up and used elsewhere and will not greatly influence the productivity growth of industry in the UK. Highly trained scientists are valuable, but they are less valuable without the assistance of those who can understand new ideas and use them extensively. The effectiveness of product and process development can be much improved by the active participation of those who will be involved in the day to day production of new products and services, and their contribution will be enhanced by better education and training.

Analysts have distinguished between three broad phases in the development of a new technology — emergence, consolidation and maturity. In the early stages of 'emergence', risks are high reflecting lack of knowledge concerning the future potential of the new technology and the difficulties of keeping control of the research results. 'Consolidation' is the phase in which the qualities and potential uses of a new technology become established. It is during this phase that the most profitable opportunities are likely to arise from the exploitation of a technology. It is also the phase which requires the greatest use of the skills and adaptability of the workforce. Countries lacking such a resource may therefore be forced to deploy scientific manpower on the 'emergence' phase of a technology and a relatively poorly trained workforce in the 'maturity' phase. Both the growth of productivity and the recorded profitability of business operations would be expected to suffer in these circumstances.

Innovation in the marketplace

Many of the papers argue that successful innovation results from the search for better means of satisfying customer needs rather more than from technological innovation. Discussions of innovation usually tend to focus upon technology, perhaps because it is widely accepted that the science base is a public good and therefore a proper target for public support and public policy. The extent to which governments could or should influence the market is much more contentious.

On the face of it, UK suppliers have every opportunity to market innovations at home, since the rate of penetration of new products such as video cassette recorders, micro computers and cellular telephones has been exceptionally high in the UK by international standards. Yet although the market is responsive, the performance of UK suppliers in these product areas has been much less impressive. Sinclair has been one of the few companies to exploit the receptivity of the UK market but, perhaps because of an early failure to articulate the necessary capabilities of marketing, R&D, and efficient, high quality volume production, Sinclair was not able to capitalise upon an early lead. Conversely, those markets which have traditionally been dominated by the public sector such as defence, telecommunications, and energy generation, have demanded high technical standards but specified equipment which did not accord with world market practice and thus tended to isolate the UK suppliers. In addition, the traditional methods of public sector purchasing tended to sap competition and entrepreneurial vigour rather than encourage it. The government should use trade policy and competition policy to maintain an open and demanding market in the UK. There is clearly a need to understand better the relationship between public purchasing and innovation; fostering competition in public tendering and developing common standards across the EC should help in this regard.

A case can be made for fiscal measures. The Japanese, for example, have stimulated innovation in their machine tool industry by permitting higher levels of capital allowances for machine tools with an advanced technological specification. The danger of selected measures of this kind is, of course, in ensuring that the specification is relevant to world market needs. In Japan the users helped draw up the specification of advanced machine tools which would be eligible for higher allowances. In this may be the essential clue for any government which is contemplating selective measures to encourage innovation; those measures should be drawn up in consultation with potential customers rather than the suppliers. But the justification for selective fiscal intervention — the market structure of the industry, the nature of the technology, the barriers to market access — should always be clear.

Stimulating innovation in industry

The papers in this book stress the importance of innovation in achieving competitive advantage but, perhaps more importantly, they draw attention to the proper objective of innovation: to satisfy the wants and aspirations of consumers. Two general lessons must be learnt if the UK's competitive position and innovatory record are to be improved. First, from the point of view of firms, innovation needs to be treated as an integral part of business activity, that is entirely consonant with firms' commercial objectives and extends far beyond narrowly defined technological R&D. Success depends on developing a wide range of capabilities in successful collaboration with other firms.

Second, from the point of view of public policy, encouraging innovation requires attention to the market environment and an understanding of the incentives to innovate facing firms. Improving those incentives by subsidy or by sponsoring collaboration and diffusion must be balanced by the maintenance of vigorous competition if the basic incentive to satisfy consumers' aspirations is be to sharpened.

References

Baumol, W J (1992) 'Horizontal Collusion and Innovation', *Economic Journal*, vol 102, no 410, pp.129–37

Ergas, H (1987) 'The Importance of Technology Policy' in Dasgupta, P and Stoneman, P (eds) *Economic Policy and Technological Performance*, Cambridge, Cambridge University Press

Geroski, P A (1991) 'Innovation and the Sectoral Sources of UK Productivity Growth', *Economic Journal*, vol 101, no 409, pp1438–51

Geroski, P A (1992) 'Vertical Relations Between Firms and Industrial Policy', *Economic Journal*, vol 102, no 410, pp138–47

Patel, P and Pavitt, K (1991) 'Europe's Technological Performance', DRC Discussion paper no 81, Science Policy Research Unit, University of Sussex

Index